It's about to get easier to teach and learn MLA style.

MLA Handbook
Ninth Edition

AVAILABLE NOW

Paperback and e-book
$22.00

AVAILABLE IN JUNE

Hardcover
$45.00

Spiral-bound
$32.00

An all-in-one resource, the *MLA Handbook* includes

- extensive guidance on creating works-cited-list entries using the MLA template of core elements
- easy-to-follow explanations of in-text citations
- recommendations for using inclusive language
- an appendix with over 200 works-cited-list entries by publication format
- updated advice on avoiding plagiarism
- paper-formatting guidelines

Visit style.mla.org/hb9 to learn more.

2020 *Composition Studies* Reviewers

Ira Allen
Wendy Anderson
Amy Anderson
Neil Baird
Christopher Ryan Basgier
Heather Bastian
Dave Blakesley
Jessie Borgman
Sheila Carter-Tod
Amy Cicchino
Richard Colby
Tom Deans
Elías Dominguez Barajas
Qwo-Li Driskill
Timothy Elliott
Michele Eodice
Kristi Girdharry
Bruce Horner
Yu-Kyung Kang
Carrie Leverenz
Susan Martens
Heather Martin
Aja Y. Martinez
Christine Martorana
Richard Matzen
Michael McCamley
Laura Rose Micciche

Michelle Miley
Jessica Nastal-Dema
Andrea Olinger
Lori Ostergaard
Jason Palmeri
Melissa Berry Pearson
Patricia Portanova
Annette Harris Powell
Margaret Price
Jessica Restaino
Jim Ridolfo
Shelley Rodrigo
Hannah J. Rule
Donnie Sackey
Jennifer Sano-Franchini
Christopher Schroeder
Ryan Shepherd
Ann Shivers-McNair
Ryan Skinnell
Trixie Smith
Natalie Szymanski
Darci Thoune
Elizabeth Vander Lei
Scott Warnock
Amy Williams
Kathleen Yancey

composition STUDIES

Volume 49, Number 1
Spring 2021

Editors
Matthew Davis
Kara Taczak

Book Review Editor
Jason Chew Kit Tham

Managing Editor
Megan Busch

Content Editors
Mike Haen
Callie Kostelich
Emma Kostopoulos
Alex McAdams
Clare Sully-Stendahl

Blog Editors
Lauren Fusilier
Megan Von Bergen

Social Media Editors
Nitya Pandey
Annmarie Steffes

Editorial Assistant
Anna Aldrich

Editorial Consultant
Bob Mayberry

Former Editors
Gary Tate
Bob Mayberry
Christina Murphy
Peter Vandenberg
Ann George
Carrie Leverenz
Brad E. Lucas
Jennifer Clary-Lemon
Laura R. Micciche

Advisory Board
Sheila Carter-Tod
Virginia Tech University

Elías Dominguez Barajas
Florida State University

Qwo-Li Driskill
Oregon State University

Susan Martens
Missouri Western State University

Aja Y. Martinez
University of North Texas

Michael McCamley
University of Delaware

Jessica Nastal-Dema
Prairie State College

Annette Harris Powell
Bellarmine University

Melissa Berry Pearson
Northeastern University

Margaret Price
The Ohio State University

Jessica Restaino
Montclair State University

Donnie Sackey
The University of Texas at Austin

Christopher Schroeder
Northeastern Illinois University

Darci Thoune
University of Wisconsin-La Crosse

SUBSCRIPTIONS

Composition Studies is published twice each year (May and November). Annual subscription rates: Individuals $25 (Domestic), $30 (International), and $15 (Students). To subscribe on-line, please visit https://compstudiesjournal.com/subscriptions/.

BACK ISSUES

Back issues, five years prior to the present, are freely accessible on our website: https://compstudiesjournal.com/archive/. If you don't see what you're looking for, contact us. Also, recent back issues are now available through Amazon.com. To find issues, use the advanced search feature and search on "Composition Studies" (title) and "Parlor Press" (publisher).

BOOK REVIEWS

Assignments are made from a file of potential book reviewers. If you are interested in writing a review, please contact our Book Review editor at Jason.Tham@ttu.edu.

JOURNAL SCOPE

The oldest independent periodical in the field, *Composition Studies* publishes original articles relevant to rhetoric and composition, including those that address teaching college writing; theorizing rhetoric and composing; administering writing programs; and, among other topics, preparing the field's future teacher-scholars. All perspectives and topics of general interest to the profession are welcome. We also publish Course Designs, which contextualize, theorize, and reflect on the content and pedagogy of a course. CFPs, announcements, and letters to the editor are most welcome. *Composition Studies* does not consider previously published manuscripts, unrevised conference papers, or unrevised dissertation chapters.

SUBMISSIONS

For submission information and guidelines, see https://compstudiesjournal.com/submissions/.

Direct all correspondence to:

> Matthew Davis, Co-Editor
> Department of English
> UMass Boston
> 100 Morrissey Blvd
> Boston MA 02125–3393
> compstudiesjournal@gmail.com

Composition Studies is grateful for the support of the University of Massachusetts Boston and the University of Denver.

© 2021 by Matthew Davis and Kara Taczak, Co-Editors

Production and distribution is managed by Parlor Press, www.parlorpress.com.

ISSN 1534–9322.

Cover art by Catalina Sepulveda.

https://compstudiesjournal.com/

composition STUDIES

Volume 49, Number 1
Spring 2021

Contents

2020 *Composition Studies* Reviewers	4
From the Editors: Marking a Year	10

At a Glance

Into the Wild: Teaching for Transfer at the Two Year College   14
Howard Tinberg, Sharon Mitchler, and Sonja Andrus

Articles

Disciplinary Lifecycling: A Generative Framework for Career Trajectories in Rhetoric, Composition, and Writing Studies   16
Laurie A. Pinkert and Lauren Marshall Bowen

Cross Postings: Disciplinary Knowledge-Making and the Affective Archive of the WPA Listserv   42
Zachary Beare

Pandemic Pedagogy: What We Learned from the Sudden Transition to Online Teaching and How It Can Help Us Prepare to Teach Writing in an Uncertain Future   60
Jennifer Sheppard

A Pedagogy of Amplification   84
Danielle Koupf

Course Design

Constellating Community Engagement in a Cultural Rhetorics Seminar   103
Maria Novotny, Claire Edwards, Gitte Frandsen, Danielle Koepke, Joni Marcum, Chloe Smith, Angelyn Sommers, and Madison Williams

Where We Are: Intergenerational Exchanges

Intergenerational Exchange in Rhetoric and Composition: Some Views from Here   119
John Brereton and Cinthia Gannett

The Intergenerational Blunder of Elitism as Fun(k)tionality, aka An
Open Letter on Choices When "Keepin' It Real Goes Wrong …"   125
Todd Craig

On Podcasting, Program Development, and
Intergenerational Thinking   130
Eric Detweiler

Intergenerational Knowledge, Social Media, and the Composition
Community: Insights and Inquiries   135
Amanda M. May

When the Family Tree Metaphor Breaks Down, What Grows?   140
Benjamin Miller

Where Would We Be?: Legacies, Roll Calls, and the
Teaching of Writing in HBCUs   144
Beverly J. Moss

Intergenerational Exchange as a Practice of Negotiation   149
Juli Parrish and Wendy Chen

A Form of Phronesis   154
Diane Quaglia Beltran

Tradition and Change   156
Victor Villanueva

Too Green to Talk Disciplinarity   160
Zhaozhe Wang

Notes on Intergenerational Exchange: The View from Here   164
Kathleen Blake Yancey

Book Reviews

Dismantling Anti-Blackness and Uplifting African American
Rhetoric: A Review Essay   170

   Rhetorical Crossover: The Black Presence in White Culture,
   by Cedric D. Burrows

   Linguistic Justice: Black Language, Literacy, Identity, and Pedagogy,
   by April Baker-Bell

   Reviewed by *Chloe J. Robertson*

Graduate Student Writing Is Graduate Student Work: A Review Essay   177

   *Conceptions of Literacy: Graduate Instructors and the Teaching of
   First-Year Composition,* by Meaghan Brewer

Graduate Writing Across the Disciplines: Identifying, Teaching, and Supporting, edited by Marilee Brooks-Gillies, Elena G. Garcia, Soo Hyon Kim, Katie Manthey, and Trixie G. Smith

Learning from the Lived Experiences of Graduate Student Writers, edited by Shannon Madden, Michele Eodice, Kirsten T. Edwards, and Alexandria Lockett

    Reviewed by Turnip Van Dyke

On African-American Rhetoric, by Keith Gilyard and Adam J. Banks   **184**

    Reviewed by Mikayla Beaudrie

Unruly Rhetorics: Protest, Persuasion, and Publics, edited by Jonathan Alexander, Susan C. Jarratt, and Nancy Welch   **188**

    Reviewed by Rebecca S. Haynes

Labor-Based Grading Contracts: Building Equity and Inclusion in the Compassionate Writing Classroom, by Asao B. Inoue   **192**

    Reviewed by Stephie Minjung Kang

Counterstory: The Rhetoric and Writing of Critical Race Theory, by Aja Y. Martinez   **196**

    Reviewed by Louis M. Maraj

Personal, Accessible, Responsive, Strategic: Resources and Strategies for Online Writing Instructors, by Jessie Borgman and Casey McArdle   **200**

    Reviewed by Kailyn Washakie

Contributors   **204**

From the Editors: Marking a Year

A year ago, we introduced the spring issue with reference to our "feelings of uncertainty, trauma, and fear" and examples of how "parts of our individual and collective well-being are challenged, compromised, and threatened" by the pandemic. A year on, those sentiments—and the inequitable dispersal of those harms—still accurately describe for many the day-to-day lived experience and general sense of the past year. The cover to this issue, composed by one of Kara's students, captures this reality from the perspective of a student: discarded masks; coffee cup stains; days, weeks, months marked off the calendar; seasons, in the window, passing by. A computer screen filled with what students have disparagingly dubbed "Zoom University."

And yet, it would seem that hope springs eternal. Amidst the difficulty, we here at *CS* found enough space for empathy and compassion: for our students, colleagues, reviewers, authors, prospective authors, and for ourselves. And we certainly received even more fellow-feeling in kind: our reviewers, whom you can find listed in the front matter, were immensely generous with their attention and effort at a time when both were surely overtaxed. *CS* authors and prospective authors were patient with feedback, decisions, and page proofs. And *CS* advisory board members were supportive, responsive, and dedicated. To those advisory board members who stayed on an extra mini-term to keep the journal afloat: we thank you. (And to those of you who, because of other commitments and difficulties, could not be the reviewers and authors you wanted to be this past year: we understand, we appreciate you, and we hope to be able to support you and work together soon.)

In addition, and as we announced last time, we're hopeful because the *CS* team has grown. This issue includes the collective efforts of Anna Aldrich, Mike Haen, Callie Kostelich, Emma Kostopoulos, Alex McAdams, and Clare Sully-Stendahl, all of whom—under the phenomenal guidance of our managing editor, Megan Busch—worked this issue into being. In addition, Nitya Pandey and Annmarie Steffes remain our fantastic social media editors. And Lauren Fusilier and Megan Von Bergen deserve special recognition: over the course of the last year, they've planned, designed, and launched *FEN Blog*, which is available at compstudiesjournal.com/blog/. There you can already find thoughtful and thought-provoking posts by Sheila Carter-Tod (centering African American rhetorics as a way to think about rhetorical knowledge in the writing classroom) and by Adam Hubrig (arguing that access isn't an achievement, but a series of "ongoing conversations and actions that address the systematic inequalities and institutional barriers that exclude disabled and other marginalized bodies"). And more are forthcoming!

We also find hope in the future of the journal. In summer 2021, we will release our second special issue, this one titled "Diversity is not Equity: BIPOC Scholars Speak to Systemic Racism in the Academy and Field." The guest editors, Ersula Ore, Kimberly Wieser, and Christina Cedillo, have been hard at work gearing up for this issue. It will be released fully online and open-access on our website this summer. We are now seeking collaborative editorial teams for a digital special issue in summer 2022, so if you have a possible topic, please submit a proposal to compstudiesjournal@gmail.com.

This Issue

No doubt, this issue kicks off with the cover: designed by Catalina Sepulveda, it is our first cover that features student artwork. (Somewhat famously for *CS* folks, Laura R. Micciche's son designed several of the colorful covers during her editorship, and we're glad to continue such a tradition in our own way.) Of the cover, Cat says:

> Studying during the pandemic has been very hard, especially online. For the most part, trying to stay engaged and motivated is more challenging than the course itself. For this piece, I wanted to portray it as realistic as possible. As opposed to an abstract form that represents the emotions of studying online, I wanted to show the mundane daily feeling of learning online. The focus of the piece is simple: a student sleeping during their Zoom lecture. However, it's the details that make the message. Marks on the wall, crosses on the calendar, cobwebs on the backpack, a broken clock, all four seasons just passing by... all represent that feeling of losing track of time, of days just merging together into an ongoing cycle of repetition. I wanted the room to be as full and cluttered as possible to resemble the year and its intensity.

At A Glance: Connections and Collaborations

This issue's At A Glance, by Howard Tinberg, Sharon Mitchler, and Sonja Andrus, draws on their work on the Teaching for Transfer (TFT) curriculum in community college settings. "Into The Wild: Teaching for Transfer in the Two-Year College" is guided by an ecological metaphor for thinking through how the TFT curriculum functions at different institutions, through different adaptations, and for different student populations. Their supplementary web text is an enormously helpful resource for exploring teacher and student experience, curricular efficacy, two-year college adaptation, implementation, and research, as well as reading within the TFT curriculum. A pdf and a video of the webtext is available here: https://compstudiesjournal.com/current-issue--spring-2021-49-1.

The Articles

The articles in this issue span a range of methods, disciplinary concerns, and time periods. The issue begins with an article by Laurie A. Pinkert and Lauren Marshall Bowen which, building on their empirical, collective work elsewhere, offers the metaphor of a "disciplinary lifecycle" as a way of understanding academic work as a process of becoming (through activities, phases, and cycles) rather than the living-out of a trajectory. Second, and very timely, is Zachary Beare's analysis of the WPA-L listserv as an affective disciplinary space. Seeing the listserv as a knowledge-making space, Beare argues that we might come to understand and value WPA-L as much for the democratic possibilities of its platform as for the tensions, disagreements, and emotional processes it can embody. Next, Jennifer Sheppard examines the results of a "hyperlocal programmatic survey" of faculty needs during adjustments to emergency online teaching in 2020. Situated within the context of scholarship on OWI, Sheppard's findings should be useful to WPAs and teachers alike: by focusing on pedagogy, connection, and logistics—in that order—programs can support instructors planning to teach online for the first time. Finally, Danielle Koupf argues for critical-creative tinkering, a practice of "reuse that infuses writing with the hands-on, experimental ethos of the makerspace," in the composition classroom. Through Koupf's analysis, tinkering becomes not only a process through which composition occurs, but also a layered opening up of invention and amplification with historical roots, among other places, in writing textbooks of the 19th Century.

The Course Designs

This issue contains one course design, and it's a substantial one: Maria Novotny, Claire Edwards, Gitte Frandsen, Danielle Koepke, Joni Marcum, Chloe Smith, Angelyn Sommers, and Madison Williams combine forces to outline and collectively reflect on a cultural rhetorics approach to a graduate seminar in rhetoric and composition. This course, focused on professional and community-engaged work at the University of Wisconsin-Milwaukee, harmonizes course design, content, and reflection with four pillars of cultural rhetorical pedagogy: story, decolonization, relations, and constellation. The resulting multivocal, reflective narrative outlines how to practice cultural rhetorics in the classroom and in a variety of communities beyond it.

Their course materials are available at https://compstudiesjournal.com/current-issue--spring-2021-49-1/.

The Where We Are Section

We are thrilled by this issue's Where We Are, which focuses on Intergenerational Exchange. We have a fabulous group of scholars in the early, mid, late, and emeritus stages of their academic lifecycles. Each contribution offers a particular way of knowing in our current moment, and, taken together, the section offers a more complex understanding of who we are as a field and how we might move productively forward together. We have organized these pieces alphabetically, but we see interesting resonances across and among the pieces: we urge you to explore and enjoy those connections.

The Book Reviews

The book reviews for this issue include two review essays: first, Chloe J. Robertson's "Dismantling Anti-Blackness and Uplifting African American Rhetoric" is a timely review focused on anti-blackness in the discipline that, when read with and against Sheila Carter Tod's post at *FEN Blog* and Mikayla Beaudrie's review on African-American rhetoric (in this issue), pays significant dividends. Second, in "Graduate Student Writing is Graduate Student Work," Turnip Van Dyke reviews three books focused on the development of graduate students. And, fittingly, Van Dyke is both a graduate student and a first-time composition teacher. The essay ends with a call for graduate students to find and support each other: we join Van Dyke in hoping you'll answer that call.

Rounding out the issue, the individual reviews take up major strands of development in the field: protest and public rhetoric, critical race theory and methodology, labor-based grading contracts, African-American rhetorics, and online writing instruction. Taken together, they are as solid a short introduction to current concerns in rhetoric and composition as you could find anywhere.

Thank you, again, to our reviewers, authors, advisory board, and editorial team. Thanks, most of all, to the *CS* subscribers, who allow our work to continue. We look forward to a brighter, more equitable, and more just future with all of you in it.

MD and Kt
Boston and Denver
March 2021

At a Glance

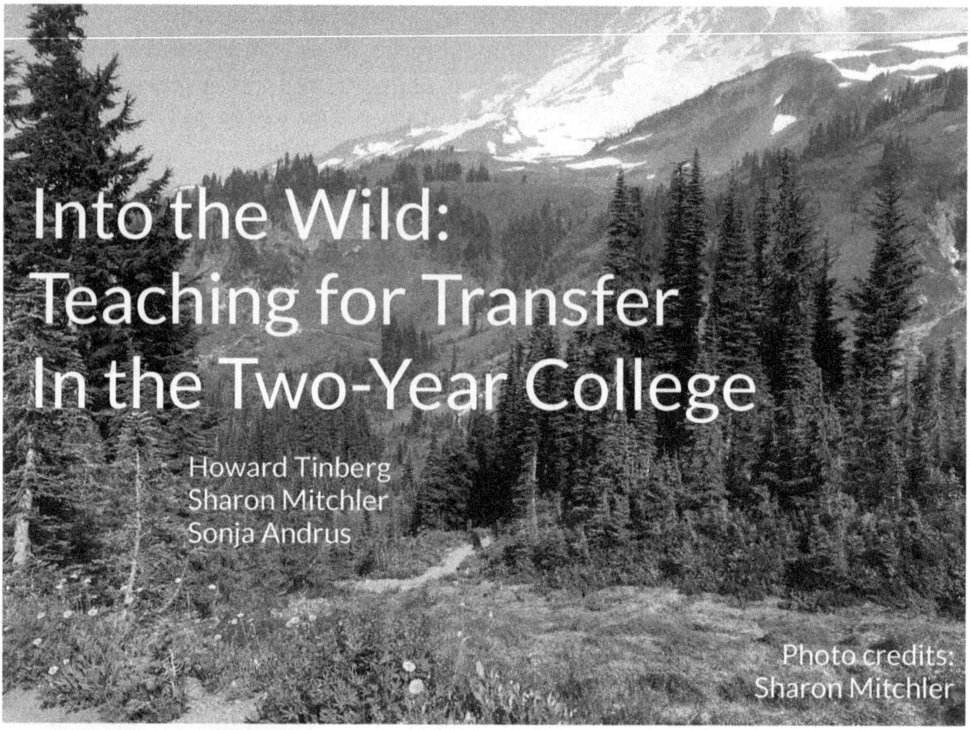

Into the Wild: Teaching for Transfer In the Two-Year College

Howard Tinberg
Sharon Mitchler
Sonja Andrus

Photo credits: Sharon Mitchler

Teaching for Transfer (TFT) is a curriculum that prioritizes the explicit transfer of knowledge developed in a writing class to other contexts in which composing is required, drawing upon these key elements: sequenced and scaffolded assignments; explicit, embedded reflection; keywords; and the development of the student's theory of writing.

Yancey, Kathleen Blake, Liane Robertson, and Kara Taczak. Writing Across Contexts: Transfer, Composition, and Sites of Writing. Utah State University Press, 2014.

Many students come to their first college course lacking confidence in their writing and reading abilities, have had little experience writing with sources, and have been given few opportunities for reflection and revision.

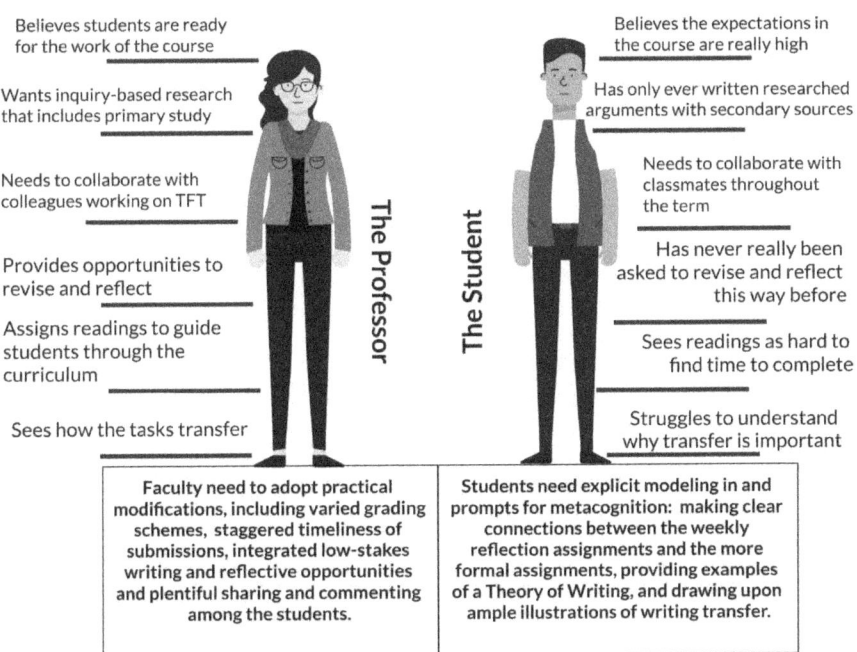

TFT works in the two-year college first-year writing classroom when the instructor takes the time to make modifications to the curriculum that can accommodate the variety of learners they have and guide them through the wilderness of learning to see what writing is, how it works, and how to use their knowledge and abilities in future writing contexts.

Articles

Disciplinary Lifecycling: A Generative Framework for Career Trajectories in Rhetoric, Composition, and Writing Studies

Laurie A. Pinkert and Lauren Marshall Bowen

In this article, we theorize the disciplinary lifecycle as an alternative to the limited metaphor of the "career arc." We argue that theorizing career trajectories as lifecycles resonates more fully with the experiences that are common to careers in rhetoric, composition, and writing studies (RCWS), thereby providing more possibilities for individuals to recognize and enact their disciplinary development across varying environments and in different phases of their careers. Further, we call for the field to better acknowledge the changing environments for disciplinary work by making visible typified but underrepresented phases in our scholarship and career development discourse.

Disciplinary Identities and Labor Realities in Rhetoric, Composition, and Writing Studies

Shaken by the COVID-19 pandemic and the worst recession in the United States since 2008 (Irwin), higher education has undergone major financial and philosophical changes, with more expected in the months and years ahead. Amid hiring freezes, staffing cuts, and furloughs; the suspension of doctoral admissions; the suspension of research and travel funding; and other disruptions to business as usual, career advisor Karen Kelsky has gone so far as to suggest that higher education is preparing for "an extinction event . . . for a whole traditional mode of operations in higher education." To be sure, the "spaces of action" (Henkel 157) in which disciplinary activities are conventionally performed were already changing, but many have now been eliminated—perhaps permanently. What does this seismic shift in an already-precarious institutional context mean for those who do, and who someday will, develop disciplinary expertise in rhetoric, composition, and writing studies? Although no one can offer a crystal-ball view into the future, we can begin to imagine what the ongoing shifts in our landscape mean for the ways we claim and support disciplinary identification with rhetoric, composition, and writing studies (abbreviated as RCWS).

In this article, we examine open-ended comments from various self-identified members of the field who responded to a large-scale survey of their activities and career timelines.[1] This survey was prompted by a collaboration between the CCCC Cross Generational Task Force and the CCCC SIG (now a Standing Group) for Senior, Late Career, and Retired Scholars. Responding to a call from task force member Louise Wetherbee Phelps in 2017, we became part of an interinstitutional, intergenerational research team eager to better understand intellectual and practical labor within the field of RCWS throughout the career, including into retirement. We wondered what activities were typical of those in RCWS, what kinds of preparation individuals received for their various activities, and how specific activities mapped onto timelines of experience.

Through explaining, questioning, rejecting, qualifying, or otherwise attempting to shape our reading of their career trajectories, survey respondents prompted us to challenge the prevailing metaphor of the career arc, which consistently haunts and constrains ways of envisioning a career in RCWS. In this article, we illustrate three facets of the career arc that make it especially problematic for RCWS and articulate possibilities for "disciplinary lifecycling" as a generative frame for theorizing, enacting, and supporting more comprehensive notions of disciplinary development throughout one's career and beyond.

Activities, Phases, and Lifecycles

Our lifecycle survey collected a range of quantitative and qualitative responses from 419 participants who self-identified as affiliated with RCWS. In this article, we focus on responses to a multi-part question, in which individuals traced and described various "phases" of their RCWS careers. To do so, they selected positions from a menu and/or wrote in additional positions that were not already listed. (See table 1 for a list of included positions.)

Table 1
Survey Categories and Positions from which Participants Selected

Categories	Positions
K-12 Education	Teacher – Elementary Level
	Teacher – Middle Level
	Teacher – Secondary Level
	Administrator
	Librarian
	Other – Please describe _____
Higher Education	Writing Fellow, Consultant, and Tutor as Undergraduate Student
	Teaching/Administrative/Research Assistant or Tutor as Master's Student
	Teaching/Administrative/Research Assistant or Tutor as PhD Student Tenured/Tenure-Track Faculty
	Non-tenure-Track Faculty
	Staff
	Administrator within a writing/literacy-related program/unit
	Administrator within a program/unit not writing/literacy-related
	Librarian
	Other Higher Education Position – Please describe _____
Employment Outside Education	Professional – Please describe _____
	Self-employed
	Non-Academic Writer
	Independent Scholar
	Other Employment Outside Education – Please describe _____
Retirement	In a Partial or Phased Retirement Program
	Retired, Working Part-time in Rhetoric, Composition, and Writing Studies
	Retired, Working Full-time in Rhetoric, Composition, and Writing Studies
	Retired, Working Part-time in a position not Writing/Literacy-related
	Retired, Working Full-time in a position not Writing/Literacy-related
	Retired, Not Working
	Other Retirement Phase – Please describe _____

When participants selected a particular position (e.g., "Teacher—Elementary Level"), this position was auto-populated into the subsequent section where participants indicated the duration of that experience and the numbers of institutions at which they held that position. Then, participants arranged their experiences into a chronology that included all positions selected or written in (see figure 1 for a sample chronology) and provided additional details about their lifecycles through a text entry box. While the chronologies identified the positions that individuals held, the open-ended comments provided affective, descriptive dimensions that narrated how these positions, as "phases" of a lifecycle, might contribute to an individual's sense of disciplinary "identity-as-position"—that is, the ways individuals represent and construct disciplinary identities through "rhetorical positioning of themselves within (or beyond) the field" (Bowen and Pinkert 258).

Fig. 1. Screenshot of a sample chronology of career phases arranged by a survey respondent.

Describing the career trajectory as a lifecycle grew initially out of our desire to capture the entirety of the career trajectory, much in the same way the Writing through the Lifespan research collaborative has driven attention toward the ways that literate activities occur and develop over lifespans and across sites ("life-wide") (Dippre and Phillips 6). Thus, *lifecycle* was initially chosen to be inclusive and lifespan-oriented; however, it also became generative for thinking about the possibilities for careers in RCWS.

In the beginning, we used the term *academic lifecycle* as we were primarily recruiting participants who were developing or applying their disciplinary expertise within academic or educational spaces. As we further theorized this lifecycle and analyzed participant responses, however, "academic" became a problematic boundary because, for example, many of our participants held concurrent positions within and beyond the academy. Further, the expertise developed in one domain was not confined to that domain: our participants described the applications of academic knowledge to community-based and business-oriented spaces and vice versa, further suggesting that divisions between "academic" and "non-academic" activities will not offer the most meaningful ways of thinking about a career in RCWS. Therefore, we found "disciplinary" to be a more capacious and accurate descriptor of the lifecycle that we aimed to understand and used the verb form *lifecycling* to connote the active, cumulative, and iterative possibility inherent in this frame.

The Career Arc: A Prevailing Metaphor to Signal Ascension, Singularity, and Early-Career Vitality

The career arc is a pervasive metaphor to describe the trajectory of experience and development in any field, depicting an unbroken rising-and-falling trajectory. In its usage, career arc evokes the dramatic arc to conceptualize the career as drama or narrative. The dramatic arc, famously theorized by German novelist Gustav Freytag, is represented as having five stages that follow a pyramid structure: introduction, rise, climax, return or fall, and catastrophe or *denouement* (Freytag 114-115). The same visual metaphor came to depict a "rising and descending staircase" image of the modern human life course, which age studies historian Thomas R. Cole notes replaced "the endless circle or *cycle* of human life" of antiquity (5) and evolved into universal set of stages in which predictable social roles would be played at specific ages (see fig. 2).

Since individuals come to envision and understand themselves through the stories they tell about their lives (Bruner), the dramatic arc can be a compelling metaphor for a career, fashioning an appealingly linear, narrative structure to the evolution of the professional self and featuring a dramatically satisfying (and thus aspirational) zenith. However, this narrative structure also limits how career trajectories are envisioned. For example, just as literacy practices become associated with—and thus deemed socially appropriate for—people of particular ages and even generations (Bowen), the career arc model may prescribe not only what activities count as part of one's disciplinary development but also the appropriate timing of those experiences over the lifespan.

Fig. 2. An example of 19th-century iconography of the human life course; Baillie, James; *The Life and Age of Man: Stages of Man's Life, from the Cradle to the Grave*; c1848; Library of Congress; https://lccn.loc.gov/2006686267 (public domain).

The career-as-arc metaphor pervades discussions about career trajectories in higher education. Although often an unnamed narrative structure, a search for actual appearances of *career arc* in *Inside Higher Ed* and *The Chronicle of Higher Education* reveals some commonalities in usage. Universally, *career arc* denotes the long view of a working life, likening the career to a marathon, for example, rather than a sprint (Stober). Occasionally, the metaphor also captures activity of deliberately crafting one's own career, allowing the "conception" of one's own arc as a viable motive for pursuing the next "higher profile, higher-paying job" (Devine). While we find longitudinal and agentive dimensions worth preserving in our ways of representing and envisioning careers in RCWS, the arc metaphor represents rare and privileged career trajectories as norms. To examine the limiting factors of this sometimes implicit but ever-present metaphor for career trajectories in RCWS, we identify three themes that survey responses evidenced.

Career Arc Limitation 1: Rendering Invisible Trajectories that Diverge from the Ascension Model

The ideal career arc is envisioned as a template of stages for career advancement from low to high levels of labor: a steady, uninterrupted ascension through institutional hierarchies, accompanied by the commensurate accrual of professional influence and power. In the context of higher education, the rising trajectory of the career arc implies that, as a career advances, the ideal professional is increasingly removed from low-status labor, which traditionally includes the teaching of first-year-level courses. David Perlmutter caricaturizes this imagined trajectory in his *Chronicle* article, "Teaching the 101": "Unfortunately junior professors are quickly caught up in this culture of prole avoidance. Many assume that their career arc is to teach more and more graduate seminars and eventually to never meet an undergraduate save the ones that serve lunch at the Faculty Club." Rarely so blatant as Perlmutter describes, an ascension-model career arc reveals itself through a tacit but pervasive institutional expectation, which can shape valuations of career phases. However, steady, upward progress narratives are particularly unrepresentative of careers in rhetoric, composition, and writing studies, which often involve regular (and willing) interaction with introductory-level students across phases of the career.

For many RCWS members, their institutional positions offer a clear challenge to this ascension orientation of the career arc because these positions do not offer opportunities for changes in labor conditions. For example, those on fixed-term appointments may not have opportunities for promotion that change institutional titles connoting prestige, or if they do have such opportunities, more prestigious titles may not change labor conditions significantly. The relevance of institutional conditions is made evident in the chronology and narrative of one respondent (white, female, from a lower middle-class background, age 65-74), who explained that, upon earning her PhD, she obtained a tenure-line faculty position at a four-year college, then moved to an adjunct position, then became full-time faculty at a tribal college that did not have a tenure track.[2] From this position, she became chair of the department. As this instance demonstrates, the idea that a successful career constitutes a climbing of institutional hierarchies does not always map well onto the institutional realities of RCWS faculty careers in which individuals may move into and out of positions that do not have a series of delineated steps to prepare them to climb to subsequent levels.

Even when individual careers seem to follow an idealized ascension, the framework upholds institutional hierarchies that are detrimental to members of our field. For example, one survey respondent who identified as a retired tenure-line faculty member and writing program administrator (white, female, from a working-class background, age 65-74) provided a lifecycle chronology that might, at first glance, appear to support an ascension model of rising upward through the institutional ranks (from graduate degree to graduate degree, to the tenure track) and away from contact with introductory-level students. However, the ascension narrative would position this participant's writing center work—because it was performed while at the graduate level—as lower-level work. Such positioning has consequences for RCWS spaces of action: if writing center administration is regularly viewed as introductory "graduate student" work, then it is less likely that institutions will assign higher-order-level value to such work, potentially contributing to the conflicts we sometimes see in hiring priorities, performance reviews, promotion, and resource management within RCWS spaces such as writing centers.

Career Arc Limitation 2: Reinforcing Industrialized Notions of Work

In addition to narrowly representing success as ascension through institutional hierarchies, the career arc also prioritizes singularity: a sense that a career's progress is measured only by the labor valued by an employing institution. In this way, the career arc sets up additional binaries: not only the high/low, up/down of career ascension, but also the in/out, on/off binary of a singular career track. Despite our own efforts to create a survey that allowed for self-description, flexibility, and space to resist the ascension imperative of the career arc, our survey design still evidenced the pervasive influence of arc's emphasis on singularity, as we imposed an insider/outsider metaphor when asking respondents to identify their current position. By marking "professional" positions as "outside the academy" and denoting "non-academic" writing as non-normative labor, we inadvertently replicated the career arc metaphor's singular focus, rendering the academic as institutionally recognizable and the non-academic as less valued, perpetuating an industrialized notion of work that counts only in service to a primary institution.

Fortunately, many respondents used the affordances of the write-in phases and the open response question to challenge an academic/non-academic boundary. For instance, a tenure-line faculty survey respondent (Latino/Hispanic/Spanish, male, poor/working poor background, age 65-74) narrated a chronology that seems to progress upward through the institutional ranks. Despite the seemingly consistent upward trajectory of the academic phases—graduate study to tenure-track position to administration—the participant explains that their employment phases overlap: "I was a short-order cook while a tenure-track assistant professor." In the career arc narrative, there's typically no place for a short order cook and no way to make sense of labor that doesn't explicitly contribute to institutional prestige, yet this participant writes this experience into visibility and calls us to find ways to understand this labor and its potential contributions to disciplinary experience. Despite our field's research that acknowledges the literacy practices present in activities that are not always understood as discursively-based (e.g., Mirabelli), we have yet to see similarly thriving research on the co-constitutive nature of such activities for experts in RCWS careers. As a field, we seem eager to validate and acknowledge literacy-based activities for our research participants but less likely to do so for ourselves.

Narrow emphasis on a single-track progress narrative occludes the economic realities of academic labor: in particular, the labor that many academics must perform to create the conditions that make RCWS work in academia possible. A tenure-line research university faculty member (American Indian or Alaska Native, female, from a poor/working class background, age 55-64) describes teaching four classes per semester at one institution while completing her doctoral degree at another—a balancing act that required 700 miles of commuting per week, but which she hoped would provide her an opportunity for promotion at her current teaching institution. Unfortunately, the university where she taught "refused to hire [her] in ten academic searches," though she did eventually move on to a full-time faculty position elsewhere.

Further, a graduate student and teaching assistant (two or more races, female, from a lower-middle-class background, age 45-54) outlines a complex chronology of thirteen phases, including undergraduate tutoring, elementary-level teaching, professional writing, self-employment, pursuing a Master's degree, teaching as non-tenure-track higher education faculty, secondary-level teaching, directing a writing center, and completing doctoral work. About this complex chronology, the respondent explains:

> The jobs I have had do not pay enough to live off of (e.g. I was full-time adjunct faculty at a R2 institution and started at $19,000 a year, raising two-children as a single mother, and with student loans); so, I have worked 2-3 jobs at a time (often working 50-80 hours a week) for over 20 years. This makes my work timeline more complex and look more broken... However, I have held many of my jobs for many years (e.g. I am still working one job for the last 18 years...).

The participant noted that seeing her jobs as distinct phases didn't seem to "reflect [her] work experience in the field of higher education." In this comment, she seems oriented toward a field of higher education, not toward a singular institution—an orientation undercut by a career arc, which is primarily vectored toward a primary institution of employment. The arc's singularity is rigidly reinforced by institutions that require reporting of outside activities through conflict-of-interest policies, which position the institution as the determinant of what kinds of labor are appropriate, when, and under what conditions, calling upon the field only in certain instances, when outside readers or external reviewers are deemed appropriate and defined most often by a notion of peer institution not a measure of disciplinary expertise.

Conversations about the traditional progress narrative of the academic career arc have already indicated that variation inevitably exists, as a diversifying professoriate demands broader recognition of successful career pathways (Segran) and leaving the academy does mean an individual has "failed" in some way (Yachnin). However, diversification is often presented as a set of discrete obstacles to be accommodated or otherwise endured: for example, the need to temporarily "stop the tenure clock" for childcare (National Academy of Sciences, National Academy of Engineering, and Institute of Medicine 31). The career arc does not readily permit us to recognize the ongoing effects that the various roles we play across social and economic domains can have on career trajectories.

Career Arc Limitation 3: De-Emphasizing Development that Occurs in Later Stages of One's Trajectory

The upward, linear movement of an idealized professional trajectory not only fails to anticipate the career paths that do not map easily onto it but also leads to predictable (and usually age-aligned) chronological phases that fail to capture one's actual career chronology. Further, the arc also obscures the latter phases of a career. Put in terms of Freytag's narrative arc, the resolution of the career arc would occur after the arc's climax—where, presumably, one has officially "made it" as a success in one's field (see figure 3). Perhaps as a consequence of the career arc vision, very little attention has been paid in RCWS or other disciplines to what happens beyond what is traditionally called mid-career, and retirement is not cast as a part of the career, at all, but the sometimes-welcome end of it.

Even those careers that move along institutionally celebrated milestones are not well-served by the invisibility of what happens after one has ostensibly made it in RCWS. Peggy O'Neill describes one outcome of this invisibility in a reflective *WPA Writing Program Administration* essay, in which she describes being in "mid-career and midlife" and feeling "bored, unsettled, unmotivated" (174)—an experience that, she soon discovered, was common among faculty who perceived themselves at a similar position in age identity and professional status. Through research on and observations of career satisfaction, O'Neill reflects on the importance of the "pivot," or meaningful, deliberate transition into what Laura Micciche calls "hypermiling" or "purposefully slowing down" in order to steer into a mid-career "U-curve" and make a "gradual arrival" in late-career (qtd. in O'Neill 179). Two things strike us as especially important about O'Neill's reflection: first, the sense that she needed to actively seek out a framework for confronting what she learned, eventually, was a common experience; and second, that she describes her trajectory as a kind of detour—a "U-Turn"—from a previous trajectory. In both points, we see laid bare both the pervasiveness of the career arc metaphor and its limitations for making sense of the latter "half" of an RCWS career: it silences and diminishes what later careers (and later life) might actually look and feel like.

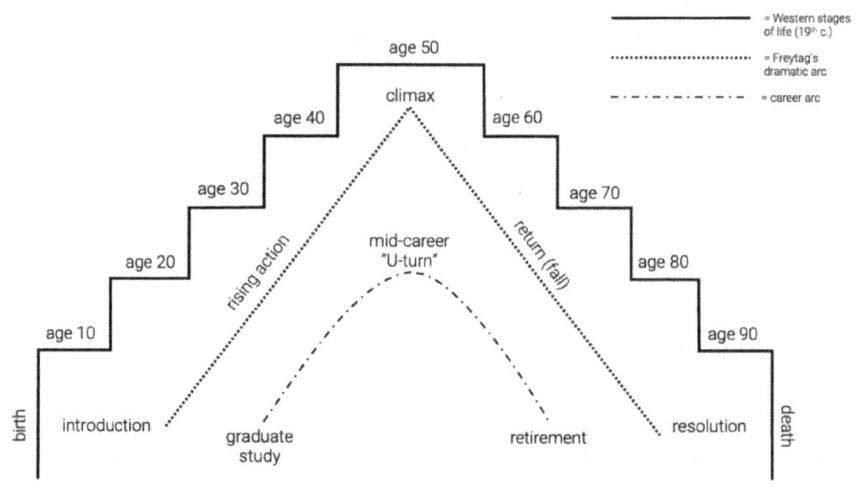

Fig. 3. Diagram illustrating the mirroring shapes of the career arc, dramatic arc, and Western iconography of the ages and stages of modern life.

These limitations, we contend, can have detrimental effects on career planning and disciplinary identity development. Some of these effects are suggested in responses to our survey, in which we dedicated particular attention to retirement as experienced and envisioned. We asked participants to identify activities they hoped to pursue or were already pursuing during retirement and to provide open-ended comments on their retirement plans or experiences. While many respondents named and identified activities they hoped to take up (from learning new skills, to engaging in community service, to continuing teaching), others were confounded by the prompt, as they did not envision career continuity following separation from employing institutions. "Do you expect people to work until they die? Isn't your survey kind of missing the point of retirement?" asked one responded. Said another, "When I leave academia, I don't plan to moonlight. I will have had enough."

For others, retirement was an altogether unknown entity, as evidenced by survey responses such as, "I haven't really thought much about this" and "I can't even imagine what I'll want to do (even though I'm no longer a spring chicken)." Across all age groups, respondents indicated a general sense of being ill-prepared for the transition into retirement, as compared with traditionally other transitions. For example, when asked about their preparation for submitting materials for promotion, 36% of our respondents reported being "very well prepared" whereas only 15% reported the same level of preparation for making decisions about retirement. One respondent (age 65-74) explained, "Perhaps like a number of other academics, I have not nurtured hobbies or other activities outside of my professional work that I am eager to have more time to pursue, and so how I will fill time productively is a current concern." Another respondent, from the same age group: "I have yet to find useful resources to help me think through my plans. Nor have I been able to identify useful steps to engage my possible plans." We believe that respondents' sense that they lack the means (or the will) to envision retirement as a phase of the career speaks to the commonplace status of career arc perspectives. The idealized career arc as an unbroken rise and unspoken decline, at best, misrepresents career trajectories as they actually unfold and, at worst, denies individuals the opportunity to envision meaningful disciplinary trajectories.

The Disciplinary Lifecycle: A Framework with Generative Possibilities

The inadequacies of the career arc have been previously identified in RCWS, particularly through feminist critique and intervention. For instance, Michelle Ballif, Diane Davis, and Roxanne Mountford's *Women's Ways of Making It in Rhetoric and Composition*, published at the beginning of the 2008 recession that marked significant and lasting changes to the academic job market, made an important effort to help women "obtain tenure-track positions," "succeed in the tenure and promotion process," and "balance career with personal endeavors" (4). This valuable work called attention to the limitations of traditional models and offered stories and strategies for not just navigating one's career but also "making it" in that career. The focus of *Women's Ways*, as the contributing authors of the "Wo/men's Ways of Making It in Writing Studies" special issue of *Composition Studies* observe, is mostly on the pathway toward securing tenure-track jobs at research-oriented universities: a pathway that seems to require a kind of "single-mindedness" about career success (Danberg 69). While this is a career path that many individuals may pursue, Loren Marquez and Christine Cucciare et al. question the focus on the tenure-track and research productivity as dominant markers of success.

We read such critique as an indication that the ascension model of the career arc is exerting a pervasive and oppressive force on individual career paths. As an abstract ideal, the arc casts real career trajectories as deviant or deficient when labor is distributed outside of institutionally-recognized activities. Familiar to many academics, including us, parenting is one such form of labor, which, in the absence of institutional policies and resources, forces many in academia to improvise what Alex Hanson calls "career killer survival kits" (35). Marquez poignantly calls for the field to further advance the work of *Women's Ways* by advocating for greater diversity in recognizing the career trajectories and accomplishments of women in RCWS:

> As women in Composition Studies who work, give, write, parent, listen, mentor, read, present, teach, publish, administer, guide, evaluate, and who are of different cultural, ethnic, and economic backgrounds, different sexual orientations, and teach at two-year, four-year, teaching, and research universities, public and private, and who care for children, parents, or loved-ones, we need to write about our ways of making it in the field to provide a broader account and fuller definition of making it. (76)

As a feminist project, these efforts to challenge the inadequacies of the traditional career arc are linked to a view of the field across more varied sites of disciplinary action, as we see happening, for example, in Amy Goodburn, Donna Lecourt, and Carrie Leverenz's edited collection, *Rewriting Success in Rhetoric and Composition Careers*. Even more crucially, we see a link to the wide and varied efforts to uncouple the work of the discipline from normative white, Western academic perspectives. In *Black Perspectives in Writing Program Administration*, Staci Perryman-Clark and Collin Lamont Craig call our attention to the "historically and politically maintained power asymmetries endemic of the ivory tower" that become "coded" into institutional practices (10-11)—asymmetries that we see inherent not only in institutions but also in the career arc with its emphasis on an idealized ascension that inheres and requires privilege, therefore making it not just difficult but impossible for those who do not have access to its entry points or institutionalized mechanisms for validation. In reflecting on her own disciplinary trajectory as a Black scholar, Sherita Roundtree further pushes us to examine such points of entry and access: "What are the gatekeeping mechanisms that become an inherent part of procedures and protocols, making it more difficult for folks like myself to access and continue doing meaningful work?" (Botex et al., n.p.).

Taking a cue from these scholars, we argue that it is not enough to critique the pervasive metaphor of the career arc by demonstrating its inadequacies and finding ways to validate ever-more varied experiences through the existing metaphor. Instead, we think it is important to work toward the imagining of new metaphors to replace the career arc because lived career trajectories rarely map well onto exponential line graphs. Further, we anticipate that new metaphors for our career trajectories can begin to erase the sometimes-unspoken, often-palpable distinctions we have internalized between the academic and the professional ("non-academic"), the novice and the expert, the institutionally-recognized and the community-oriented. Toward this end, we offer disciplinary lifecycling as a generative frame. Like the career arc, it can speak to a desire for a lifespan narrative and an image that not only explains but also visualizes possibilities for career development. Yet unlike the arc, its dimensions are malleable enough to retract and stretch with the kinds of variance that mark careers in RCWS. In what follows, we outline disciplinary lifecycling as a framework of possibility that is more responsive to the realities of labor in RCWS.

Visualizing the Lifecycle: Foregrounding Microcycles and Spaces of Action

When we say lifecycling, readers may immediately conjure an image of the biological lifecycle in its simplest form: a circular model of progress through specific phases of an organism's lifespan, from inception to reproduction (see fig. 4). While we see resonances between disciplinary lifecycling and the biological lifespan, our lifecycling model centers on the development and regeneration of disciplinary knowledge (not the individual species as in a biological model). Therefore, a single loop in a disciplinary lifecycle represents disciplinary knowledge (fig. 5, panel A) that is sometimes accumulated, building in effect over time, and sometimes immediately transformative, like threshold concepts that open new, irreversible ways of thinking (Meyer and Land 74).

Over time and across contexts, a person's lifecycle can be represented by a series of loops or microcycles, in which disciplinary knowledge is conceived and regenerated through a range of activities and practices that make up the ongoing process that we call *lifecycling* (fig. 5, panel B). We do not represent these microcycles as a line of progressive development that eventually curves its way to a clean, closed loop when expertise is attained, as this approach would leave microcycles incomplete when the spaces of action in which disciplinary knowledge is developed or applied is removed or rendered invisible. Rather, we see the microcycles emerging as an already-complete loop that enlarges according to the transformative effect of the disciplinary knowledge developed within it.

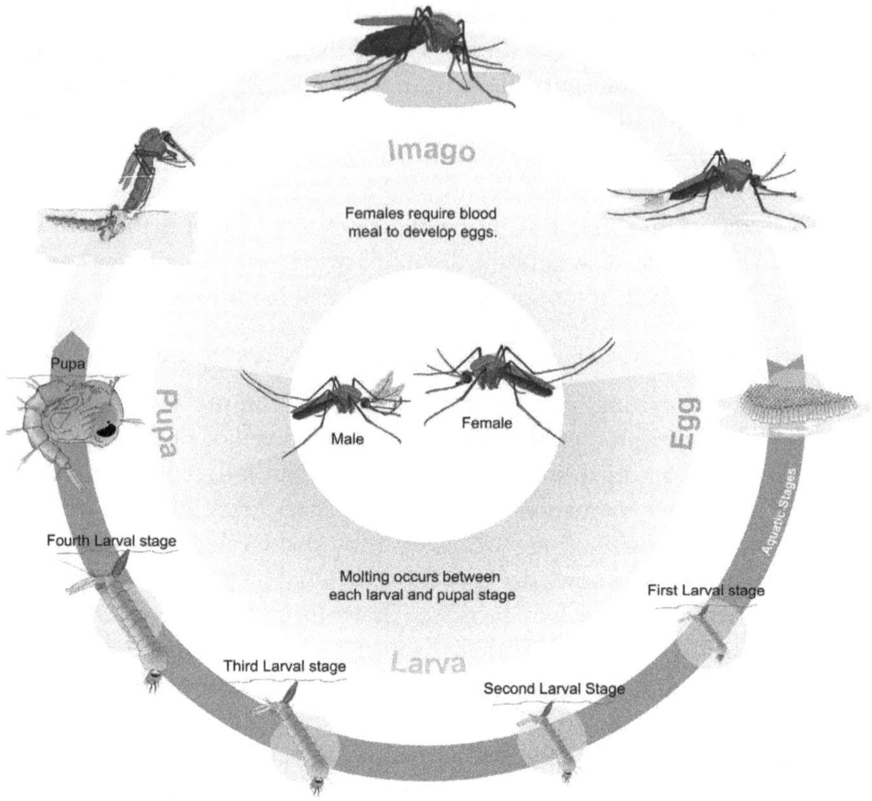

Fig. 4. Sample Biological Lifecycle Visualization; Mariana Ruiz Villareal; "Culex Mosquito Lifecycle"; Wikimedia Commons; July 1, 2020. commons.wikimedia.org/wiki/.

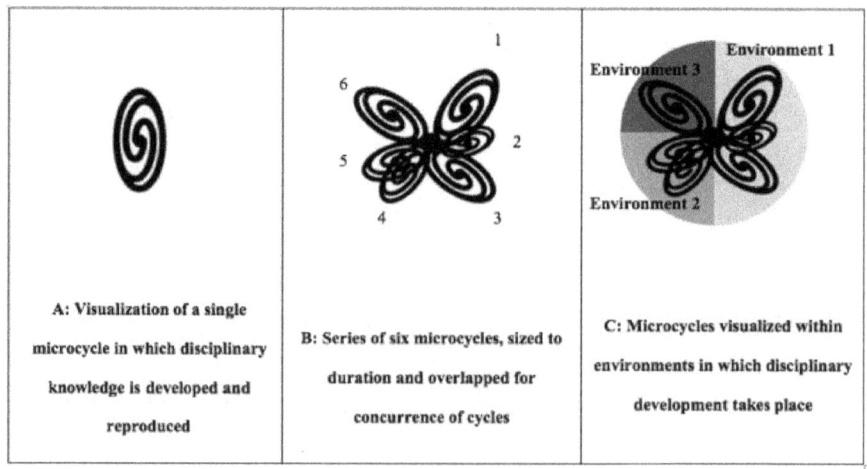

Fig. 5. Diagram illustrating disciplinary lifecycling.

Within this framework, we use environment to name the places (physical and virtual, social and individual) in which disciplinary activities occur. However, these places—institutions, organizations, homes, community organizations, etc.—are not accessed or experienced equitably by all individuals. Therefore, we differentiate environments—the places in which our activities occur—from spaces of action—those particular environments in which individuals experience agentive possibilities for disciplinary development. The interactivity of environments with disciplinary knowledge development might be represented by a shaded background in figure 5, panel C. Environments certainly provide a background for disciplinary activity that is necessary to acknowledge but an environment shared by two individuals does not necessarily indicate equal access to a space of action. As we discuss in an interview-based study of disciplinary identity (Bowen and Pinkert), spaces of action, which are created by organizational contexts, position responsibilities, reporting structures, and so forth, are essential for ongoing development and application of disciplinary expertise in phases such as retirement. Here, we extend our thinking to include spaces of action as a key component of disciplinary lifecycling, as they can constrain or make possible disciplinary development within a single microcycle and across multiple microcycles. Moreover, shifting access to one space of action may have impact on another. A brief example from our interview study is illustrative: in retirement, Michelle Lewis (a pseudonym) felt that academic conferences, once a key space of action for her, no longer served this function as she lacked continued access to a corresponding institutional space. She explained, "why do I want to go and hear all the latest and greatest . . . when I have no writing center to go back to with this information?" (Bowen and Pinkert 264). Thus, the transformative effect of a microcyle and, therefore, its size in relation to other microcycles is related to one's *transformative access* to the "networks of power" (Banks 45) that can enable environments to emerge from the background as spaces of action.

The representations of lifecycling we provide are messier than the career arc, with its even curves and singular lines. However, this variation is not the side effect of a career gone awry, as the career arc would suggest. Disciplinary knowledge is refined in overlapping experiences, such as being a faculty member and a graduate student simultaneously, and in social realities, such as abruptly changing locations to pursue a job nearer family or take on another position that better meets one's financial needs. The loops and layers are essential to understanding our careers amid their gendered, racialized, socialized, institutionalized realities: if we aim to envision what's likely and possible for RCWS experts and to more inclusively represent career trajectories, we must develop a frame that allows for the contours, the backgrounds, the variations, and the repetitions. To begin such acknowledgment, we discuss three possibilities through which lifecycling can offer a frame that isn't limited by the narrow perspectives inherent in the career arc.

Disciplinary Lifecycling Possibility 1: Recognizing Individual Variance in Disciplinary Development

In contrast to the career arc's emphasis on ascension, often signaled by the expected pursuit of increasing salaries or increasing prestige of position type, lifecycling thwarts *a priori* hierarchies that privilege one phase (with its accompanying microcycles) over another. For example, pursuing a graduate degree after gaining professional experience connotes neither ascension nor decline. Instead, it signals a new phase in which disciplinary knowledge is developed and applied. In this way, lifecycling diverges from the career arc in which the speed and height to which you "climb" to the next "level" is favored, while any continuation of the same activity can be perceived as a plateau, and thus as a deficiency. By recognizing the interrelations within individuals—their knowledge and their labor—a disciplinary lifecycling model can make visible often-overlooked phases in which disciplinary knowledge is acquired, honed, applied, revised, and transformed.

By working against the reliance on a presumed upward trajectory, lifecycling opens the possibility for developing a more realistic and discipline-specific understanding of the typified experiences of the disciplinary lifecycle in rhetoric, composition, and writing studies. In the participant-generated chronologies, shown in table 2 below, all of the participants share experience as Master's Degree Students, as Graduate Assistants during their master's degrees, and as Higher Ed Administrators. Additionally, three of the four chronologies trace their earliest disciplinary development to their undergraduate experiences as a student or a writing fellow, tutor, or consultant and include experience in non-tenure-track positions within higher education. But the chronologies vary significantly in the timing of these experiences. This maps onto what we already know about the variance in individuals' career trajectories: individuals may hold positions before pursuing a doctoral degree, after obtaining a doctoral degree, or concurrently with their graduate work. Such variation highlights the reality that, even when participants experience the same position types within RCWS, these positions are sequenced and contextualized differently, necessarily shaping individuals' development and application of disciplinary expertise. Disciplinary lifecycling makes space to acknowledge the varied ways that individuals encounter and develop disciplinary knowledge through practice, advanced study, teaching, research, and so on.

Table 2
Four Participants' Lifecycle Chronologies

Participant A Administrator in a program/unit not writing/literacy-related; white, male from a working class background, age 35-44	Participant B PhD-level teaching, admin, or research assistant; two or more races, female, from lower-middle-class background, age 45-54
1. Bachelor's Degree 2. Professional 3. Master's Degree 4. Graduate Teaching, Admin, or Research Assistant (Master's level) 5. Higher Ed Staff 6. PhD 7. Self-employed 8. Graduate Teaching, Admin, or Research Assistant (PhD level) 9. Higher Ed Non-Tenure-Track Faculty 10. Higher Ed Tenured/Tenure-Track Faculty 11. Higher Ed Administrator within a writing/literacy-related program/unit 12. Higher Ed Administrator in a program/unit not writing/literacy-related	1. Undergraduate Writing Fellow, Tutor, or Consultant 2. Teacher—Elementary Level 3. Tech 4. Professional 5. Grant writer as well as journalism 6. Self-employed 7. Master's Degree 8. Higher Ed Non-Tenure-Track Faculty 9. Teacher—Secondary Level 10. Graduate Teaching, Admin, or Research Assistant (Master's Level) 13. Higher Ed Administrator in a program/unit not writing/literacy-related 11. Writing Center Director 12. Graduate Teaching, Admin, or Research Assistant (PhD level)
Participant C Tenure-line faculty; American Indian or Alaska Native, female, from a poor/working class background, age 55-64	**Participant D** Administrator within a writing/literacy-related unit; Latino/Hispanic/Spanish, male, from a poor/working poor background, age 65-74
1. Bachelor's Degree 2. Undergraduate Writing fellow, Tutor, or Consultant 3. Self-employed 4. Master's Degree 5. Graduate Teaching, Admin, or Research Assistant (Master's level) 6. Higher Ed Administrator in a program/unit not writing/literacy-related 7. Non-academic writer 8. Edited medical books, including one about diagnosis at the molecular level 9. Higher Ed Staff 10. Higher Ed Librarian 11. PhD 12. Training in using computers in composition 13. Higher Ed Non-tenure-Track Faculty 14. Higher Ed Tenured/Tenure-Track Faculty	1. Military, personnel clerk, short-order cook, computer operator (prior to the existence of personal computers) 2. Associate's Degree 3. Bachelor's Degree 4. Master's Degree 5. Graduate Teaching, Admin, or Research Assistant (Master's Level) 6. Graduate Teaching, Admin, or Research Assistant (PhD Level) 7. PhD 8. Higher Ed Tenured/Tenure-Track Faculty 9. Department Chair, Associate Dean, Director of American Studies 10. Higher Ed Administrator within a writing/literacy-related program/unit

Disciplinary Lifecycling Possibility 2: Allowing for Concurrent Applications of Disciplinary Knowledge Within and Across Spaces of Action

Lifecycling also offers an opportunity to recognize the cross-contextual mobility of RCWS disciplinary expertise, as well as the broader variability of spaces of action in which disciplinary expertise can be developed and applied. This provides an important contrast to a linear, single-minded focus on disciplinary activity only occurring within institutionally-recognized spaces of action (e.g., for our survey participants: institutions of postsecondary education, academic conferences, academic journals, etc.).

Demonstrating the wide-ranging applications of RCWS expertise, survey respondents often included in their chronologies those jobs which earned them income during the phases of undergraduate and graduate study. For example, a full-time community college staff member with teaching, administrative, and/or technological responsibilities (white, female, from a working-class background, age 55-64) describes her entrance into an RCWS career lifecycle after being nominated to be a writing tutor when she enrolled in her local community college at the age of 40. Before then, she had worked primarily in retail and as a medical receptionist, the latter of which continued to sustain her financially throughout her bachelor's and master's degree programs, until she eventually landed a full-time position as a writing center director. Another RCWS member, a tenure-line faculty member at a research university (white, male, from a working-class background, age 35-44) shared that he had worked as a private writing tutor during his PhD program, which "doubled" the income he earned as a graduate teaching assistant. From his personal experience, this respondent offered a hypothesis: "I expect that recent students in rhet/comp have expanded prolifically into the service (gig) economy of such affective labor."

Another way our survey respondents addressed the variation in the domains in which their expertise is valued was to provide counterevidence of the traditional distinction between academic and non-academic career paths. A doctorate-holding participant (white, non-binary, from a lower middle-class background, age 55-64) represented what they perceived to be a disciplinary overlap between two traditionally distinctive careers. This participant presented a career chronology that begins with the completion of a PhD program (which included teaching experience) followed by several years as a non-tenure-track faculty member at two different institutions. Eight years after earning their PhD, the respondent describes "return[ing] to my original field, being a liberation theologian/preacher/writer/minister in the Presbyterian Church, USA"—a line of work the respondent anticipated pursuing for "five to ten more years." Although the survey did not tell us precisely how the disciplinary intersections of these two fields of work—theology and writing studies—were experienced, we can see an alignment of interests across both fields within in their lifecycle, and we can imagine the possibility that skills, dispositions, and experiences of lifecycle phases are informed by, and carried outward into, other phases throughout the lifecycle. For example, although the respondent notes that they are no longer in a higher education context, they did indicate current engagement in activities that are not far-flung from traditional academic/RCWS work, including teaching, lecturing and speaking publicly, and "writing poetry, prose poems, and spiritual inspiration in published books, journals, and [a] spiritual/social justice blog." In this case, the application of writing or rhetorical expertise is not described as a means of financial necessity but rather as an integrative experience.

In another survey response, a tenure-line faculty member at a community college (white, male, from a lower-middle class background, age 65-74) described what the traditional career arc model would represent as two distinct career paths—yet, in actuality, the two career trajectories were co-dependent. Commissioned to the military in the early 1970s, this respondent explained that the US Army sponsored his master's degree so that he would be able to teach at West Point—which he did, on a part-time basis, while still active in the military. Retired from the Army after 27 years of service, the respondent spent three years "as a technical writer and adjunct" before shifting to full-time faculty positions, first at a regional master's institution and finally at a community college. The respondent plans to retire from teaching in "another year or two." In addition to challenging traditional visions of retirement, this respondent's account challenges the facile separation of "academic" and "non-academic" work, as the non-academic employer functioned as a sponsor and beneficiary of the academic trajectory of his career.

Disciplinary lifecycling encourages greater recognition of concurrence and multiplicity that is already common to RCWS careers and that may become more exigent for RCWS experts' career trajectories in the near future. Students who specialize in rhetoric, composition, and writing studies often enter positions that demand their expertise, but which may not be identifiable by a title that differentiates their *writing* expertise from other domains (social media developer, project manager, user experience specialist, etc.). By recognizing that RCWS disciplinary knowledge and labor realities do not always align in ways that acknowledge and promote the articulation of disciplinary identity development, the lifecycle framework can prompt participants to trace meaningful trajectories that acknowledge disciplinary knowledge and disciplinary labor within and beyond a singular employer.

Lifecycling Possibility #3: Creating the Possibility to Trace Typification Throughout Disciplinary Development

A lifecycle model not only creates space for variance in the timing and type of experiences that make up RCWS disciplinary development but also avoids the conflation of chronological age with developmental stage, as illustrated previously in figure 3. If career phases in RCWS mapped onto chronological age, then we might expect Participant D (table 2), who identified as being age 65-74, to have the highest number of phases in their career or to have experienced some traditionally prestigious phases that others of a lesser age have not. However, what we see in the survey results is that at varied ages, members of the disciplines are participating in a range of activities, which reinforces the inadequacy of an ages-and-stages-style ascension model and the continued need for a frame that acknowledges and affords disciplinary development throughout one's lifespan. The recognition that disciplinary development does not progress, start, or stop at predictable stages of a career or ages of a lifespan resists the tendency to dismiss later stages of the career—including retirement—as irrelevant, such that a perceived sense of "U-Turn" in mid-career, or a sense that disciplinary development must end at retirement, no longer holds. Such a shift in perspective aligns with interviews with retired members of RCWS who completed this survey, all of whom operated at a remove, either entirely or in certain particulars, from their pre-retirement academic institutions. Many retirees seek new spaces of action in which to apply and extend their disciplinary expertise and are able to extend their disciplinary identities into what would be considered non-academic sites, including political organizations, community reading groups, and even in grandparenting activities (Bowen and Pinkert 262).

Lifecycling affords opportunities to trace typification without ossifying as another ages-and-stages arc, which not only prescribes the stages, but also the timing of those stages over a lifespan. Identifying the typified experiences emerging across multiple trajectories yields, we think, two important opportunities: (1) to identify phases—like retirement and self-employment—that are common but are, as of yet, underrepresented in the field's scholarly and professional development agendas; and (2) to trace the shifting morphology of RCWS careers over time, amid changing spaces of action.

Reinventing Our Conceptions of the Career in RCWS Through Disciplinary Lifecycling

If we aim to recognize more fully the realities of intellectual labor within RCWS, reinventing our conceptions of the career through the metaphor of the lifecycle is not just possible but necessary. George Lakoff and Mark Johnson's *Metaphors We Live By* argues that metaphors are "not just a matter . . . of mere words" but reflect and reify cultural conceptual systems (6). Jonathan Alexander, Karen Lunsford, and Carl Whithaus have recently argued for "an analysis of the dominant metaphors of a given field of study" to consider how such metaphors operate as Burkean "terministic screens" that "*determine* and condition how scholars are approaching, understanding, and analyzing their objects of study" (107). Nedra Reynolds enacts such careful examination of dominant spatial metaphors in composition, such as locating the teaching and researching of writing in contact zones, at the boundary, or on the frontier, or lamenting the location of composition in the trenches, at the margins, or even in the basement (28). Such metaphors, however, not only determine how we perceive our discipline (as Reynolds notes) and how we perceive our objects of study (as Alexander et al. note) but also how we perceive ourselves and others as disciplinary experts—and, in turn, how we enact our career trajectories and support the career trajectories of others. We believe that visual and spatial metaphors have played a crucial role in our discourse on disciplinary development: the career arc haunts and constrains how careers in rhetoric, composition, and writing studies are theorized, enacted, and supported.

In terms of theorizing RCWS careers, the shift away from the linear, ascension-emphasizing career arc toward the lifecycling frame recognizes that disciplinary/intellectual development must be oriented within a lifespan perspective that is life-long and life-wide—that is, across domains and contexts—up to and including multiple generations (Dippre and Phillips 6). This imperative isn't just for those who spend their careers in places other than the academy (e.g., technical writers or copyeditors) but also for those who labor in spaces traditionally conceived of as academic or educational because rhetorical expertise is developed and applied across such boundaries, and lifecycling is aimed at marking individual regeneration through disciplinary knowledge-making activity wherever it occurs. We see great possibility for further theorization of the regenerative nature of lifecycling and the interconnectedness of generations, which aligns with our disciplinary understandings of writing, research, teaching, administration, service, activism, and so on as means of creating opportunities for future individuals and activities.

New ways of envisioning careers, we contend, support new possibilities for individuals to enact them. Even before the pandemic, shifting realities of intellectual labor in institutions of higher education—in which the age of austerity and retrenchment presses postsecondary writing programs to "make do with less" (Scott and Welch 5)—are already rendering some privileged academic spaces of action less accessible in the short-term and less sustainable in the long-term. In a field in which a high percentage of members already develop and apply expertise in contingent positions, the neoliberal privatization and destabilization of higher education have significant consequences for RCWS career paths. Alongside other crucial responses, including resistance through labor equity advocacy (Kahn et al.) and adaptation through forging multi- and interdisciplinary institutional relationships (Matzen and Abraham), we propose disciplinary lifecycling as a metaphor that makes possible a new vision for careers in RCWS (and beyond) that responds to the disciplinary knowledge and labor realities of our field.

Consider two data points, likely familiar to readers of *Composition Studies*: (1) According to State Higher Education Finance data, the proportion of US public higher education institutions' revenues coming from student tuition (called "student share") has increased from 20.9% in 1980 to almost 50% in 2019, as states become less and less invested in supporting higher education as a public good. Historically, student share rises during periods of economic recession and levels off afterward but does not return to pre-recession proportions (SHEEO); (2) The 2020-2021 hiring season for faculty positions in Rhetoric, Composition, and Technical Communication marks a historic low, with listings down by more than half from the previous hiring season (Ridolfo). Exemplified in these two trends is a clear exigence for those who seek academic positions, in particular: individuals who are entering the discipline will need to be both proactive and nimble in their enactments of disciplinary identity, as the institutions (environments) to which the work of the field is traditionally attached continue to narrow access to the spaces of action in which transformative disciplinary development can occur. Moreover, the changes in landscape—shifts away from singular employers, institutionalized markers of prestige, and predictable chronologies—aren't characteristic only of those working in education but are also experienced by writing and rhetoric experts who work across a range of contexts (Tigar; Kahn). Given our participants' backgrounds, this article has focused on lifecycling's possibilities for RCWS members working in educational/academic contexts, but the disciplinary lifecycling model, which recenters career development on relationships to the discipline rather than employing institutions, may yield important ways to conceive of disciplinary development across RCWS career tracks that have been traditionally differentiated not by the kinds of expertise needed within them but by the perceived academic or professional environments in which they were performed.

The shift from institution to discipline necessitates, in turn, a shift in how members of the discipline support one another. We believe that lifecycling can point the way toward career development practices that are more responsive to the current and future realities of disciplinary labor. When viewed from a lifecycling standpoint, development can and must include closer attention to typified phases that are currently under-represented. Further, lifecycling and corresponding research efforts can shift focus productively away from traditional emphasis on currently-less-common, privileged phases and their related microcycles and instead build a career path vision that acknowledges, recognizes, and values common phases more fully. Lifecycling will not eliminate the pressures exerted by the institutions in which we enact our disciplinary knowledge, perform disciplinary activities, and, in cases of employment, draw our incomes; but it can help us to challenge the values of those institutions as the status quo for measuring career success and development.

Finally, our shift away from a focus on the institutions to the discipline leads us to consider the generative work lifecycling can do beyond traditional boundaries. What spaces of action currently elide our view? How might we support members of RCWS across a greater range of domains? In considering such questions, RCWS can be open to fundamental pragmatic changes in how we mentor, recruit, promote, and recognize members of our field—changes that, we believe, would lead to more inclusive and equitable career development within the discipline.

Notes

1. Participants were recruited through e-mail announcements on disciplinary listservs such as the ATTW-L, WPA-L, WAC-L, WCenter-L, and ARWS-L and through flyers at disciplinary conferences such as CCCC.

2. Tenure-line is used to describe both tenured and tenure-earning respondents.

Works Cited

Alexander, Jonathan, et al. "Toward Wayfinding: A Metaphor for Understanding Writing Experiences." *Written Communication*, vol. 37, no. 1, 2020, pp. 104-131, doi.org/10.1177/0741088319882325.

Ballif, Michelle, et al., editors. *Women's Ways of Making It in Rhetoric and Composition*. Routledge, 2008, doi.org/10.4324/9780203929841.

Banks, Adam J. *Race, Rhetoric, and Technology: Searching for Higher Ground*. Lawrence Erlbaum, 2006, doi.org/10.4324/9781410617385.

Botex, Sharieka, et al. "Academic #BlackLivesMatter: Black Faculty and Graduate Students Tell Their Stories." *Constellations*, no. 3, 2020, constell8cr.com/issue-3/academic-blacklivesmatter-black-faculty-and-graduate-students-tell-their-stories/.

Bowen, Lauren Marshall. "Age Identity and Literacy." *enculturation*, no. 31, 2020. enculturation.net/age_identity_and_literacy.

Bowen, Lauren Marshall, and Laurie A. Pinkert. "Identities Developed, Identities Denied: Examining the Disciplinary Activities and Disciplinary Positioning of Retirees in Rhetoric, Composition, and Writing Studies." *College Composition and Communication*, vol. 72, no. 2, 2020, pp. 251-281.

Bruner, Jerome. "The Narrative Construction of Reality." *Critical Inquiry*, vol. 18, no. 1, 1991, pp. 1-21, doi.org/10.1086/448619.

Cole, Thomas R. *The Journey of Life: A Cultural History of Aging in America*. Cambridge UP, 1992.

Cucciarre, Christine Peters, et al. "Mothers' Ways of Making It—or Making Do? Making (Over) Academic Lives in Rhetoric and Composition with Children." *Composition Studies*, vol. 39, no. 1, 2011, pp. 41-61, compositionstudiesjournal. files.wordpress.com/2019/02/39n1.pdf.

Danberg, Robert. "On (Not) Making It in Rhetoric and Composition." *Composition Studies*, vol. 39, no. 1, 2011, pp. 63-72, compositionstudiesjournal.files.wordpress.com/2019/02/39n1.pdf.

Devine, William F. "Carpetbagging Coach's Last Lesson." *Inside Higher Ed*, 10 Jan. 2014, www.insidehighered.com/views/2014/01/10/penn-state-coachs-departure-evidence-college-sports-exploitation-essay.

Dippre, Ryan J., and Talinn Phillips, editors. *Approaches to Lifespan Writing Research: Generating an Actionable Coherence.* WAC Clearinghouse/UP of Colorado, 2020. wac.colostate.edu/books/perspectives/lifespan/.

Freytag, Gustav. *Freytag's Technique of the Drama: An Exposition of Dramatic Composition and Art.* Translated by Elias J. MacEwan, Scott, Foresman, & Co., 1900. *Internet Archive,* archive.org/details/freytagstechniqu00freyuoft.

Goodburn, Amy, et al., editors. *Rewriting Success in Rhetoric and Composition Careers.* Parlor Press, 2013.

Hanson, Alex. "Career Killer Survival Kit: Centering Single Mom Perspectives in Composition and Rhetoric." *Composition Studies,* vol. 48, no. 1, 2020, pp. 34-52. compositionstudiesjournal.files.wordpress.com/2020/06/hanson.pdf.

Henkel, Mary. "Academic Identity and Autonomy Revisited." *Governing Knowledge: A Study of Continuity and Change in Higher Education: A Festschrift in Honour of Maurice Kogan,* edited by Ivar Bleiklie and Mary Henkel, Springer Netherlands, 2005, pp. 145–65. doi.org/10.1007/1-4020-3504-7_10.

Irwin, Neil. "The Pandemic Depression Is Over: The Pandemic Recession Has Just Begun." *New York Times.* 3 Oct. 2020, www.nytimes.com/2020/10/03/upshot/pandemic-economy-recession.html.

Kahn, Faisal. "How Is the Gig Economy Changing the Future Jobs Landscape: The Global Economy Is Changing with the Changing Demographics." *Medium.* 18 Dec. 2018, medium.com/technicity/how-is-the-gig-economy-changing-the-future-jobs-landscape-bd032a26f737.

Khan, Seth, et al., editors. *Contingency, Exploitation, and Solidarity: Labor and Action in English Composition.* WAC Clearinghouse/UP of Colorado, 2017. wac.colostate.edu/books/perspectives/contingency/.

Kelsky, Karen. "The Professor Is In: Stranded on the Academic Job Market This Year?" *Chronicle of Higher Education.* 17 Apr. 2020, www.chronicle.com/article/the-professor-is-in-stranded-on-the-academic-job-market-this-year/

Lakoff, George, and Mark Johnson. *Metaphors We Live By.* 1980. U of Chicago P, 2003.

Marquez, Loren. "Narrating Our Lives: Retelling Mothering and Professional Work in Composition Studies." *Composition Studies,* vol. 39, no. 1, 2011, pp. 73-85. compositionstudiesjournal.files.wordpress.com/2019/02/39n1.pdf.

Matzen, Richard N., and Matthew Abraham, editors. *Weathering the Storm: Independent Writing Programs in the Age of Fiscal Austerity.* UP of Colorado / Utah State UP, 2019. doi.org/10.7330/9781607328957.

Meyer, Jan H. F., and Ray Land. *Overcoming Barriers to Student Understanding: Threshold Concepts and Troublesome Knowledge.* Routledge, 2006.

Mirabelli, Tony. "Learning to Serve: The Language and Literacy of Food Service Workers." *What They Don't Learn in School: Literacy in the Lives of Urban Youth,* edited by Jabari Mahiri, Peter Lang, 2004, pp. 143-162.

National Academy of Sciences, National Academy of Engineering, and Institute of Medicine. *The Arc of the Academic Research Career: Issues and Implications for U.S. Science and Engineering Leadership: Summary of a Workshop.* National Academies P, 2014. doi.org/10.17226/18627.

O'Neill, Peggy. "U-Turns, Pivots, and Gradual Arrivals: Navigating Midlife and Mid-Career in Academe's Changing Landscape." *WPA: Writing Program Administration*, vol. 40, no. 2, 2017, pp. 174-179.

Perlmutter, David D. "Teaching the 101." *The Chronicle of Higher Education*, 8 Sept. 2004, www.chronicle.com/article/teaching-the-101/.

Perryman-Clark, Staci, and Collin Lamont Craig, editors. *Black Perspectives in Writing Program Administration: From the Margins to the Center*. NCTE, 2019.

Reynolds, Nedra. *Geographies of Writing: Inhabiting Places and Encountering Difference*. Southern Illinois UP, 2004.

Ridolfo, Jim. "Market Comparison." *Rhet Map: Mapping Rhetoric and Composition*. 2021, rhetmap.org/market-comparison/.

Segran, Elizabeth. "What Can You Do with a Humanities Ph.D., Anyway?" *The Atlantic*, 31 Mar. 2014, www.theatlantic.com/business/archive/2014/03/what-can-you-do-with-a-humanities-phd-anyway/359927/.

State Higher Education Executive Officers Association (SHEEO). *State Higher Education Finance (SHEF) Report: AY 2019*, shef.sheeo.org/report/.

Stober, Katharyn L. "Why You Should Job Search Like a Runner." *Inside Higher Ed*, 17 Jul. 2017, www.insidehighered.com/advice/2017/07/17/practical-tips-improving-performance-and-building-endurance-runner-also-apply-job.

Scott, Tony, and Nancy Welch. Introduction. *Composition in the Age of Austerity*, edited by Nancy Welch and Tony Scott, Utah State UP, 2016, pp. 3-20.

Tigar, Lindsay. "The Evolving Role of Writers in the Gig Economy: Growing Your Freelancing Skill Set (1 of 5)" *ClearVoice*. 7 Feb 2019, www.clearvoice.com/blog/evolving-role-of-writers-in-the-gig-economy/.

Yachnin, Paul. "Humanities PhD Grads with Non-academic Jobs Could Shake Up University Culture." *The Conversation*, 7 Jan. 2020, theconversation.com/humanities-phd-grads-working-in-non-academic-jobs-could-shake-up-university-culture-127298.

Cross Postings: Disciplinary Knowledge-Making and the Affective Archive of the WPA Listserv

Zachary Beare

As the future of the WPA Listserv (WPA-L) remains uncertain, this article reflects on the ways the WPA-L has functioned as an important site of disciplinary knowledge-making and emotion work for the field of composition studies. It examines the potential of the listserv format for democratizing participation in the enterprise of disciplinary knowledge-making and examines how perspectives and lifeworlds of a diverse field have come into contact on the platform. Such a dynamic showcases tensions, ongoing dialogue, and emotionally felt perspectives not often visible in (or sometimes erased from) traditional sites of scholarly publication.

On April 28, 2021, Barry Maid, the longtime administrator of the WPA Listserv (WPA-L) wrote to the list announcing that upon (or shortly before) his retirement on May 15, 2021, all listserv operations and posting privileges would be (at least temporarily) suspended. This unexpected announcement occurred at a turbulent time in the listserv's history. Many had been questioning the usefulness of the platform and some had already suggested dissolving it entirely, arguing the hostility, racism, and sexism exhibited on the listserv left it unredeemable. Over the last several years, I have seen the WPA-L referred to on Twitter and Facebook as, among other things, "a dumpster fire," "a car crash you can't look away from," and "an irredeemable cesspool of everything that is toxic in the academy." I understand where these characterizations come from and why so many have questioned whether the listserv could remain a productive site of conversation and resource sharing. Like many others, I have been shocked and infuriated by messages and conversational turns that have taken place in heated threads. I am thinking, for instance, about the discussion of Vershawn Ashanti Young's CFP for the 2019 Conference on College Composition and Communication that (d)evolved into a debate over the legitimacy of codeswitching and codemeshing; about Michelle LaFrance's brave calling out of a culture of mansplaining on the listserv and the clumsy, sexist commentary that resisted her apt charge; and about the shouting match about Heterodoxy and whether rhetoric and composition as a field suffers from a lack of viewpoint diversity that inspired dozens of messages in early 2019. I am also thinking about the terrifying moment in which an anonymous user going by the name "Grand Scholar Wizard" wrote in to the list. Not only did this anonymous troll dismiss the significance of points being made by scholars of color as they engaged in a dialogue about issues raised in Asao Inoue's 2019 CCCC Chair's Address, this person did so under a moniker clearly inspired by racist and white supremacist rhetorics. These and similar threads have been examined, both directly and indirectly, in several recent publications, including in a *CCC* article by Marnie Twigg, a symposium in *Writing Program Administration* edited by Michelle LaFrance and Elizabeth Wardle, and in a book chapter by John Trimbur. These threads were also discussed extensively in a "Where We Are" dialogue published in *Composition Studies* in fall of 2019 between the recently-formed WPA-L Working Group and founders of the nextGEN listserv. While there was clear overlap in the philosophies of these groups, their responses could be read as a tension between reformers and revolutionaries, the former who sought to remedy the many problems of the WPA-L and the latter who suggested an exit and new build would be more appropriate and safer for many.

I saw the appeal of both of these responses. I read the threads inspiring these reactions—and the backchannel commentaries about them across social media—with great interest. I have been thinking about the listserv and its disciplinary functions for several years. While I understand why these moments inspired some to unsubscribe and to dismiss the value of the listserv entirely, these moments, rough as they were, further cemented my belief that the WPA-L should be seen as an important archive of disciplinary knowledge-making, one warranting further attention. To be clear, this article is not an apologia for the listserv or the many members who have rightly been called out for their complicity in systems of racism and sexism in its threads; rather, it is a rumination on the types of knowledge and experience that could be encoded and archived through a digital platform that, at least theoretically, allowed a broader cross section of the discipline equal voice and opportunity for contribution. Specifically, I argue the listserv has functioned as an archive of affects, an archive of the felt impressions and vibrating emotional intensities surrounding the field's work and the experiences of its members.

The WPA-L as a Site of Disciplinary Communication and Knowledge Making

It is strangely difficult to research the extant scholarship on the WPA-L, because while there has been very little scholarly work focused specifically on the listserv, the platform and its conversations are referenced across hundreds of articles, book chapters, and monographs, most often as a site of invention or inspiration. Scholars discuss conversations on the WPA-L that motivated or supported their inquiries and the developments of their projects. In its twenty-eight-year history, the WPA-L has served as an invaluable resource not only for writing program administrators but also for teachers and scholars of composition and rhetoric at all levels and from all institutional contexts who have used the space to dialogue about issues of the discipline. The WPA-L has been a central clearinghouse for disseminating CFPs for conferences, special issues, and edited collections; for advertising jobs, programs, workshops, and events; for distributing surveys and recruiting research participants; and for gaining, sharing, and making knowledge. In perhaps the only piece of published scholarship to examine knowledge-making on the WPA-L, Huiling Ding utilized a grounded approach to analyze posts from October of 2005 and identified nine categories of knowledge-making activities regularly occurring on the listserv. Ding writes, "the notable content generated via the list identifies this technology-mediated communication as a valid platform for intellectual contribution and innovation, in doing so expanding concepts of scholarly knowledge making as formal only" (118). Ding showcases the importance of informal knowledge-making taking place on the list, especially with the sharing of personal experience. Ding, however, does not consider the affective context shaping and performed through that work, which is also archived on the list. Examining the WPA-L archive reveals that knowledge-making is not just informal, tacit, and experiential; it is also emotionally loaded and felt, shaped by the affective contexts surrounding and inspired by the work.

After all, during its nearly three decades, the WPA-L has functioned as a site of conversation and community building. Members of the list celebrate promotions and publications, they mourn the deaths of scholars in the field, and they engage in storytelling about their personal and professional lives. It might be easy to forget this now in the age of social media and constant connection, but historically, these emotionally loaded relational functions of the listserv have been important for the field of composition and rhetoric because, as so many of our disciplinary histories have argued (Crowley, S. Miller, North), the short history of the field has regularly been marked by experiences of marginalization and struggles for legitimacy. These emotional experiences shape the work. Additionally, because practitioners in the field have often been isolated as the only (or one of only a few) composition and rhetoric specialist(s) in their home departments and because many in the field increasingly lack access to conferences (or sometimes even access to journals) due to funding constraints, institutional locations or adjunct or contingent statuses, the WPA-L has often been an essential way for individuals to find allies and advocates and to feel connected to the discipline and its current conversations, research, and political objectives.

The WPA-L archive is a unique site to study because it is one of the only places where one can witness members of the discipline respond to and dialogue about issues en masse and in time. In the listserv archives, one can go back and read the emotional responses to elections, to the 9/11 terrorists attacks, to natural disasters, and to a whole host of cultural and disciplinary events. These conversations on the WPA-L are fascinating because the back-and-forth communication allows one to see numerous voices literally *in conversation*, and through that conversation, to see ideas developed, revised, confronted, contradicted, dismissed, and even attacked. With such a conversational dynamic, one is able to occasionally witness ruptures and breakdowns in the disciplinary civility typically characterizing published accounts of the field. These emotionally charged moments afford glimpses into the felt-realities of listserv participants and allow readers to witness theoretical discussions and generalizations about the field come into sharp contrast with the material circumstances and personal narratives of specific members of that field. Additionally, these listserv discussions are important for the field to confront because, in many ways, they have been the most open and publicly accessible accounts and representations of its field. Unlike the disciplinary conversations taking place behind the journal subscription paywalls of our field's publications or in the air-conditioned meeting rooms of our field's increasingly unaffordable conferences, the WPA-L and its archives have been freely and publicly accessible to anyone with an internet connection.

Just what counts as disciplinary knowledge-making in the field of composition and rhetoric has long been a contentious issue, one inspiring debates about what exactly "scholarly activity" looks like. These debates are often connected to larger conflicts about the purpose of the discipline. Often, this debate comes down to a tension between seeing composition and rhetoric as a pedagogically focused discipline and seeing it as a theory-building enterprise with an empirical research agenda. This is, of course, a false binary, but it has remained a tension active on the WPA-L. Each vision inspired conversation threads, and the varied perspectives often came to a head in heated moments on the listserv.

While the suggestion that the field's focus should extend beyond the domains of practice and pedagogy need not necessarily construct a hierarchy where pedagogy is positioned as the less significant form of intellectual work, that pattern often is inscribed, especially in the ways forms of intellectual work are rewarded with economic incentives and also with other forms of capital like publication, community prestige, and, of course, tenure and promotion. Such a division is even more fraught when considering its connections to issues of labor and institutional location, further dividing non-tenure track members and tenure track members of the field, and further separating the teaching-oriented work of both tenure and non-tenure track two-year institution faculty from the work of research and theory-building expected of tenure-track university faculty. These divisions have been further magnified in the rather dismal employment landscape of today's academy, where "full- and part-time adjuncts, graduate students, and postdoctoral fellows account for well over three fourths of all faculty appointments" (Schmidt). And a recent MLA report shows that closer to our own disciplinary home, "60 percent of faculty in English Department work off the tenure track" and "in two-year colleges, the figure rises to approach 80 percent of English instructors." In such an environment, the division between the practice-oriented pedagogical vision of the field and the theoretical and empirical research visions of the field become entangled in questions of privilege, access to resources, and employment security.

In *Constructing Knowledges*, Sidney I. Dobrin posits that "the debate [between theory and practice] emerges from a young field attempting to establish its identity. It is a political, philosophical issue, an issue . . . of where one stands. This becomes political and philosophical in that individual participants in the field must determine how the debate affects their participation—what knowledge they privilege" (26). The problem with Dobrin's characterization is its implication that both sides exist on a level playing field, and wherever "one stands," one might be able to be heard (and heard in a way that is counted and legitimized). In fact, this debate is more complicated. It is not just a problem of how to define the field; it is also a question of who gets to decide how it is defined and where such definitional work gets to be done, a question of who we remember to involve in these discussions. The very positionality of individuals in relation to this debate can sometimes prevent them from being a part of the conversation about what knowledge is privileged, especially in restricted locations of disciplinary discourse (like the pages of the field's academic journals). This makes examination of these debates on (at least slightly) more open, diverse, and democratic platforms like the WPA-L important. As Holly Hassel and Joanne Baird Giordano have argued in "Occupy Writing Studies: Rethinking College Composition of the Needs of the Teaching Majority," "not enough has been said in scholarly conversations about marginalization of open-admission and two-year campuses from professional dialogues even though such campuses are sites of engaging and essential work where almost half of all college students start their postsecondary educations" (117-118). Hassel and Giordano demonstrate convincingly that peer-review practices shaping participation in official platforms of disciplinary knowledge-making—whether in publication or presentations at the national conference of the field— often disadvantage two-year specialists. Even conferences—sites of disciplinary knowledge-making typically thought of as more open and accessible to individuals than the publications of the field—are found to be exclusionary in their study. At the time Hassel and Giordano published their article, they point out that of the 184 proposal reviewers named in the program for the

Conference on College Composition and Communication, only 4 (2%) were from two-year campuses.

The marginalization of teaching-focused members of the discipline is, of course, not a new problem. Speaking over 30 years ago (and relying on a problematic metaphor of indigeneity), Stephen M. North began his *The Making of Knowledge in Composition* by directly addressing the conversation about who is granted the right to speak and who has been silenced in debates about disciplinary identity and purpose:

> Composition has grown tremendously—has, really, *become* a field. But while this growth has been exciting, it has often seemed chaotic and patternless as well, and has had . . . major liabilities. The first is that the new investigators have tended to trample roughshod over the claims of previous inquirers, especially the 'indigenous' population that I will call the Practitioners. In other words, much of what especially teachers, and to lesser extent writers, have claimed to know about writing has been ignored, discounted, or ridiculed—so that, despite their overwhelming majority, they have been effectively disenfranchised as knowledge-makers in their own field. (3)

I want to be clear that I condemn the overly casual parallel North constructs between indigenous populations and practitioners, especially reading his words now, at a moment when the discipline is reckoning with ongoing marginalization of BIPOC scholars in our own field. However, North's language of disenfranchisement is important, for it points to the way a majority of disciplinary members are not often granted the power, privilege, or access to share their knowledge or to take part in the shaping and defining of the field in ways that are recognized (a problem continuing today). Though organizations like CCCC, NCTE, CWPA, and others have articulated commitments to represent the voices and interests of members of the profession whose primary role is to teach, a look at the individuals leading such organizations and a look at who is published—and even afforded the ability to present at conferences—reveals that there remains a major problem of representation. As North argued decades ago, and as Hassel and Giordano demonstrate more recently, the "overwhelming majority" remains too often left out of the (more legitimized sites of) conversation. Thus, it is crucial to investigate parallel sites of disciplinary knowledge-making and conversation where a wider array of voices have been able to actively participate, platforms like the WPA-L. It is also crucial to consider how this broader disciplinary history shapes the emotional context and content of the conversations in these potentially more democratic venues.

Indeed, frustrations with what is privileged in official spaces of disciplinary knowledge making and tensions between research and practice regularly have erupted on the listserv in ways that reveal the affects shaping these conversations and the individually felt experiences of individuals. In fact, I see these tensions at play in many of the recent heated threads on the WPA-L. Given the still-heightened emotions surrounding those threads, though, perhaps turning to a slightly older example would be useful. In March of 2015, a thread emerged on the WPA-L responding to Adam Banks's CCCC Chair's Address entitled "Funk, Flight, Freedom." The WPA-L's discussion of Banks's address began relatively innocuously. Participants discussed the emotional impact of the talk and began unpacking its implications, especially Banks's call to "retire" the essay as the dominant genre we teach. At the same time, though, a parallel, more heated conversation developed questioning the very premise of the initial conversation—the premise that the essay (and print-based prose of students more broadly) continues to be a key form and intellectual concern of the field of composition and rhetoric. This was challenged early in the discussion in a response from Fredrik deBoer, the most active thread contributor (both in terms of number of messages and numbers of words). At that time of this discussion, deBoer was completing his PhD at Purdue University and was on the academic job market. deBoer responded to the discussion, explaining, "I was surprised to see so many react to the speech on Twitter as a call for the field to abandon the essay as a principal [sic] intellectual concern. That abandonment happened long ago. After all, how many panels at that very conference had anything to do with the essay, or with writing instruction in general?" (deBoer "Re: Video of Banks' Talk?"). DeBoer's responses to the thread focused on what he saw as a disciplinary move away from print-based composition and writing pedagogy, a move that unfairly disadvantaged doctoral students like himself who have focused on such work. In this moment—when deBoer had just been on the job market—the listserv functioned as an outlet for him to express his frustrations with the field and to speak back to the very people that might (or might not) have been hiring him, an opportunity graduate students on the market are typically not afforded.

deBoer's assertions were, of course, rightly challenged by several other listserv contributors, who pointed to the substantial body of scholarship in the flagship journals of the field that is focused on student writing and writing instruction. Kathleen Yancey, who at that time was relatively fresh from her tenure as editor of *College Composition and Communication* and thus had a personal stake in this conversation and deBoer's controversial charge, provided probably the most direct rebuttal to deBoer's argument, calling it "a pretty large overstatement" and then providing a list of articles that had appeared in *CCC* in the previous years as a counter to his assertions.

Outside of the listserv, deBoer's claims have also been refuted by empirically-based research projects, perhaps most notably by Benjamin Miller's dissertation *The Making of Knowledge-Makers in Composition,* an ambitious project examining 2,711 dissertations in composition and rhetoric published between 2001 and 2010. Miller specifically references deBoer's listserv claims about the lack of dissertations in the field focused on student writing and writing instruction. Counter to this assertion, Miller reveals dissertations centered on the teaching of writing actually accounted for the largest cluster of texts in his large study (nearly one-third). Miller discusses the significance of his findings in relation to the comments from deBoer:

> Needless to say, heated email messages are not often known for their high standards of evidence; they are not refereed articles, and deBoer and others may have been simply glib in declaring the presence or absence of certain dissertation topics. Even so, claims like this were repeated and repeatedly grounded only in anecdote. My study, and future distant reading projects like it, provide a means of checking anecdotal impressions against a wider scope, rendering them either falsifiable or defensible. (70)

While it might be tempting to use research from scholars like Miller to simply dismiss and then disregard the arguments of deBoer in this listserv thread (or even to disregard the value of platforms like the listserv), I would argue that Miller's words help highlight an important function of the listserv as an archive of disciplinary knowledge-making. It is an archive of those "anecdotal impressions," those felt claims that might not survive the referee process. And those "anecdotal impressions" have impacts. They give a window into the feelings of the discipline or at least the feelings of members of the discipline. This is important and something worth paying attention to, for it might help us consider and think about how we relate to one another within this field, how and why divisions develop, and how we might better understand the psychological and emotional dimensions of the discursive and professional landscapes we traverse.

While these emotionally charged debates might be read as disciplinary problems, others have argued that such debates about knowledge-making are central to the discipline's success, rapid growth, and even core identity. In *Constructing Knowledges,* Dobrin argues that "in order for rhetoric and composition (or any field, for that matter) to evolve, debates concerning useful knowledge must proliferate" (19). Dobrin positions the debates within the field of composition and rhetoric as dramatically different from those of other disciplines, arguing that our field, unlike others, is at its most productive when it does not reach any sort of consensus or resolution. Near the end of his book, Dobrin makes this point even more firmly, arguing that "as composition has searched for identity among this transformative amalgam of knowledge and within the academy, the theory debates have produced many advances in the field's recent and rapid evolution" (155-156). Even a cursory look at the dynamic and often heated nature of the WPA-L conversations illustrates that these ongoing debates have remained a characteristic of the life of the discipline. And if, as Dobrin argues, this sort of antagonistic theory-building is central to the field's evolution and distinctive disciplinary identity, then disciplinary sites like the WPA-L are imperative to study because the nature of the medium facilitates such back-and-forth dialogue.

If debate about identity and knowledge without resolution is, in fact, our field's mandate and a key feature of its success and identity as a discipline, the question becomes how such work should be conducted. Dobrin argues that since "the *debate* has become crucial for all scholars on all sides" that "the responsible position compositionists [should] take in this debate is not one of moderator, not one of having answers, but one of teachers and scholars who must participate in practice and who must engage that practice through theory" (26). Thus, Dobrin suggests that compositionists need to engage in practices of genuine inquiry, continually participating in conversations about and reflecting on their practices and conceptions of the discipline. Dobrin helps to explain the importance of such work in his earlier discussion of the nature of theory:

> Most often theory is organic, receptive to new observations, additional facts, further speculation. Theory accounts for experience and allows new experience to alter or contribute to the evolution of that theory. Theory provides a framework within which one can operate, ask questions, even alter or refine principles of that theory based on new experience, new observation. That is, theory does not allow itself to stagnate. It pushes and pulls its way to understanding how a set of phenomena, a field, a body of knowledge, operates. (8-9)

I like Dobrin's account of organic theory-building and knowledge-making because it so closely resembles how really good conversations in the WPA-L archives progress. In those moments, queries are sent out, and they are met with narratives of experience and citations of research and existing theory. Individuals come together, wrestle with ideas, and share resources. And importantly, the participants in these conversations are diverse, coming at posed questions from a range of institutional contexts and perspectives, allowing more disciplinary stakeholders to participate in the knowledge-production of the field, not just those whose job titles specifically position them as "scholars" or "researchers." Then, in light of what is shared, original posters and responders alter and refine their ideas, often rethinking their positions. In such moments, you see individuals push on, resist, and expand their ideas and the ideas of the discipline in light of other voices.

Who Gets to Author a Discipline? (And Who Doesn't?)

Still, the type of in-time and actively dialogic knowledge-making and theory-building found in the listserv archives is not what is usually imagined when one thinks about official histories and narratives of field, and it is important to question why this is, to consider the forces shaping whose voices are invited, recorded, heard, archived, and remembered and to explore the politics behind who gets to author a discipline and, perhaps more importantly, who doesn't. It might be more accurate to talk about the "politics" of these issues as political economies and material conditions that shape access, membership, status, power, and (abilities to make) contributions to the discursive landscapes of the discipline. In *Terms of Work for Composition*, Bruce Horner reflects on the material realities enabling and constraining participation in authorized forms of disciplinary knowledge-production. Drawing on A. Suresh Canagarajah, Horner argues that "while scholars have long recognized the 'sociality' of scholarly 'knowledge-production,' they have typically ignored the material constraints on such production" (223).

Horner makes clear that the ability to participate in disciplinary knowledge-making (at least in traditionally legitimized ways) is, largely, a function of privilege, and specifically privilege mediated by material realities, arguing quite convincingly that "lack of the availability to meet these 'nondiscursive' requirements makes it difficult for scholars to materially produce, send, and have their writing read by journals and publishers" (224). Horner calls on the field to recognize and confront the significance of "the small percentage of the field's membership represented by the authorship of published essays and the lopsided (over two to one) ratio of male to female authors in scholarly journals" (225). And in addition to the troubling gender disparity that Horner points to, we should also be cognizant of the lack of representation of scholars of color, contingent faculty, and faculty in non-research roles.

Especially important for my work in this article, Horner's text also showcases how our failure to attend to material realities shaping participation in official spaces of disciplinary knowledge-making both emerges from and further contributes to a product-based mindset. Horner describes this as a "commodified view of scholarship" and theory-making (225). Theory and knowledge, thus, become treated as consumable products rather than as generative and dynamic processes of idea-building. Perhaps this provides some explanation of why we might not ordinarily think about conversations from the WPA-L archives as knowledge-making and theory-building; their ongoing, in-process nature feels counter to our typically commodified and product-based conceptions of such work.

A more typical product-based conceptualization of disciplinary knowledge-making is illustrated in projects such as Maureen Daly Goggin's *Authoring a Discipline*, which looks to the more exclusive and legitimized sites of knowledge-making (in her case, the major journals in the field) as a means of conducting disciplinary historiography. Given the fact that only a small percentage of the field publishes in scholarly journals, though, her choice in methodology, likely inadvertently, furthers the marginalization of some members of the field, neglecting entire segments of the discipline. Her project also continues to work under the type of product-focused conceptualization of knowledge-making that scholars like Horner have troubled.

Goggin "show[s] how journals, as one legitimating instrument of disciplinarity, function in a dialectical relation with a discipline" (xiv), explaining she elected to study journals and editors because they "provide an important window on disciplinary discursive practices" (xv). Further, Goggin argues journals function as one of the most important gatekeeping mechanisms of the field and play a central role in determining which avenues of inquiry, methodologies of investigation, and forms of scholarship are valued and centered in the field's attention. I certainly agree with Goggin's claims about the importance of journals in shaping a discipline, but I wish she did more to reflect on the *problems* of that reality. Moreover, though I admire Goggin's interest in "how journals . . . function in dialectical relation with the discipline" (xiv), it seems difficult to do that work, when, as Horner argues, so many disciplinary voices and perspectives are not represented in the pages of journals.

This problem seems doubly troubling given Goggin's decision to exclude from her analysis journals focused on specific subject areas or those journals with missions focused on serving narrower audiences or research/pedagogy areas in the profession. Goggin gives as examples journals focused on the work of writing center specialists or those teaching at two-year colleges as those that were excluded from analysis. Given that writing center professionals and two-year college teachers continue to be marginalized within our already-marginalized discipline, her choice inevitably skews the image of the "discipline" and its relation to the scholarly journals she studies. Goggins' argument for looking at "journals created to serve a broad and diverse readership on a wide range of topics" seems to be hinged on a conception of the field as diverse but which still sees itself as a cohesive community, and that sort of community mindset can blind one to divisions, tensions, and marginalizing practices within groups (xvi).

The actual tensions, debates, and sometimes emotion-filled shouting matches that have taken place on the WPA-L help resist overly simplistic conceptualizations of the discipline as a cohesive community on which product-focused conceptions of knowledge-making like Goggin's tend to rely. This, paired with the in-time and in-relation-to-others theory-building that has occurred on the WPA-L, is what makes the archive so interesting to study. It is one of the few places one can glimpse theorizing in action. And, as I have said before, the WPA-L archive is an important site to investigate because it is one of the few places where individuals, whose material realities might prevent them from contributing to restrictive locations of disciplinary knowledge-making like scholarly journals, can have a voice. It is a site where individuals who might not have material support or extensive time have been able to dialogue with individuals who do have those luxuries. It is a site where we get a greater cross section of the discipline and where access to knowledge and knowledge-making is, at least slightly, more democratized.

Jeanne Gunner reflects on this democratization of access in her essay "Disciplinary Purification: The Writing Program as Institutional Brand," describing a "flattening of status" that occurs on the WPA-L (630). Gunner explains that on the listserv, "claims to special professional standing or authority are out of bounds (with a few carefully regulated exceptions), and community members, regardless of disciplinary knowledge or orientation, are interpellated as professional equals" (630). Gunner's comments about this "flattening of status" point to yet another reason why the WPA-L archive is such a rich and important site of study: it is one of the few disciplinary locations where individuals with very different levels of authority come together to dialogue on topics. Though disciplinary power and academic celebrity certainly shape the discourse of the listserv (a fact that can be clearly seen by looking at the numbers of replies that different users' threads receive), the WPA-L has been a location where full professors and graduate students, folks from two-year colleges and R1 institutions are all, at least theoretically, allowed the same voice.

Understanding the WPA-L through Theories of Affect in Digital Spaces

In her essay, Gunner posits that the "even playing field" found on the WPA-L is, at least partly, "produced by the listserv's *lingua franca*, which cloaks professional and economic inequality in a shared conversational, informal style" (630). While the informal communication style of the listserv may flatten status, it also likely has allowed conversations to reach emotional intensities not often seen in more formal and traditional sites of disciplinary knowledge-making, something Gunner acknowledges, arguing "the WPA listserv offers a useful environment in which to observe affective discourse" (630). Working in the tradition of Gunner, I am interested in examining the ways the affect-infused discourse of the WPA-L allows for ruptures in disciplinary convention, and because of that, I would argue that affect must be considered as a significant force shaping and mediating projects of disciplinary knowledge-making and theory-building (and the reception of those projects). As Laura R. Micciche argues in "More Than a Feeling: Disappointment and WPA Work," there is "an affective context [which] circumscribes how we work—how we function on a daily basis, how we envision the possibility of creating changes, and how we develop a sense of efficacy and purpose in our work lives" (443-444). Micciche explains "emotion, like reason, is a vital component in the construction of knowledge and in the everyday activity of social life" (436). Expanding on this point, she argues that "the interconnections between politics and emotion . . . elucidate the way emotional needs call forth political theories" and that "they can also show us how a given culture system produces emotional dispositions for its subjects" (436). Following Micciche's lead, I argue that affect is a vitally important lens through which to examine the processes of invention, response, reflection, and revision that take place in the WPA-L archives. Scholars who have theorized affects in digital spaces can help us understand these dynamics and how they are shaped by technologies of composing and the spatial and temporal relationships they facilitate.

Reflecting on the role of affect in knowledge-making in their essay "Towards a New Epistemology: The 'Affective Turn,'" Athena Athanasiou, Pothiti Hantzaroula, and Kostas Yannakopoulos encourage readers to think about what "the sociality of emotions and affectivity means in terms of multiple temporalities and historical changes in local and global power configurations" (5). Their call to historicize and consider affect as situated within power-knowledge relations pairs nicely with Horner's argument for continually recognizing the material conditions and political economies which shape the enterprise of knowledge-making. And Micciche's work provides a bridge between these two ideas with her insistence on remembering that "our work practices are embedded in a social framework composed not only of economic and professional issues, but emotional ones as well" (452). As Micciche explains, "emotions express the valuations of a community, [and thus,] descriptions of how we work must address the way emotion structures our professional activities," the ways emotion shapes our relations with others in the field, and how emotions become intimately engaged with issues of power and privilege (452).

Given that much of the theorization of affect and emotion has focused on issues of embodiment and corporeality, it may seem strange to discuss affect's impact on disciplinary knowledge-making on an online platform like the WPA-L, but as Patricia Ticineto Clough makes clear in her introduction to *The Affective Turn*, there is increasing interest in the function and circulation of affect in virtual, disembodied spaces:

> Affect is not only theorized in terms of the human body. Affect is also theorized in relation to the technologies that are allowing us both to "see" affect and to produce affective bodily capacities beyond the body's organic-physiological constraints. The technoscientific experimentation with affect not only traverses the opposition of the organic and the nonorganic; it also inserts the technical into felt vitality, the felt aliveness given in the preindividual bodily capacities to act, engage, and connect—to affect and be affected. The affective turn, therefore, expresses a new configuration of bodies, technology and matter. (2)

Clough's discussion of technologically mediated affects also allows for a reflection on the ways that different platforms and genres of mediated communication might encourage more and less visible (or visibly embodied) affects. For instance, email-based platforms (like the WPA-L) because of their less formal discourse conventions and the speeds at which messages are sent, can embody affect in ways that other forms of written communication (like journal articles and monographs) cannot. They can also draw on and express affect through different semiotic tools. The repetition of letters, the use of emoticons, and the inclusion of images and hyperlinks, for instance, are common in email communication. These varied resources point to what Sara Ahmed has described as "the emotionality of texts" in *The Cultural Politics of Emotion*. Ahmed uses the term as "one way of describing how texts are 'moving,' or how they generate effects" (13). Ahmed's reference to "movement," too, can be its own indicator of affect on the WPA-L (both in how responders to listserv queries quote and juxtapose comments for specific rhetorical purposes, and also for how the speed, acceleration, and deceleration of responses [as evidenced in time stamps] can be indicative of affect, sometimes indicating that conversation is "heating up").

Adi Kuntsman also addresses this notion of affects as moving through textual and digital spaces in *Digital Cultures and the Politics of Emotion*. Kuntsman describes what she calls the "affective fabrics of digital cultures" and argues for seeing digital spaces as "archives of feelings" (6). In many ways, Kuntsman begins to theorize how affectively loaded texts, those messages we craft and send out into the world, have lives of their own and do affective work beyond us (sometimes much to our chagrin). Kuntsman explains that archives of emotion are "always open to (re)emergence" and recirculation (7), explaining that "digital sites are never still: emails going viral, 'sharing,' postings and re-postings on social networks, and many other examples of circulation call our attention to the work of emotions *as they move*" (7).

The themes of re-emergence and re-circulation of ideas and affects are interesting to consider in relation to the WPA-L, especially in the age of screenshots and back-channel conversations on other social media platforms. In recent years, I've seen comments from the listserv being discussed on other platforms (especially Twitter), and often see evidence that such outside discussion draws people to the listserv threads, too. Also, because people have subscribed to the listserv in different ways (with some people following the list in time as messages are sent and others getting regular digest versions), readers likely experienced the emotional intensities of threads and the movements of ideas and discussions in dramatically different ways. Likewise, list members who had been active for a long time (and thus had longer memories of the discursive landscape) likely reacted differently to regularly reoccurring threads of discussions than new subscribers. And then there is the larger question of how the nature of the medium—the digital interface and the (varying degrees of) asynchronous communication—impact idea sharing and affective response differently than they might in real life. Considering this question in their essay "Contagious Bodies: An Investigation of Affective and Discursive Strategies in Contemporary Online Activism," Britta Timm Knudsen and Carsten Stage suggest that "the Internet creates a range of milieus where the ability to affect and be affected is altered compared to face-to-face communication and non-digital media," and they argue that "the Internet's deterritorialization of communication, the possibility of a high degree of immediacy and personal interactivity simply engage the making of new types of environments, where collective affective processes can be quite intense despite the lack of a common physical space" (149). They argue that "the affective potential of the Internet in other words is its intertwinement of *immediacy* (the users relate to events as they occur), its *loosening of spatial constraints* (the users can be situated all over the world) and its *interactivity* (the users can communicate with each other as individuals)" (149).

While the loosening of spatial constraints also exists with scholarly publishing and other forms of traditional academic knowledge-making, the immediacy and direct interactivity of the WPA-L archive makes it an especially important location for examining a discipline like composition and rhetoric and its spirited debates about identity and objectives. While traditional forms of academic knowledge making are slow processes that allow individuals distance from ideas, on listserv threads, responses sometimes follow in under a minute. And while we might interact with other scholars through processes of citation in our published writing, we typically depersonalize those interactions by "responding to an argument" or "taking issue with a point of view" more so than addressing or reacting to a particular person. In listserv discussions, though, the affective intensity and stakes of these interactions are heightened.

The in-time nature and personal tone of discourse keeps individuals attached to their ideas to a degree that doesn't seem to happen as much with published scholarship. The nature of the listserv also presented the possibility that one might be met with a deeply personal counternarrative or that one might face a public with a very different interpretation of an issue at hand (or even that you might be scolded or publicly chastised). Making knowledge in that space has had a different felt dimension.

To Forward or Reply: A Conclusion

In the wake of recent crises on the WPA-L and now with Barry Maid's announcement of its (at least temporary) suspension of operations, it is possible the platform has outlived its usefulness or that its functions are now being fulfilled primarily by other digital spaces. I now see many of the requests for materials and advice that used to come through on the WPA-L now being shared on Facebook and Twitter. During the COVID-19 global pandemic, I expected the listserv to explode with threads about pedagogical solutions, implications for promotion and tenure, and challenges presented for WPA work and TA preparation. Some of those threads were started, but I saw a lot more happening on other platforms and in groups like Pandemic Pedagogy and Pandemic Writing Pedagogy on Facebook. Part of this shift is surely generational. Email and listservs are older technologies that feel at odds with the increasingly mobile composing practices most of us rely on now. But I also think part of this change is connected to affect and emotion. When one posts on Facebook or Twitter, one typically has more control over who reads and responds to a message. There is more possibility for insulating yourself with like-minded individuals, more social filtering available, more ability to shut down threads. There are affordances to this, but there are also constraints and costs. In their defense of reforming the WPA-L published in *Composition Studies*, the WPA-L Working group reminded readers and the nextGEN respondents that the WPA-L has "long served as a unique place that allowed for interactions on professional issues across rank, geography, institution, and specialization" but acknowledge "facing many challenges in [their] efforts to revise the WPA-L toward what [they] perceive as its potential" (204). The success of that intellectual project will inevitably be shaped by the affects of the moment and by the individually felt emotions of the players involved. Regardless of its future, the WPA-L will exist as an archive of the affects that brought our field to this moment of deliberation about where and how we should talk to one another.

Works Cited

Ahmed, Sara. *The Cultural Politics of Emotion.* Routledge, 2004.

Athanasiou, Athena, Pothiti Hantzaroula, and Kostas Yannakopoulos. "Towards a new Epistemology: The 'Affective Turn." *Historeind,* vol. 8, 2009, pp. 5-16.

Banks, Adam. "Ain't No Walls behind the Sky, Baby! Funk, Flight, Freedom: The 2015 CCCC Chair's Address." *College Composition and Communication,* vol. 67, no. 2, 2015, pp. 267-279.

Canagarajah, A. Suresh. "Non-discursive Requirements in Academic Publishing, Material Resources of Periphery Scholars, and the Politics of Knowledge Production." *Written Communication,* vol. 13, no. 4, 1996, pp. 435-472.

Clough, Patricia Ticineto. Introduction. *The Affective Turn: Theorizing the Social,* edited by Patricia Ticineto Clough, Duke UP, 2007, pp. 1-33

Crowley, Sharon. *Composition in the University: Historical and Polemical Essays.* U of Pittsburgh P, 1998.

DeBoer, Fredrik. "Re: Video of Banks' Talk?" *WPA-L.* Arizona State University. 25 Mar. 2015. https://lists.asu.edu/cgi-bin/wa?A1=ind1503&L=wpa-l#211 Accessed 18 Nov 2020.

Ding, Huiling. "A Case Study of the Impact of Digital Documentation on Professional Change: The WPA Electronic Mailing List, Knowledge Network, and Community Outreach." *Complex Worlds: Digital Culture, Rhetoric, and Professional Communication,* edited by Adrienne P. Lamberti and Anne R. Richards, Baywood 2011, pp. 117-129.

Dobrin, Sidney I. *Constructing Knowledges: The Politics of Theory-Building and Pedagogy in Composition.* State U of New York P, 1997.

Goggin, Maureen Daly. *Authoring a Discipline: Scholarly Journals and the Post World War II Emergence of Rhetoric and Composition.* Lawrence Erlbaum, 2000.

Gunner, Jeanne. "Disciplinary Purification: The Writing Program as Institutional Brand." *JAC,* vol. 32, no. 3/4, 2012, pp. 615-643.

Hassel, Holly, and Joanne Baird Giordano. "Occupy Writing Studies: Rethinking College Composition for the Needs of the Teaching Majority." *College Composition and Communication,* vol. 65, no. 1, 2013, pp. 117-139.

Horner, Bruce. *Terms of Work for Composition: A Materialist Critique.* State U of New York P, 2000.

Knudsen, Britta Tim and Carsten Stage. "Contagious Bodies: An Investigation of Affective and Discursive Strategies in Contemporary Online Activism." *Emotion, Space and Society,* vol. 5, no. 3, 2012, pp. 148-155.

Kuntsman, Adi. "Affective Fabrics of Digital Cultures." *Digital Cultures and the Politics of Emotion: Feelings, Affect and Technological Change,* edited by Athina Karatogianni and Adi Kuntsman, Palgrave MacMillan, 2012, pp. 1-17.

LaFrance, Michelle and Elizabeth Wardle, editors. "Building a Twenty-First-Century Feminist Ethos: Three Dialogues for WPAs." *Writing Program Administration,* vol. 42, no. 2, 2019, pp. 13-36.

Micciche, Laura. "More than a Feeling: Disappointment and WPA Work." *College English,* vol. 64, no. 4, 2002, pp. 432-458.

Miller, Benjamin. *The Making of Knowledge Makers in Composition: A Distant Reading of Dissertations.* 2015, City U of New York, PhD Dissertation.

Miller, Susan. *Textual Carnivals: The Politics of Composition.* Southern Illinois UP, 1991.

North, Stephen M. *The Making of Knowledge in Composition: Portrait of an Emerging Field.* Boynton/Cook, 1987.

Schmidt, Peter. "AAUP Proposes Giving Contingent Faculty a Much Bigger Role in College Governance." *Chronicle of Higher Education,* 28 June 2012.

Trimbur, John "Composition's Left and the Struggle for Revolutionary Consciousness." *Writing Democracy: The Political Turn in and Beyond the Trump Era,* edited by Shannon Carter, Deborah Mutnick, Stephen Parks, and Jessica Pausek. Routledge, 2020, pp. 27-50.

Twigg, Marnie. "Last Verse Same as the First? On Racial Justice and 'Covering' Allyship in Compositionist Identities." *College Composition and Communication,* vol. 71, no. 1, pp. 7-30.

"Where We Are: Dialogue and Disciplinary Space." *Composition Studies,* vol. 47, no. 2, pp. 203-210.

Yancey, Kathleen. "Re: Video of Banks' Talk?" *WPA-L.* Arizona State University. 25 Mar. 2015. https://lists.asu.edu/cgi-bin/wa?A1=ind1503&L=wpa-l#211 Accessed 25 Feb 2019.

Pandemic Pedagogy: What We Learned from the Sudden Transition to Online Teaching and How It Can Help Us Prepare to Teach Writing in an Uncertain Future

Jennifer Sheppard

> This article reports on findings from a hyperlocal programmatic survey on writing instructors' experiences in moving teaching online during the coronavirus pandemic. It highlights key challenges instructors reported, including a need for strategies addressing increased workload; a desire for greater experience with pedagogy- rather than technology-driven instruction; a plea for attention to personal/professional well-being; and concerns about the increased attention needed to address logistics in digital teaching. The article contextualizes these local challenges within larger scholarly conversations about online writing instruction (OWI) and offers a series of pedagogical and professional best practices relevant for future online and hybrid teaching. It concludes with a discussion of the limitations of this project and directions for future research.[1]

From the widespread illness and death due to COVID-19 and the resulting stay-at-home orders to the extraordinary protests against racial injustice, 2020 was a time of historic tumult. It was also a time of massive change to the education system at all levels. While distance education generally and the work of scholars in online writing instruction (OWI) in particular have continued to expand over the last two decades, only a small minority of teachers and institutions were prepared for the abrupt transition to fully online instruction. As one *Chronicle of Higher Education* article described the experience, Pandemic spring 2020 was "pedagogical triage," not the careful, deliberative work normally required to design online teaching and learning (Bessette et al.).

Although there is much uncertainty about how ongoing pandemic concerns and the large-scale online teaching precedent now set will affect higher education in coming years, it is important to document this experience and the significant impact it has had on composition instructors and their pedagogies. This article begins by examining the spring 2020 perspectives of instructors in one large writing studies program. Reflecting on responses to an anonymous departmental survey about workload and pedagogical choices in the sudden shift to online teaching, I highlight key challenges instructors reported and contextualize these local experiences within larger scholarly conversations about OWI.

While responses to this survey echo many issues raised previously by OWI scholars, on a local level, they also illustrate what the rapid shift looked like in practice for both individual instructors and a program as a whole that was largely new to offering online writing instruction. After offering a set of practical pedagogical suggestions for addressing some of these concerns in future online and hybrid teaching, I conclude with a brief discussion of limitations of the survey and some directions for future research.

What We Can Learn from the Suddenly Online Experience of Spring 2020

Like almost all of higher education, the writing studies department at my large urban public university made the abrupt, mid-semester switch to teaching all courses online in March 2020 due to the COVID-19 pandemic. Following a week of what campus administrators called an "instructional pause," our department's 90 instructors and the roughly 7,000 students we were teaching transitioned into various synchronous and asynchronous forms of virtual teaching.[2] Prior to this change, our department offered only about 15% of our courses at a distance and about the same percentage of our faculty had completed training for online teaching.[3]

Near the end of the spring 2020 semester, we shared some of our challenges and successes in a virtual faculty meeting and began to think about the potential for being online again in the fall. To help us better understand everyone's online classroom experiences and the ways we might support one another moving forward, an ad hoc committee was tasked with designing a short, anonymous survey via Google Forms.[4] Our intentions were twofold: to understand if, where, and how workload had increased so we could find ways to ease that strain; and to identify professional development needs related to online writing instruction to better prepare for future virtual teaching. As shown in the appendix, we crafted a 10-question survey and received responses from 47 of our 90 instructors.

In addition to documenting a significant spike in the number of hours instructors spent preparing for and interacting with students, our committee also saw four professional and pedagogical themes emerge in the survey results: an appeal for strategies to address the increased workload; a desire for greater experience with pedagogy- rather than technology-driven instruction; a plea for attention to personal/professional well-being; and a need for attending to increased logistical concerns in digital teaching. In the sections that follow, I discuss these four online teaching challenges by drawing on existing scholarship in OWI. While a rich body of research and professional organization guidance has emerged over the last two decades, many instructors and programs have remained largely unfamiliar with these contributions, even during the pandemic's widespread transition online.

Although our survey provides a snapshot of the experiences of faculty in one local context, these findings confirm the significance and applicability of prior work in OWI. Reports from a variety of popular press, social media, and professional venues suggest that many of the challenges our faculty faced were shared widely by instructors both in writing studies and across higher education. Documenting these experiences will contribute to a record of local studies examining the educational impact of the pandemic spring 2020 and the larger trend toward more online course and program offerings. Findings from our survey illustrate how OWI scholarship can inform theory and practice not just in our specific writing program, but across the broader composition field. Additionally, these findings highlight new directions for future research.

Four Professional and Pedagogical Themes That Emerged from Our Survey

Workload Considerations for Faculty and Students

In trying to understand how workload may have increased during the shift to online teaching, one question our survey asked was: "In your best estimation and in relation specifically to online teaching, how much additional time ABOVE your normal preparation did you spend planning, teaching, grading, or communicating in the SPRING semester with students per working day since our transition to online teaching?" Given a scale from 0-6+ hours, half of our 47 respondents reported they spent *at least an additional four hours per course per day* over their normal teaching preparation. With a course load of five classes per semester, each capped at 30 students for our full-time lecturers, this was a substantial workload addition.[5] Put simply, as one participant noted in response to a later question, "We must not underestimate the time this takes ... This work has been worthwhile, and my teaching will be much better for it. But if we care about good pedagogy, we must realize that course development takes a MASSIVE amount of time."

In an open-ended question intended to unpack the quantitative question above, our survey asked respondents, "What are the top 2-3 things you are spending additional time on that you would not in teaching a face-to-face course?" Without time for advanced preparation, many instructors commented that they attempted to port in-person class activities, major projects, and due dates into the online setting without much adaptation. That is, they largely sought to fill in their regular meeting days with recorded lectures, live Zoom sessions, and required discussion board posts intended to track student "attendance" and participation. One third of instructors left comments indicating that they felt overwhelmed and burned out from this approach as they tried to respond to every post, draft, email, and request for virtual appointments.

Although the sudden shift to online teaching did not include the pre-course planning that is often cited (Borgman and McCardle; Darby and Lang; Morris and Stommel; Pallof and Pratt; Warnock) as the most significant time investment for new online instructors, survey respondents identified a number of other activities that made their teaching experiences so time-intensive. Comments highlighted instructors' curricular efforts such as redesigning course schedules, creating asynchronous presentation materials, and conducting lectures via Zoom. Additionally, several noted the extra time required for setting up and doing virtual conferencing, communicating with whole classes and individual students, responding to discussion board posts, managing student groups/interactions, and generally trying to replicate activities previously accomplished in an in-person setting.

The mid-term, unexpected transition to online teaching was certainly a part of this heavy workload. Planning that might previously have been accomplished over several weeks or months was compressed into a few days. OWI and broader distance education literature highlight the front-loading work of designing syllabi, scheduling, and curricular materials prior to the start of a course. Without a doubt, teaching online adds extra time to pre-course planning and daily preparation. While teaching in fully online or hybrid environments shares many pedagogical similarities with in-person instruction, it also involves other affordances and constraints that require time for reimaging teaching and learning.

However, even with such advanced preparation, work during the term is hardly light. Just as in an in-person course, the day-to-day preparation, interaction with students, and feedback on their writing in an online course requires constant attention. By its nature as an online, always-accessible activity, OWI students and instructors often have unrealistic expectations about availability and response times, adding to a sense that the work is never done. As Borgman and McArdle discuss,

> At the start, an instructor new to online teaching may feel very overwhelmed and working harder may seem like the answer. Many new and seasoned online instructors will jump into online instruction with zealous enthusiasm ... but this can be counterproductive and sets unrealistic expectations for students while creating an impossible standard for instructors to uphold in the long run. (Borgman and McArdle 54)

Survey respondents echoed these observations, commenting on the vastly increased number of student emails they received and their attempts to maintain contact during the chaotic pandemic semester. As one instructor noted, "Chasing after students to turn in assignments and fulfill course requirements was very time consuming. Being compassionate and flexible was necessary and the best way under the circumstances, but it was a lot to ask." Another commented, "Setting up group work and discussion is incredibly time-consuming, and monitoring and responding to 30 plus groups even more so."

While both the quantitative and qualitative portions of our survey indicated instructors greatly increased their workload, including their efforts to offer extra empathy and support to students during the pandemic semester, it will be critical for successful online teaching in the future to find ways to maintain quality educational experiences without instructors burning themselves out. As one example, Borgman and McArdle highlight the importance of crafting a realistic, practical approach to online teaching. Besides their emphasis on building attentive, personable relationships with students, they focus on strategic prioritization in the design, instruction, and administration of their courses. In explaining this focus, they write: "[P]lanning a responsiveness strategy for your administrative style, course design, and instruction is essential for success as an online instructor … [Y]ou need to set expectations with your students … in order to create a process of response that is doable and works for you in the long run" (65-66). A critical take-away in thinking about the workload of teaching online is that instructors need to develop intentional, manageable approaches that attend to both student learning and instructor well-being.

Pedagogy-driven Instead of Technology-driven Online Teaching

Many instructors who were new to online teaching as a result of COVID-19 initially assumed that their biggest priority was gaining more technical experience. Like most institutions, our campus underwent a short hiatus in instruction to give faculty time to transition their teaching online. During this pause, our campus-wide instructional technology department made numerous learning management systems (LMS), Zoom, and other technical training webinars readily available. While most department instructors availed themselves to some of these offerings, many soon realized that the basic mechanics of our LMS (for those who weren't already using it) and applications like Zoom were relatively easy to use.

Prior scholarship in OWI (Borgman and McArdle; Kastman Breuch; Selfe; Warnock) has shown that while technological issues are important concerns for instructors, the work of teaching online, especially for first time instructors, should be more profoundly shaped by pedagogical considerations. The final three questions in our survey investigated these ideas. In the first, we asked participants what resources, training, or other assistance would be most valuable in easing their workload to teach future online classes. We provided a list of possibilities and asked them to mark all that applied. While responses indicated a desire to learn more about the upcoming (pre-planned) campus transition from the Blackboard LMS to Canvas and what we called "other technologies beyond the basics for teaching and/or student work (e.g., podcasts, YouTube videos, screencasting, and/or web- or texting-based applications, etc.)," 76% of participants marked an interest in learning more about "online pedagogy (e.g., strategies for creating student-student and student-faculty interactions, producing accessible materials, etc.)."

A desire for pedagogical rather than technological support was further demonstrated by the two open-ended questions that closed our survey. These questions asked about the top two or three things participants were spending additional time on and what other information they would like the department to know about their online teaching experiences. The most striking take-away was that instructors really wanted to know not just how to use relevant applications, but how to transform in-person classroom practices, such as creating community and encouraging engaged student participation, into ones that worked in online spaces.

Since its emergence in the early 1980s, the field of computers and composition has examined the intersection of technology and the teaching of writing in in-person, hybrid, and online contexts. While these scholar-teachers have often been enthusiastic explorers of new technologies, they also have a long history of critical interrogation of how these technologies both shape and are shaped by pedagogy. Perhaps the most central mantra has been that pedagogy, not technology, should drive teaching (Cook; Johnson and Arola; Selfe; Warnock; Warnock and Gasiewski). This belief is echoed in OWI literature and professional organization position statements such as those from the Global Society of Literacy Educators (GSOLE) and the Conference on College Composition and Communication (CCCC) where they remind readers that "An online writing course should focus on writing and not on technology orientation or teaching students how to use learning and other technologies" (CCCC *A Position Statement*).

One of the most revealing comments in our survey focused on the perceived need to redesign curriculum and pedagogy around available technologies. This was most notable in regard to feeling an implicit pressure to utilize synchronous teaching modalities and technologies such as Zoom. As one respondent commented, "I am not comfortable using Zoom for 'live' class meetings; therefore, I hope we will be given the option to teach asynchronously instead of synchronously." Despite there being no explicit requirement or even encouragement to use Zoom, it was part of nearly every email, IT department webinar, Teaching

Center message, and listing of online resources shared across campus. This comment highlights an important point in the technology vs. pedagogy debate. Rather than making classroom decisions based on pedagogical commitments, student needs, workload considerations, and other concerns, many teachers felt an unspoken pressure to try to mirror the experience of their in-person classrooms through live video presentations and class discussions. While Zoom and other synchronous technologies can certainly support specific pedagogical goals, the important point here is that decisions about whether or not to use them should be based on an instructor's teaching goals and learning outcomes, rather than their technological abilities to replicate an in-person structure that isn't always superior.[6] Particularly with the teaching of writing, there can be a number of benefits to an asynchronous, hybrid, or low-tech approach.

In his 2009 book, *Teaching Writing Online: How and Why*, Scott Warnock advocates for the important role asynchronous activities can play in online writing instruction. One benefit he notes is the way this mode can encourage conversation among a greater diversity of students as they have time to think about and respond to complex ideas. Rather than the rapid pace of an in-person or live virtual discussion and the hesitations some students have about contributing while on the spot, asynchronous opportunities can relieve some of the pressure students feel about adding their voices and ideas (69-70). Additionally, for composition instructors specifically and for other faculty wanting to support development of critical, discipline-specific writing practices more broadly, asynchronous discussion takes place through writing. Not only does this increase the quantity of the writing students do, the interaction with their peers *through writing* offers greater opportunities to develop such practices as audience awareness, clarity, persuasion, use of sources, and more.

Beyond the pedagogical decisions about whether to use a synchronous or asynchronous format or about whether to use a specific tool such as Zoom, instructors need to attend to other social, economic, and privacy considerations relating to their students. While live video conferencing applications can help to create a sense of presence and classroom community in online spaces, they also come with significant potential downsides. One concern is that technologies, such as Zoom, can be bandwidth-intensive and often work best on laptops/desktops rather than mobile devices. As the long-discussed digital divide persists, uneven access to technology and internet connectivity can replicate systemic inequality in the education system. As educators, we need to be attentive to which technologies we use so that we support the success of all our students rather than perpetuating various forms of privilege and gatekeeping.

Further, others (Finders and Muñoz; Sonnemaker) have suggested that Zoom and similar video-based synchronous technologies literally open a portal into students' living spaces in ways that can violate privacy, highlight socio-economic inequities, and put them (or those they live with) at risk. Although the survey comment noted above seems like a straightforward choice between modalities, the work cited in this section illustrates just a few of the many considerations that should play a role in instructors' choices about technology so that student participation can be maximally-inclusive and equitable. The key point here is not that any of these tools are inherently problematic, but that instructors should think first about pedagogical considerations, learning goals, and student realities rather than starting with available technologies.

Personal and Professional Well-being in Teaching Online

One of the most striking findings from our survey was the personal and professional toll teaching exclusively online took on instructors. While increased workload was certainly part of this, responses also included comments about feelings of depression, isolation, and even despair. In response to the survey question asking about what instructors would like the department to know about their online pandemic teaching experience, approximately 25% of respondents wrote about missing connections with individual students and larger in-person communities of learners. While half of our survey respondents had prior experience teaching some of their courses online, many of them wrote about the sense of disconnection when all of their courses went online. As one of these OWI-experienced respondents reported, "I've taught a limited number of classes online for several years and enjoyed it. I actually advocated that the department offer more courses online. No more … I found the constant mediation (via technology) depressing. I felt totally disconnected from my students, who simply didn't exist for me as people at the end of the semester."

While it has not been a central focus of research, considerations of the social, personal, and emotional impact on instructors do come up in OWI literature, even among strong proponents. As Palloff and Pratt warn, "Online there is a greater possibility for a sense of loss … loss of contact, loss of connection, and a resultant sense of isolation. Consequently, attention should be paid to the intentional development of presence" (31). Similarly, Conceição and Lehman remind readers that "the online environment is elusive" and we can lose a sense of closeness with our students (11). No longer are instructors able to rely on eye contact, body language, and the nuance of voice to help us connect with students. No longer can students linger after class or casually drop by an instructor's office in the same ways that allow for casual conversations and the building of community. As a result, many online instructors can feel a lack of engagement that may have been central to their in-person teaching experiences.

Although social and emotional issues have typically been discussed from a student perspective, our survey suggests that concerns over (lost) interpersonal connection and classroom community can be equally important for instructors. More than a decade ago, Palloff and Pratt focused on the concept of "social presence" and the key role it can play in reducing "social distance between all participants" and making the online teaching/learning experience feel more "human" (12). More recently, Borgman and McArdle, highlighting the emotional aspects of writing, note that "When writing instruction moves online, connecting with students proves more challenging" (18). Creating a sense of classroom community is not only central to the learning experience of students, but also to the personal and professional well-being of teachers. Although rethinking how to build interpersonal connections in online classroom settings is complex, I will offer some practical recommendations in the final section of this article.

Pedagogies of Logistics

When asked what two to three tasks instructors spent additional time on in the online COVID-19 spring, survey respondents reported a wide range of activities. One common thread, though, was logistical planning and correspondence with students. This included "creating 'detailed' notes for each slide in a PowerPoint presentation," "data entry" in the LMS, "answering emails," and "organizing my thoughts into well written paragraphs instead of loose outlines." Of particular note, though, was the effort expended to write clear, explicit instructions, the need to send multiple reminders to students about due dates (with one person referring to this as "hand-holding"), and answering a flood of individual student questions via email. While many respondents saw this work as essential to supporting student success in an online setting, others implied that attending to these logistical details was a time drain that took away from the "real" work of teaching.

Many of the challenges instructors faced were, of course, the result of the abrupt, unexpected shift to the online environment. As many OWI scholars have suggested, much of successful online teaching is preparation, particularly on the front-end of the course design process. Time for developing materials, outlining regular procedures for submitting assignments and interacting with classmates, and pre-loading some content into an LMS would have reduced many of these issues. Attending to logistical concerns as pedagogy is so critical in online teaching that it is outlined in twelve examples of effective practice in the CCCC position statement on online writing instruction. For example, the statement advocates for the use of explicit, text-centric, plain language in instructions and for the use of "redundancy and repetition" in explaining concepts (CCCC *A Position Statement*). As the CCCC statement, along with many OWI scholars, stress, there is a significant need for detail, clarity, and redundancy in communication with students.

The work of writing teachers in helping students develop a diversity of contextually-, generically-, and rhetorically-savvy writing practices is complex. Conveying the logistics that scaffold students' learning of these practices is similarly challenging, but it is a core part of our responsibility. As nearly every readiness survey for students planning to take an online course emphasizes (Darby and Lang xxi), students need to be able to work independently, to navigate course materials, and to understand how to take initiative in their learning experiences. However, an essential responsibility of faculty is to facilitate this learning through clear communication and organization. Such work is not hand-holding or "just" clerical, but rather, is a key pedagogical orientation that helps to structure students' day-to-day and term-long learning. It works to highlight specific expectations about their efforts and offers them pathways into being more intentional about the activities they undertake. It also provides critical feedback as students check their own understandings of what is happening and demonstrates instructors' attentiveness to their learning needs. And, perhaps just as importantly, clear, consistent communication models writing practices that attend to rhetorical purpose and audience awareness. Although survey respondents' experiences with increased logistical communication was likely heightened due to the general disorientation caused by the pandemic, attention to these concerns will remain critical to OWI pedagogy and student success.

Moving Beyond Pedagogical Triage: Some Recommendations and Best Practices for Teaching Writing Online

There is a rich body of existing scholarship on online writing instruction. I have drawn on a few of these important pieces above but certainly can't fully represent the field's breadth and depth. What I will do here, though, is highlight a few recommendations and pedagogical practices intended to address concerns raised in our survey. These are meant as practical take-aways for OWI pedagogy, course planning, and day-to-day instruction, especially for instructors or programs that are new to teaching in online modalities.

Managing Workload

Any way you approach it, online instruction requires significant time. It takes thoughtful planning, regular interaction, and a willingness to make adjustments on the fly. However, this doesn't mean that instructors have to work to the point of burnout. Making a few strategic choices can streamline instructors' workloads and make experiences more productive for learners. Here are a few suggestions:

- Outline schedules with at least the key milestones/due dates *before* the term begins. While it makes sense to leave space for student contributions to course design, as well as our own adjustments to learning needs, a well-planned schedule is a crucial starting point in any online course (Darby and Lang; Warnock). Not every moment of a course needs be mapped but providing students with significant milestones upfront can, as Borgman and McArdle suggest, help instructors to "create an open and accessible space that allows for student success" (67).
- Consider using a consistent weekly schedule (e.g., a synchronous session early in the week, asynchronous/collaborative work later in the week, and/or all work being due by Sunday at 11:59 p.m.). As Warnock suggests, "Because students in an OW course do not have the built-in structure of attending class every two or three days, you should create repetitive, predictable deadlines to help them feel anchored to the weekly work in the course" (143). If students have a set routine for participation, they are more likely to get work accomplished and to do it on time. This approach also helps instructors manage their own schedules by knowing when they will have student work to respond to.
- Outline clear guidelines and boundaries about when and how you will be available. Because so much of our lives are online now, it is easy to expect instantaneous replies. Several respondents in our survey reported that students emailed requests for feedback or Zoom appointments late at night and expected responses by morning, leaving both instructors and students frustrated. Establishing clear rules about availability and in what timeframe students can expect to hear back is important (Borgman and McArdle; Conceição and Lehman). Besides being consistent for students, it can help instructors feel like they aren't always on the clock.
- Keep any presentations short, whether recorded or live, and focus on a few key ideas rather than trying to cover everything. Studies show that videos longer than 20 minutes rarely get watched all the way through and that videos that are six minutes or shorter are ideal (Guo et al. 44). This is not because students have short attention spans, but because this type of learning doesn't require active engagement with the content. Even when you have a lot of material to cover, best practices suggest chunking information across several shorter videos (Douglas 0:35-1:27). This kind of micro-lesson allows instructors to capture students' attention and convey the most

important points while also reducing time instructors spend recording and editing long videos.
- Be strategic about time. We need to approach our workloads in ways that are manageable while prioritizing what's most important from pedagogical and learning outcome perspectives. We should focus our energies on activities we see as most valuable for students' writing development and make choices to reduce or eliminate activities that might be seen as busy work. Rather than requiring assignments to account for students' time in a one-to-one ratio (such as when they would typically attend an in-person class), we should strive for purposeful activities that scaffold learning for larger projects. As Heidi Harris highlighted in a recent Keynote address on OWI, "less is more" when we focus not on counting student contributions but, instead, on helping them to "attend, organize, and integrate" the knowledge and practices of our courses (Harris 11:11-18:00).

Beginning from Pedagogy, Not Technology in Online Instruction

When the CCCC put out its *Position Statement of Principles and Example Effective Practices on Online Writing Instruction* in 2013, chief among their recommendations was that "An online writing course should focus on writing and not on technology." These understandings of the pedagogical complexity of teaching online are echoed by scores of other scholars who write about the critical importance of focusing first on writing pedagogy and student learning (Selfe), creating community (Palloff and Pratt), incorporating opportunities for both low- and high-stakes writing activities (Warnock and Gasiewski), devising methods for instructors to be accessible and responsive to students (Borgman and McArdle), leveraging technologies, modalities, and resources in strategic ways (Hewett and Ehmann; Mick and Middlebrook), and supporting diverse student learners (Gos; Miller-Cochran; Oswal). A commonality in all of this work is that pedagogical commitments, not technological capabilities, should be the driving force in designing online writing courses. In working from this central tenant, I offer the following recommendations for planning online writing instruction:

- Begin by reflecting explicitly on pedagogical commitments. As Darby and Lang argue, "when you backward design a college course, … [you] should begin the course-planning process by focusing first on the most essential goals that we have for our students" (8). Only then, should instructors move on to developing course content and methods for delivery. In keeping with this approach, instructors might start by asking what is central from teaching an in-person course to carry over into the online classroom. Once disciplinary and pedagogical commitments have been identified, it is then time to think about specific technologies that can help achieve these goals.

- Consider the learning outcomes and experiences that are integral for student learning. As outlined by the CCCC *Principles for the Postsecondary Teaching of Writing*, the primary goal for college composition courses is to help students develop critical approaches to reading, analysis, and writing. Often, this is done not through lecturing, but through activities that have students negotiate different perspectives by discussion with peers and through their own writing, which help them think about rhetorical considerations, such as addressing varying audiences and utilizing credible, persuasive evidence. OWI instructors can begin with identifying *what* these goals are rather than feeling pressured about *how* goals will be accomplished through specific modalities (synchronous/asynchronous), LMS features, and other technologies/applications.

- Remember that a fundamental principle of our work as writing teachers is inclusivity and helping students develop communication practices that will support their successes in a variety of academic, professional, and personal contexts. To do so, we need to make our courses accessible to all in terms of both content and technology (CCCC *Principles*; GSOLE). There is a constant evolution in what is considered the next best tool, but not all students nor faculty will have the hardware, software, connectivity, and digital literacies necessary to access it. Although comprehensive data about technology access for both students and instructors in higher education remains scarce, anecdotal evidence from the popular press and social media groups such as the Higher Ed Learning Collective make clear that both access and digital literacy skills among students and faculty are radically uneven. As one example from the *Chronicle of Higher Education* outlines, faculty and students in many rural, tribal, and two-year college settings face significant issues of access to computers and internet connectivity (McMurtrie). The range of pedagogical considerations related to technology is complex, but keeping these at the forefront of planning is essential. One small strategy for being more technologically inclusive is to offer an informal survey about these issues at the beginning of any online course and then to make adjustments based on student realities. Another strategy is to prioritize reliance on technologies that require low bandwidth, that are open source, and that are easy to learn or intuitive to use.

- Build in opportunities for students to contribute to course design and choice of technologies. As Greer and Harris argue, "using UX [user experience] principles in OWI invites students to participate" in making choices about course design and technology use, thus "moving them from passive recipients to active shapers of course design and content" (17). By taking a UX approach, such as asking students to brainstorm and develop learning activities from their perspective or offering them opportunities to propose and use everyday technologies in the classroom, students can feel more engaged because they have a voice in how a course is designed. Although such openness in instructional planning is a challenge because it necessarily leaves space for student input on course activities, "a user-centered mindset returns students to the center of the conversation" so that "teachers and students, not technology, shape learning experiences" (23).
- Understand that students, especially those who experienced the suddenly online COVID-19 spring, can be uncomfortable with taking online classes. As many OWI scholars (Griffin and Minter; Palloff and Pratt; Warnock and Gasiewski) argue, not all students are a good fit for learning in online environments and may take online courses out of necessity rather than by choice. As instructors, we can design our courses in ways that ease their concerns and set them up for success. One way to start this process is by crafting a short statement for syllabi about teaching commitments and how the course is designed as a supported, manageable learning experience. Instructors can also make transparent the reasoning behind instructional decisions (Darby and Lang), helping students to know what they will be doing and why. Lastly, instructors can plan for ways to accommodate student realities and convey this willingness to be adaptable to the class.

Creating Connection, Improving Personal/Professional Well-being, and Reducing (Online) Social Distance

As Borgman and McArdle emphasize, "… online writing instruction doesn't have to be impersonal or isolating just because you never get to actually meet in person. In fact, being personal is one of the most important things you can do as an online writing instructor in order to forge connections with your students" (18). Building interpersonal relationships not only helps students to be active participants in our learning communities, it helps us as instructors to feel connected as well. Further, this sense of social presence for instructors and students alike can help to reduce isolation when we are physically separated and can create a sense of accountability as we know others are interacting with our ideas and work. Here are a few suggestions:

- Provide an instructor introduction. Just as they would in an in-person class, students want to know more about the instructors that will facilitate their learning. Besides building ethos around one's background as an instructor, introductions help students see instructors as more accessible (Darby and Lang; Warnock). Introductions can include a few personal details (such as pets or hobbies) and/or a simplified description of a teaching philosophy.
- Encourage student introductions. This common activity, whether in-person or online, helps to break the ice, highlight shared interests, and build community. It can also serve as a good foundation for participation and the value of discussion as it gets students talking in a low-stakes way. Students can post a short bio, create a personal introduction on a discussion thread, or share other details that can help develop a sense of presence. Availability of student-created introductions helps instructors and students to put names to faces and to have fewer interpersonal barriers in communication.
- Do short, informal conversation starters on a regular basis. Instructions can make space for informal conversation by, for example, sharing a favorite meme or photo that represents how the weekend went or a song at the top of everyone's playlist or anything else that is quick, informal, and gets students talking to one another. Erica Stone argues that while small questions "may seem trivial, personal conversations like these help connect coursework to the outside world" (Stone 1:10:26-1:10:30). Ideas for these activities abound online, but the point of doing them is connection and community building so that everyone feels less distant.
- Make explicit requirements for establishing and maintaining social presence. By setting expectations about the kinds of engagement instructors want in the course and then modeling that for students, they can help to encourage a greater sense of presence and involvement (Borgman and McArdle). This can be included in syllabi and activity directions, but it can also be reiterated more informally throughout the term. This helps students see that beyond a course requirement, being socially present has the benefit of connecting them with others.

Approaching Logistics as Pedagogical

On the surface, logistics and class housekeeping seem relatively mundane and straightforward. However, without an in-person setting where students often seek quick clarification before, during, or after class, details need to be communicated more explicitly. Conveying information about scheduling, assignments, due dates, and similar subjects are not just course management details, but important elements of a pedagogy committed to students' success. They help students organize their time, understand requirements, and make connections between different components of our classes. As Borgman and McArdle argue, this work is "architecting" the user (student) experience and is a critical part of supporting student learning outcomes (3). Here are a few strategies:

- Recognize that clarity in language is critical but isn't as easy to write as it might appear. As anyone who has taught (or done) the infamous technical communication assignment to write directions for making a peanut butter and jelly sandwich can tell you, writing out every step of a task is harder than it seems. As writers strive to be explicit, they also need to balance these efforts with concision. This is the central challenge of any written communication sent to students and is a critical component of any online course. Recognize the importance of this communication task and take time to do it well as it connects to student success.
- Send a weekly message. One place where clear, concise messaging can be especially useful is in a weekly plan sent to students outlining upcoming activities. While students should have a syllabus and schedule they can check at any time, consistent updates previewing the week's work and due dates brings this information into the short-term and helps students incorporate it into their workflow. As Darby and Lang remind us, "… online learners are often unaware of the level of self-direction it takes to persist and succeed in a class" (149). Instructors can help students become better at directing their own learning and achieving course outcomes through consistent messaging.
- Consider conveying key information in multiple ways for redundancy and clarity. As above, being explicit in communication and directions can be challenging and sometimes we don't anticipate where students will run into problems. One approach to addressing this is to convey critical information, like project instructions, in multiple ways. Redundancy, such as presenting instructions in a synchronous discussion, providing written directions, and creating

a short video or annotated written walkthrough, can help ensure that students see and take in information.

Limitations and Directions for Future Research

The four themes that emerged from our department survey highlight a number of important considerations for writing instructors and programs as we continue teaching writing online in a future beyond the pandemic. These findings reinforce the work of OWI scholars who have offered theoretical and practical frameworks for navigating the pedagogical challenges in online settings.

Because of its focus on a local context and its small sampling of instructors, this survey had a number of limitations. Beyond its limited scale, the survey also primarily captured the experience of non-tenure line instructors with exceptionally high teaching loads, including many without extensive backgrounds in composition studies. Further, participants in this survey teach students in a large, urban, public university. While our campus is racially- and socioeconomically-diverse, the context of our geographical setting and student population is hardly universal and representative. And, finally, this survey and the online teaching experience on which it was based was conducted in the midst of a once-in-a-lifetime (we hope) pandemic. Faculty and students were often working under not just difficult, but sometimes tragic conditions. How large-scale OWI might look and feel when people are not struggling with issues of illness, unemployment, living/working/sharing space with and/or caring for family or roommates 24/7 will likely be significantly different.

Still, while the survey reported here has these and other limitations, it also points to several directions for future research. Among the most critical is a need to find out more about how the ensuing year of training, planning, and teaching online changed (or didn't) faculty's perceptions and pedagogical practices once the abrupt shift in spring 2020 was over. What did faculty and programs learn about what worked from a pedagogical perspective? What additional professional development and ongoing support was undertaken and what is still needed? How did online teaching work in a variety of contexts, such as in courses with low, discipline-recommended enrollment caps and in departments that serve highly diverse student populations and/or those that are located in rural, marginalized, or technologically underserved communities? In what ways did (and does) online teaching offer means to reimagine or extend the discipline's critical work in developing anti-racist pedagogies and writing practices and in addressing other social justice concerns? And, importantly, what can researchers learn from students about their online educational experiences? In what ways did they feel challenged, supported, or stretched beyond their capacities, and how can we evolve our curricula, pedagogies, and priorities to meet their learning needs? As the long-term implications of the pandemic for higher education unfold over the coming years, both local and large-scale studies examining questions like these will be critical in addressing our disciplinary priorities in the context of online writing instruction.

Conclusion

In a joint statement responding to the COVID-19 pandemic released on June 26, 2020, the Council of Writing Program Administrators and the Conference on College Composition and Communication reminded teachers and institutions of the high stakes surrounding writing instruction in higher education. We should be particularly attentive to whichever in-person, hybrid, or online form our instruction takes, they argue, because "Nearly all college students take a first year writing course, one that can serve as a 'gatekeeper' for access to other courses across the curriculum, to upper-division writing course requirements, to graduation, or to other curricular options" (CWPA and CCCC). As a result, our pedagogical decisions, both programmatically and in individual courses, should remain focused on our "core principles" of effective writing instruction and should be "acutely sensitive to the way that they may affect" access to higher education, student retention, and academic progress (CWPA and CCCC). Although we will continue to experience instructional and pedagogical challenges as we move between in-person and online teaching in the months and years ahead, our professional commitments and the choices we make in relation to technology will be central to our students' success as writers.

In reflecting on instructors' experiences in the local context of this survey and offering some practical recommendations, it is my hope that faculty and programs across the field can build on their already existing writing pedagogies and commitments to student success to create productive online teaching and learning experiences. By focusing first on our disciplinary commitments and then considering how we can use technology to support those values through our pedagogical practices, we can develop online instruction that is mindful of our working conditions and that engages and supports students in becoming better writers no matter the modality in which we interact with them.

Notes:

1. I want to thank my departmental colleagues for their responses to the survey discussed here. I also want to offer a special thanks to Jamie Madden and Amber Anaya for the detailed conversations we had about the findings and the implications they have for our online writing instruction workload.

2. As context, my department of 90 faculty is staffed largely by full-time (35%) and part-time (55%) lecturers who teach up to five courses a semester at our institution (with some teaching additional courses at the many two-year schools in our area). Lecturers hold MAs or MFAs in composition or a variety of writing-aligned (e.g., English or creative writing) disciplines and typically have one- or three-year employment contracts. Tenure-track faculty, who teach between one and four courses per term, depending on administrative assignments, make up only 10% of our instructors. Additionally, we employ a varying number of graduate teaching associates each semester who serve as instructors of record for their own courses.

3. For various administrative and political reasons pre-pandemic, my department previously required certification prior to any online teaching assignment and enrollment in such training was intentionally restricted to a small number of instructors. Access to training certification and online teaching assignments was a point of tension in our department prior to the pandemic. For a fuller discussion of these local challenges and choices, see my forthcoming article in *Research in Online Literacy Education*, "Cultivating a Shared Vision: Crafting a Communal Policy and Pedagogical Guidelines for Online Writing Instruction."

4. I checked with the institutional review board at my university and was advised that I did not need human subjects approval to write about these findings because the survey was undertaken as a program assessment. No personally identifiable information was collected as part of the survey, no one is identifiable in this manuscript, and the survey/responses are not accessible nor searchable online for those not involved with the department committee who collected this information.

5. Our department has advocated to administrators for years for a reduction in enrollment caps to be in line with recommendations of no more than 20 students per writing course set by the Council of Writing Program Administrators (WPA) and the Conference on College Composition and Communication (CCCC). Teaching up to 150 students per semester was already an intense workload prior to COVID-19 and certainly exacerbated the toll taken on instructors in the shift to teaching online.

6. The standardized student learning outcomes for our department's three required lower division writing courses underwent substantial updating and revision in 2017-2018 in line with disciplinary work in rhetoric and composition. While all faculty have pedagogical freedom to choose how those goals are achieved in their classrooms, their curricula must be shaped to these learning outcomes.

Works Cited

Bessette, Lee. S., et al. "5 Myths about Remote Teaching in the Covid-19 Crisis." *The Chronicle of Higher Education*, 1 May 2020. https://www.chronicle.com/article/5-Myths-About-Remote-Teaching/248688

Borgman, Jesse. C., and Casey McArdle. *Personal, Accessible, Responsive, Strategic: Resources and Strategies for Online Writing Instructors*. WAC Clearinghouse, University of Colorado Press, 2019. https://wac.colostate.edu/books/practice/pars/

Breuch, Lee-Ann Kastman. *Faculty Preparation for OWI. Foundational Practices of Online Writing Instruction*. Parlor P, 2015, pp. 355-393. https://wac.colostate.edu/books/perspectives/owi/

Conceição, Simone C. O., and Rosemary. M. Lehman. *Managing Online Instructor Workload: Strategies for Finding Balance and Success.* Jossey-Bass, 2011.

Cook, Kelli Cargile. "An Argument for Pedagogy-Driven Online Education." *Online Education: Global Questions, Local Answers,* edited by Kelli Cargile Cook and Keith Grant-Davie, Baywood P, 2005, pp. 49-66.

CCCC. *Principles for the Postsecondary Teaching of Writing,* 2015, https://cccc.ncte.org/cccc/resources/positions/postsecondarywriting.

---. *A Position Statement of OWI Principles and Effective Practices,* 2013. http://www.ncte.org/cccc/committees/owi* CWPA and CCCC. *CWPA and CCCC Joint Statement in Response to the COVID-19 Pandemic.* June 26, 2020, http://wpacouncil.org/aws/CWPA/pt/sd/news_article/309074/_PARENT/layout_details/false.

Darby, Flower, and James M. Lang. *Small Teaching Online: Applying Learning Science in Online Classes.* Jossey-Bass, 2019.

Douglas, Kerrie. *Video Best Practices for Online Instruction: Lecture in Segments.* Purdue Engineering Education, 2019. https://www.youtube.com/watch?v=aRIrmnKz6tc

Finders, Margaret, and Joaquin Muñoz. "Cameras On: Surveillance in the Time of COVID-19." *Inside Higher Ed.* March 3, 2021. https://www.insidehighered.com/advice/2021/03/03/why-its-wrong-require-students-keep-their-cameras-online-classes-opinion

Global Society for Online Literacy Educators (GSOLE). *Online Literacy Instruction Principles And Tenets.* https://gsole.org/oliresources/oliprinciples

Gos, Michael. W. "Nontraditional Student Access to OWI." *Foundational Practices in Online Writing Instruction,* edited by Beth Hewett and Kevin E. DePew, Parlor P, 2015, pp. 315-352. https://wac.colostate.edu/books/perspectives/owi/

Griffin, June, and Deborah Minter. "The Rise of the Online Writing Classroom: Reflecting on The Material Conditions of College Composition Teaching." *CCC,* vol. 65, no. 1, 2013, pp. 140-161.

Greer, Michael, and Heidi Skurat Harris. "User-Centered Design as a Foundation for Effective Online Writing Instruction." *Computers and Composition,* vol. 49, September 2018, pp. 14-24.

Guo, Philip. J. et al. "How Video Production Affects Student Engagement: An Empirical Study of MOOC Videos." *Proceedings of the First ACM Conference on Learning @ Scale,* March 2014, pp. 41-50, https://doi.org/10.1145/2556325.2566239.

Harris, Heidi Skurat. "Teaching Small." *OWI Symposium August 2020: Small Online Writing Instruction,* August 4, 2020, (5:30-21:21), https://drive.google.com/file/d/1Puu2MNox3L8QQApbZJhk24gWDJIvV4cp/view.

Hewett, Beth. L. and Christa Ehmann. *Preparing Educators for Online Writing Instruction: Principles and Processes.* NCTE, 2004.

Johnson, Lucy, and Kristin. L. Arola. "Tracing the Turn: The Rise of Multimodal Composition in the U.S. *Res Rhetorica,* vol. 3, no. 1, 2016, pp. 98-104.

McMurtrie, Beth. "Students Without Laptops, Instructors Without Internet: How Struggling Colleges Move Online During Covid-19." *The Chronicle of Higher Education.* April 6, 2020, https://www.chronicle.com/article/students-without-laptops-instructors-without-internet-how-struggling-colleges-move-online-during-covid-19/

Mick, Connie S. and Geoffrey Middlebrook. "Asynchronous and Synchronous Modalities." *Foundational Practices in Online Writing Instruction,* edited by Beth Hewett and Kevin E. DePew, Parlor P, 2015, pp. 135-154. DOI: 10.37514/PER-B.2015.0650.2.03

Miller-Cochran, Susan. "Multilingual Writers and OWI." *Foundational Practices in Online Writing Instruction,* edited by Beth Hewett and Kevin E. DePew, Parlor Press, 2015, pp. 291-307. Parlor P. DOI: 10.37514/PER-B.2015.0650.2.09

Morris, Sean. M. and Jesse Stommel. *An Urgency of Teachers: The Work of Critical Digital Pedagogy.* Hybrid Pedagogy Inc, 2018.

Oswal, Sushil. K. "Physical and Learning Disabilities in OWI." *Foundational Practices in Online Writing Instruction,* edited by Beth Hewett and Kevin E. DePew, Parlor P, 2015, pp. 253-289. DOI: 10.37514/PER-B.2015.0650.2.08

Palloff, Rena. M. and Keith Pratt. *Building Online Learning Communities: Effective Strategies for the Virtual Classroom,* 2nd ed. Jossey-Bass, 2007.

Selfe, Cynthia. *Creating a Computer-Supported Writing Facility: A Blueprint for Action.* Computers and Composition, 1989.

Sonnemaker, Tyler. "As Zoom Classes Take Over During the Pandemic, Edtech Companies Provide a Lifeline, but Only for Schools and Parents Willing to Surrender their Students' Privacy." *Business Insider.* Oct. 13, 2020, https://www.businessinsider.com/virtual-learning-privacy-tech-teachers-parents-schools-student-data-2020-10.

Stone, Erica. M. "Building Community in the Online Writing Classroom." *OWI Symposium: Small Online Writing Instruction.* August, 4, 2020, 1:05:45-1:11:35, https://drive.google.com/file/d/1Puu2MNox3L8QQApbZJhk24gWDJIvV4cp/view

Warnock, Scott. *Teaching Writing Online: How and Why*. NCTE, 2009.

Warnock, Scott. and Gasiewski, Diana. *Writing Together: Ten Weeks Teaching and Studenting in an Online Writing Course.* NCTE, 2018.

Appendix

Department Online Workload Survey

This short survey (5-10 minutes) is designed to assess faculty increased workload concerns required by online instruction, identify topics for future professional development, and uncover resources faculty will need to teach online.

Please complete and submit the survey by Friday June 5 so that we can best help all our teachers prepare for teaching a full semester online. Thank you!

Please choose the option that best describes your position in the department:
- Tenured/Tenure Track Faculty
- Lecturer
- Teaching Associate

Please indicate the number of classes you expect to teach in the department in Fall 2020
- 5
- 4
- 3
- 2
- 1
- 0

Please indicate the number of course preps you expect to have in the department in Fall 2020
- 5
- 4
- 3
- 2
- 1
- 0

Had you taught online prior to Spring 2020
- Yes
- No

How much additional time did you spend preparing for and implementing the transition from face-to-face courses to online courses in March?

- 0-2 hours per course
- 2-4 hours per course
- 4-6 hours per course
- More than 6 hours per course

In your best estimation and in relation specifically to online teaching, how much additional time ABOVE your normal preparation did you spend planning, teaching, grading, or communicating in the SPRING semester with students per working day since our transition to online teaching?
- 0-2 hours per course
- 2-4 hours per course
- 4-6 hours per course
- More than 6 hours per course

How much additional time do you anticipate you will spend preparing for and implementing the transition in Fall 2020 from teaching face-to-face courses to online courses?
- 0-2 hours per course
- 2-4 hours per course
- 4-6 hours per course
- More than 6 hours per course

In your best estimation and in relation specifically to online teaching, how much additional time ABOVE your normal preparation do you anticipate to spend planning, teaching, grading, or communicating in the FALL semester with students per working day in order to teach online?
- 0-2 hours per course
- 2-4 hours per course
- 4-6 hours per course
- More than 6 hours per course

What resources, training, or other assistance would be most valuable in easing your workload to teach classes online in the fall? (Please mark all that apply)
- Blackboard Basics (making announcements, creating assignments, grading assignments, generating discussion threads)
- Canvas Basics (navigating Canvas, understanding Canvas' differences from Blackboard, creating, posting, and accessing assignments and documents, grading assignments, generating student discussion, tracking final grades)
- Slide Presentation applications (using PowerPoint and Google Slides)

- Web Conferencing 101 (using applications like Zoom to hold conferences, record lectures, host live class meetings)
- Online Pedagogy (e.g. strategies for creating student-student and student-faculty interactions, producing accessible materials, do I embrace or abandon quizzes?, etc.)
- Other technologies beyond the basics for teaching and/or student work (e.g. podcasts, YouTube videos, screencasting, and/or web- or texting-based applications, etc.)
- Other

What are the top 2-3 things you are spending additional time on that you would not in teaching a face-to-face course?

What other information would you like to tell the department about your experiences teaching online?

A Pedagogy of Amplification

Danielle Koupf

This article argues that the intersection of invention and style is a rich site for rhetorical study, for amplification, and for critical-creative tinkering, a process of writing new versions of an old text. At this intersection, writers can tinker to amplify an existing text and thus work to continue or begin anew the inventive process. To illustrate these outcomes, I recover two exemplary exercises from nineteenth-century textbooks, where exercises in tinkering find many promising precursors. Revealing such precursors in the nineteenth century furthers work by scholars, such as Lucille M. Schultz, who have discovered innovation in instructional materials of this period. After analyzing exercises by R. G. Parker and Virginia Waddy, I extend my lens beyond the Western rhetorical tradition and forge connections between tinkering and African American and Indigenous rhetorical traditions. I then highlight an exercise in tinkering from my first year writing classroom in which students amplified a passage from Walker Percy's "The Loss of the Creature." Upon sharing and analyzing examples of student tinkering, I conclude by weighing the benefits and drawbacks of teaching amplification, reasoning that in pedagogical rather than performative contexts, amplification can reaffirm invention.

In his 1899 rhetoric *The Practical Elements of Rhetoric*, Amherst professor John F. Genung defines rhetorical amplification as "the final process of composition" (285).[1] He explains that upon creating a plan for writing, ideas "are expressed only in germ. They need to be taken up anew and endowed with life; to be clothed in a fitting dress of explanatory, illustrative, and enforcing thought. This is the office of rhetorical amplification" (285). Gideon O. Burton, on his long-running website *Sylva Rhetoricae*, identifies amplification as "a central term in rhetoric, naming a variety of general strategies as well as some very specific procedures or figures of speech." Moreover, "amplification names an important point of intersection within rhetoric where figures of speech and figures of thought coalesce. That is to say, means for varying and repeating kinds of expression (figures of speech, or *copia verborum*) overlap with means for developing ideas or content (the figures of thought, or *copia rerum*)" (Burton). Genung acknowledges this intersection in calling amplification "the meeting-ground of invention and style" (285). This meeting-ground, I argue, is a rich site for rhetorical study, a site where I see the writer stretching, extending, or building upon a text. In taking what already exists and giving it greater attention, the writer practices what I call *critical-creative tinkering*.

Critical-creative *tinkering*, or *tinkering* for short, is a practice of reuse that infuses writing with the hands-on, experimental ethos of the makerspace (Koupf). It recasts writing as a material practice linked with discourses of crafting and making in which texts are open to manipulation and adaptation. Students write *inside* an existing text by adding, subtracting, substituting, rearranging, combining, and reformatting. They do not adopt a step-by-step procedure but rather an open-ended approach. Still, one change will typically demand another and so on. What results is not necessarily an improvement over the original text, though it may be; instead, it is an alternative—a new version. Tinkering proliferates possibilities, making it a prime tool for achieving amplification.

When tinkering to amplify an existing text, invention does not only continue, as Genung suggests, but may also begin anew—moving the writer in a new, unexplored direction. I contend that amplification is not always "the final process of composition," as Genung had it, but sometimes just the beginning. In fact, Genung concedes this point when he writes of the composer who amplifies,

> Having determined on his plan, let him surrender himself fearlessly to the current of his thought; let him be filled and fired with it *anew*, as if it had not been coldly analyzed. Nor should he be the slave of his own prearranged plan of discourse; that is, he should not let it chill the glow of his thinking. The mind often works more vigorously in amplification than in planning; and so the progress of actual composition may suggest a better arrangement of some points. If so, *let the work of planning be reopened*; and let not the writer shun the rewriting and rearranging thus necessitated. (286; emphasis added)

In this article, I demonstrate that tinkering with a text to amplify it is a productive invention strategy, both for persisting with an old composition and for jumpstarting a new one.

My experiences teaching tinkering have demonstrated that students who tinker achieve both critical and creative gains. They come to a greater understanding of both writing in general and the source text in particular by inhabiting that text, by dwelling inside it; tinkering is thus a critical practice. At the same time, tinkering creates new text and provides students with opportunities to try stylistic techniques in the source text; it is generative and therefore creative. At its core, tinkering is a process of inventing from preexisting materials, of patching things together, of reuse and bricolage.[2]

I have found many tinkering exercises in nineteenth-century rhetoric and composition textbooks, particularly in composition books designed for schools rather than colleges and universities. I recover these early cases of tinkering to establish a history of tinkering and to continue identifying invention as an outcome of nineteenth-century exercises. More than repetitive drills, these exercises provide substantive practice in style and invention. Lucille M. Schultz argues, "...nineteenth-century writing instruction in the schools was a site for tremendous pedagogical innovation—and, in fact, [. . .] it was in the schools that composition instruction as we know it had its beginnings" (6). She demonstrates how nineteenth-century composition books anticipate more recent trends in writing instruction, including free writing, sentence combining, and the importance of practice. I add to this list critical-creative tinkering. Associating nineteenth-century exercises with tinkering furthers Schultz's work of revealing innovation in textbooks designed for schools and extends scholarship reinforcing that grammar and style work serve invention (Blakesley; Butler; Stodola).

My research into the nineteenth century has uncovered two remarkable exercises, one in R. G. Parker's *Progressive Exercises in English Composition* and another in Virginia Waddy's *Elements of Composition and Rhetoric with Copious Exercises in Both Criticism and Construction*, two books most likely designed for schools (Parker is identified as a grammar school teacher and Waddy as a high school teacher on their title pages. While it is difficult to know who actually consulted the books, we can infer that they were designed for school audiences). Though I focus on just two exercises, the procedures associated with tinkering pervade nineteenth-century rhetoric and composition textbooks, as students are constantly tasked with rearranging phrases and sentences, substituting words and phrases, adding to short essays and stories, and transforming one kind of writing into another. Yet Parker's and Waddy's exercises in particular—certainly not isolated examples—display the critical and creative elements necessary to qualify an exercise as true tinkering.

Lessons from the nineteenth century are themselves amplified as I move beyond the Western rhetorical tradition and identify resonances among tinkering, African American rhetorical traditions, and Indigenous composing practices. I build a web of relations to show that tinkering and the larger maker movement are not new: they have antecedents both across history and across cultures. In fact, my own exercise in tinkering encouraged students to forge such connections themselves by amplifying a paragraph from Walker Percy's "The Loss of the Creature." After analyzing student responses to this exercise, I conclude by weighing the benefits and drawbacks of teaching amplification, which in exaggerated form may merely pad a text, providing the "fluff" (in my students' words) necessary to reach a word or page minimum. I contend that in a pedagogical rather than performative context, amplification—even when it produces "fluff"—is not a detriment, but an aid to learning and invention.

Nineteenth-Century Rewriting Exercises and Their Precursors

Schultz has argued convincingly that *exercise* in the nineteenth century "did not mean low-level activity, signifying repetition. Nor did it refer to easy-answer questions and fill-in-the-blank drills" (164). She continues, "'exercises' suggested a pedagogy based on practice, the use of performance-based (as opposed to recognition-based) activity to improve one's level of fitness in composing, not unlike today's use of exercise to signal a means of enhancing fitness or strength or musical proficiency" (164).

Schultz foregrounds exercises that asked students to invent in response to a prompt such as a picture or question. These contrast with what I have identified as another common form of exercise, which I call *rewriting exercises*. In nineteenth-century rhetoric and composition textbooks, students constantly practice rewriting. Rewriting exercises call upon students to combine, rearrange, substitute, add, and delete and in this way are reminiscent of tinkering. Importantly, though, some more than others help students achieve both the critical and the creative ends of true tinkering.

Rewriting exercises did not originate in the nineteenth century, nor in the Western rhetorical tradition. It is difficult to establish the exact origins of rewriting exercises, but antecedents can be found in classical models and across cultures. I argue that rewriting (or retelling, in an oratorical context) has been central to the history of rhetorical education. It appears, for example, in Quintilian's imitation exercises, in the progymnasmata, and in copia. Ian Michael glosses these connections in noting that transposition, prosing (i.e., turning poetry into prose), and sentence variation "are all derived from the teaching of rhetoric but they lost their coherence as the skills of rhetoric were fragmented and separately taught" (279). He continues, "These practices were taken over by grammarians and used for general linguistic training; but they were also recommended by teachers of composition and *belles lettres*" (279). Despite any loss of coherence, these exercises were widely diffused and applied to a range of literacy goals. Their wide applicability explains in part why they appear with such frequency across literacy texts.

Quintilian's imitation exercises are part of a larger curriculum that also includes the older practice of progymnasmata (Kalbfleisch), a set of graduated writing exercises that often featured rewriting or retelling. Students would recast a fable, retell a story backwards or from the middle, and explain the significance of a saying or deed, a task that involves paraphrase. Students would complete these exercises in preparation for crafting longer works in the future; as Jeanne Fahnestock explains, the progymnasmata was "an early tradition of compositional exercises that isolated and practiced the units from which longer discourses could be built" (278). This tradition in fact supported rewriting as a literacy strategy: "Even if students never used the precise formulas for the individual exercises again, they would learn that the composition of any extended text was a matter of combining smaller, separately formed, and recombinable modules. Composition was an art of *bricolage*" (Fahnestock 379).

The rewriting exercises are perhaps most strongly linked to the practice of copia, often tied to Quintilian and Erasmus. Though it can refer to a rhetorical figure, *copia* also signifies a pedagogy that develops variety of expression by requiring students to rewrite the same sentence or idea in multiple ways. As Fahnestock explains, "Students learning Latin wrote different versions of the same statement in order to increase their command of vocabulary (through synonyms) and syntax (through alternate phrasing)" (395). Likewise, nineteenth-century rhetoric and composition textbooks, including those by William Williams, William Swinton, and Virginia Waddy, often include a section on "variety of expression" that delineates ways to generate variety by substituting phraseology or by rearranging syntax. In his sixteenth-century textbook *De Copia*, Erasmus famously rewrote the sentence "Your letter pleased me greatly" 200 times to demonstrate methods for generating variety. Similar, yet abbreviated, undertakings appear in the nineteenth century—for instance, Swinton rewrites "The whale is the largest animal" in twelve varieties to demonstrate how to recast a sentence, before asking students to do the same (53).

When adapted in the nineteenth century, the rewriting exercises are emblematic of a general shift from a pedagogy of mental discipline to a pedagogy of practice. Jean Ferguson Carr, Stephen L. Carr, and Lucille M. Schultz have defined mental discipline as "the theory that the mind had certain faculties in need of disciplined training" (7), and in rhetorical instruction, it surfaces in repetitive practices of memorization and recitation. The abstract, theoretical work associated with mental discipline gradually gave way to more concrete practice with applied skills like writing, first in the schools around the 1830s and then in the colleges around the end of the Civil War (Carr et al. 9).

Despite involving actual writing instead of recitation and memorization, nineteenth-century exercises in some ways continued to demonstrate the influence of mental discipline. Carr et al. concede that "By century's end, although the discourses of 'mental discipline' often yielded to discourses that valorized 'the practical' as an educational goal, the desire to exercise or cultivate the mental faculties never completely disappeared" (8). Students are frequently asked to carefully study and understand a passage before rewriting or paraphrasing it, as though they will grasp its meaning through sheer brute force. A disciplined approach creeps into paraphrase exercises especially; note how Waddy instructs students here: "The paraphrase of another's thought requires the closest attention to every detail—strict criticism of the words and patient analysis of the grammatical features of expression" (297). Even when practice is a clear goal, it is possible to read rewriting exercises as repetitive tasks that drill students in textual operations: again and again, students must contract, expand, combine, substitute, rearrange, and transpose. I challenge this reading by connecting rewriting exercises to the critical and creative outcomes associated with tinkering.

Two Nineteenth-Century Exercises in Amplification

R. G. Parker's 1832 *Progressive Exercises in English Composition* was "enormously popular" and "among the first to emphasize practice," according to Schultz (21). Among its many rewriting exercises is "Lesson XXII: Narration Amplified," which, I suggest, offers a classical take on amplification. The model presents a two-sentence narration about the legend of Damon and Pythias labeled "Short narrative," a four-sentence elaboration labeled "Same story amplified," an 18-sentence elaboration labeled "Same story more amplified," and finally, a 29-sentence elaboration labeled "The same story still more amplified" (40-43). In imitation of this model, teachers would presumably provide a short narration from their own resources, and students would emulate the model to amplify the given narration by several degrees.

Parker's lesson accords with *copia*, or abundance, a class of amplification that involves "any method of staying on a topic by finding relevant material" (Fahnestock 394). Fahnestock explains that "Narratives are easy sites for *copia*, since they are elastic depending on the amount of detail provided" (398). Parker's lesson, by providing an extensive model, proves Fahnestock's point about the elasticity of narration. It shows that achieving this elasticity requires rhetorical invention and stylistic resourcefulness.

Imaginative, inventive work is necessary in moving from one level of amplification to the next. Students would have to imagine the steps involved in the action of the initial short plot, and they would have to invent the dialogue that might have taken place between the characters. While by no means inventing from scratch, students here are not engaging in Genung's "final process of composition," as the mere presence of different levels of amplification suggests that invention is ongoing—persisting but also beginning again and again. Presumably, students would be well-versed in whichever short narrative was provided, allowing them to use their memory to aid invention—remembering the details of the story and then amplifying them. We cannot assume that students always had the narrative in front of them; I suspect that they may have known it from memory, or at least instructors expected that they did. At the same time, students would have to draw upon their skills in style: synonymy, restatement, repetition, and embellishment.

Completing this exercise, I suggest, engages students in an early form of critical-creative tinkering. On just a surface level, it requires the moves associated with tinkering: rewriting through adding, combining, substituting, and possibly rearranging. Students write *inside* a given text: they insert new writing within the short narrative, stretching it in each successive version. Yet on a deeper level, Parker's exercise shares with tinkering the development of invention and style through rewriting. Students employ invention by imagining the scene, characters, and dialogue in the narration while experimenting with new stylistic techniques, such as synonymy, repetition, restatement, and any others that they may observe in the model and then imitate. Students tinker by generating new text—the creative element in critical-creative tinkering. Additionally, students would, ideally, come to understand whichever narration a teacher assigned through tinkering with it again and again—the critical element in critical-creative tinkering. Thus, this exercise serves not only to develop students' writing skills but also to enhance their comprehension of material for reading and memorization.

A more unusual and innovative exercise in amplification appears in Virginia Waddy's 1889 text *Elements of Composition and Rhetoric with Copious Exercises in Both Criticism and Construction*. This exercise is printed in a chapter on "Prose Composition," within a section on "Exercises in Paraphrase and Composition," under the heading "Development XIX." From these markers, I suggest that one goal of this exercise is to help students develop, compose, or generate text—that is, to invent. The exercise reprints Alfred Tennyson's two-stanza, eight-line poem "Requiescat" with these directions: "Weave into this a story of some one well known to you, and whose home you may suppose this 'fair cottage' to be; change the character, if necessary, to suit your purpose. In thus introducing narration, do not forget that the theme is principally descriptive, and that you should aim to produce a vivid picture of the scene" (329). The poem begins with the statement "Fair is her cottage in its place"—hence, Waddy's instructions to imagine "this 'fair cottage.'" Yet in the second stanza, it becomes a meditation on peaceful death, in keeping with the meaning of requiescat: "A wish or prayer for the repose of the soul of a dead person" ("Requiescat, *n.*"). Waddy's directions ignore the somewhat morbid content of the poem, creating instead an opportunity for students to use their skills in imagination and description to amplify the short text—to extend, embellish, and personalize it.

As in Parker's clearly marked amplification lesson, in Waddy's exercise students expand upon provided material by using their invention and memory. Students must add (or "weave into this") a story of someone they know, requiring them to use their imagination and their ability to recall a person and his or her home. Weaving additional material into the poem facilitates critical-creative tinkering. Students who complete this exercise not only generate new writing but also come to understand the source text in a different way through interacting with it. They relate the poem to their own lives, imagine the scene through comparing it with an actual person and his or her home, and manipulate language to gain writing skills. The verb *weave* is remarkable in that it implies that although this exercise falls under the heading of prose composition, to complete it students must write within the poem itself. This interactive element is in keeping with tinkering, which asks students to write within their own writing, a peer's writing, or a published piece. Furthermore, the term *weave* places this exercise firmly within the realm of tinkering, with its connection to discourses of crafting and making.

This exercise is especially innovative in reimagining writing as a material activity in which multiple genres and modes (poetry, description) can intertwine. In fact, I haven't found anything quite like it in other nineteenth-century composition books. Similar exercises exist, yet none involves actually weaving into an existing poem a student's own inventions (see Harvey 83; Metcalf and Bright 37; Shaw 76, 81; and Tarbell and Tarbell 74). In no other exercise that I've encountered do students actively intertwine their writing with an existing piece of text.

Imagining what might result from Waddy's exercise suggests that it would share its spirit and characteristics with several writing traditions. It might resemble a lyric essay or braided essay that combines poetry with prose and intertwines disparate strands of thought—in this case, a personal example along with the poem. In this way, the resulting text would also resemble early fanfiction, adding one's own voice to an established piece of literature or artistic production. At the same time, it would loosely incorporate the moves associated with Gerald Graff and Cathy Birkenstein's *They Say/I Say* and Joseph Harris's *Rewriting*, in establishing first what Tennyson had to say in his poem and then inserting the student's own point of view. Though not constructing an argument, the student would follow a line of thinking similar to what these two instructional texts promote: first acknowledging another author's voice (Tennyson's "they say"), then adding one's own voice ("I say"), in this case to forward (in Harris's words) Tennyson's perspective. Finally, on a material level, I see in Waddy's exercise a relationship to scrapbooking, which Ellen Gruber Garvey has shown to be an especially popular practice in the nineteenth century, one that involves weaving together previous writing (a newspaper clipping, for instance) with one's own embellishments (an autograph or inscription, for example).

With scrapbooking comes a larger connection between tinkering and other hands-on, material methods of composing, which stretch well beyond the nineteenth-century context in which I have until now situated this project. Tinkering resonates across rhetorical traditions.

Tinkering and Amplification across Rhetorical Traditions

An emphasis on reusing, rewriting, and intertwining existing materials extends beyond the Western, predominantly White rhetorical tradition represented in the textbooks that I have studied. In scholarship on African American and Indigenous composing practices, I see resonances with tinkering: a shared focus on intervening in existing texts, enacting a hands-on approach to making things, and composing across time and in relation to others. Recognizing these resonances bolsters my argument that tinkering and related makerspace practices are not new but rather, extend multiple rhetorical traditions.

In his study of African American rhetoric and multimedia, Adam J. Banks foregrounds interrupting and intervening in existing texts ("the scratch") as key moves in both Hip Hop and his own writing. I see in Banks's description of the scratch the practice of purposefully composing inside a given text observed in tinkering, in Parker's amplification exercise, and in Waddy's experiment with "weaving":

> The scratch is an interruption. It breaks the linearity of the text, the progressive circularity of the song. It takes the listener or reader back and forth through the song, underneath the apparatus that plays it, either to insert some other song or for the sheer pleasure of the sound of the scratch itself. What was noise, what was seen as the sign of a broken record or stylus, an unwelcome interruption in the continual march of text, groove, history, became a purposeful interruption, became pleasurable, became a way to insert other voices in a text, to redirect one's attention. (1-2)

Hip Hop composing processes serve Banks not only as conceptual or metaphorical models for writing but also as practical techniques. He explains here how, like a remix, his book loops, spins, layers, and repeats:

> I use the theoretical or conceptual work that the mix, remix, and mixtape do as lenses or ways to contextualize my study of a wide range of black multimedia rhetorical practices. So the chapters here cohere and yet they don't; they flow and yet they cut to other tracks, other conversations, looping in other voices in what might seem to be idiosyncratic ways. Some quotes get looped repeatedly, to serve a function like that of the sample—foundational ideas I borrow and build on that are too important for a single reference. And the prose itself spins, develops in circular ways at times, working through lay-

ering and repetition as well as through linear argument. In those ways, I hope this book models the mix and remix and becomes a kind of mixtape of its own. (7)³

Like the student who tinkers or weaves, Banks layers and loops existing materials (quotations, references, and concepts) to build something new (a scholarly monograph). He uses repetition to amplify "foundational ideas [. . .] too important for a single reference" (7).

Banks warns against dropping remix concepts into our scholarship without careful attention to the traditions from which they emerge. His work thus encourages me to trace tinkering's precursors beyond the nineteenth-century Western rhetorical tradition. In his book, Banks enacts this himself in calling the DJ a digital griot. He explains, "The storyteller and preacher are oft-studied griotic figures in African American culture. The DJ as a griotic figure has received much less attention. The DJ has taken up many of these roles and has been grounded in many of these oral and folklore traditions for decades, sometimes completely under the radar" (19). The griot is a "time binder," a "keeper of history, master of its oral tradition, and rhetor extraordinaire" (23). Viewing the DJ as a griot underscores that he or she is enmeshed in collaborative networks connecting past to present. His or her remix is not an individual composition but a community effort across time and space, as Kristin L. Arola argues in her work on composing as culturing.

Arola critiques treatments of remix in composition studies that continue to focus on the product and the individual despite the collaborative reuse in remixing preexisting materials. She turns to American Indian composing practices to refocus on process and community over product and individuality. She forwards "a process-based approach to making, one that acknowledges that a writer never composes in isolation. There is no authentic self who produces original works, instead there are writers who exist in relation to one another, draw from one another, and produce within ecologies of meaning" (280). Arola tells a story of a man creating a waterdrum for a sick boy and reflects, "I share it here for the purposes of illustrating how existing objects (logs, deerhide, water) are used with great intention in order to create something new. This composing process very carefully acknowledges the relations that existed before the composer entered the scene, while also acknowledging the relations the composer hopes to bring into existence" (280). Arola concedes that students are not crafting waterdrums in their writing classes, yet her analogy helps concretize the notions of composing with preexisting materials and of forging connections across time that are central to rewriting practices like tinkering and remix.

Banks and Arola each urge composition scholars to continue acknowledging the web of relations in which we and our practices are situated and to contribute to that web by building ever more connections. While I shed light on both tinkering and two remarkable nineteenth-century exercises, I recognize, too, that these innovations harken back to longstanding traditions of making. Thus I situate my own experiments with tinkering, an example of which follows, both within and beyond a Western rhetorical tradition.

Critical-Creative Tinkering to Amplify Walker Percy

In my first year writing seminar on the theme "Rewriting," students began the semester with Walker Percy's 1975 essay "The Loss of the Creature." A mainstay of David Bartholomae and Anthony Petrosky's reader *Ways of Reading*, "The Loss of the Creature" argues that our views of tourist destinations and our educational experiences are occluded by the institutions designed to help us see them. Percy's primary example is the Grand Canyon. Students typically grasp the gist of Percy's essay on a first read, yet tinkering with it can help them achieve a deeper understanding and make connections across time to their own experiences. Tinkering is an essential stage in my sequence of assignments on Percy's essay, as it provides a stepping stone from reading the essay to writing a new essay about it; students get inside Percy's essay beginning with a single substitution. They interrupt and intervene in the text, echoing Banks's "scratch." As in Donald Murray's "internal revision," discovery accompanies rewriting, but importantly, in both tinkering and "the scratch," rewriting is not confined to revising just one's *own* text.

After practicing Harris's coming to terms with Percy in a discussion board post or reading response, students tinker with Percy's essay by substituting "the Grand Canyon" with a place they have visited or an experience they have had. My instructions read, in part:

> For this assignment, you will tinker with the long paragraph beginning with "Why" on p. 459-460 of "The Loss of the Creature." Start by replacing the words "the Grand Canyon" in the first sentence with some other thing or place you've experienced. Then, rewrite the rest of the paragraph, sticking closely to the original text, but making changes based on your initial substitution of "the Grand Canyon." Try rearranging, substituting, adding, deleting, and combining both words and sentences.

The initial substitution necessitates further substitutions and additions as students elaborate on, or amplify, the story they have begun sharing. The content of the tinkering exercise can then become the basis for the next assignment, in which students relate a story of struggling to see or experience something due to the presence of a "symbolic complex" as Percy describes it. Students can then choose to amplify this story further still in a longer essay concluding the unit in which they more fully come to terms with, forward, and counter Percy's ideas.

In proceeding from a brief tinkering exercise to a longer story and finally to an even longer essay, this sequence of assignments shares its series of amplifications with Parker's exercise. The tinkering exercise in particular overlaps too with Waddy's exercise in that students must write within an existing piece of literature, incorporating their own experiences through both invention and memory. Students weave into Percy's paragraph their own nascent story, both to understand Percy's text in a different way (the critical aspect of tinkering) and to generate new writing (the creative aspect). They must recall an experience from their own lives while using their imagination and invention to mold that story to the template Percy provides. Students who tinker in this way become crafters, and composition becomes crafting. As Kristin Prins puts it, "untrained crafters can make their own discoveries, if they have the time and space to play. This play is part of the work—the writing and revising and rewriting and revising that we would recognize in FYC classes" (159). Tinkering exercises such as this one contribute to a makerspace ethos in composition classes, encouraging discovery, play, and experimentation.

A typical response to this tinkering exercise, written in 2018 by a student named Robert, begins with substituting *Victoria Falls* for *the Grand Canyon*. All changes appear in brackets:

> Why is it almost impossible to gaze directly at [Victoria Falls] under [natural] circumstances and see it for what it is—as one picks up a strange [shell] from [the beach] and gazes directly at it? Seeing the [Falls] under approved circumstances is seeing the symbolic complex head on. The thing is no longer the thing as it confronted the [natives]; it is rather that which has already been formulated—by [Facebook, Instagram posts, Snapchat filters, and the words *Victoria Falls*.]

More than replacing the Grand Canyon with Victoria Falls, Robert has made significant changes by updating Percy's examples of "picture postcard, geography book, tourist folders" with "Facebook, Instagram posts, Snapchat filters." Along with other students, Robert found that Percy's examples of the symbolic complex have become outdated and that social media has amplified the effects that Percy noticed in 1975. In class, many students argued that images posted via social media give viewers preconceived notions of tourist destinations so that when they visit them, their actual experiences may not match up to the hype produced online. (The counterpoint to this argument, we discovered, is that without social media and other forms of promotion, viewers may never know to visit these sights at all.) In his reflection, Robert noted, "Percy's ideas of people being held to this 'preformed complex' was seen with postcards in his time and now is very relevant today with social media. Overall, I would say that this process of tinkering allowed me to see that Percy's ideas are a lot more applicable, and that he truly had a vision for his time period and the time periods to come." This reflection demonstrates the critical component of tinkering, as Robert made connections between Percy's time and our own and thus achieved a deeper understanding of the arguments in "The Loss of the Creature."

Later in his paragraph, Robert replaces Percy's original use of the pronouns him/his/he to describe his imaginary "sightseer" with gender-neutral pronouns them/their/they. Percy's "If it does so, if it looks just like the postcard, he is pleased; he might even say, 'Why it is every bit as beautiful as a picture postcard!'" (460) becomes for Robert "If it does so, if it looks just like the media post, they are pleased; they might even say, 'This will make a great Instagram post!'" These small but meaningful changes show that tinkering has led Robert also to pay close attention to choices of language and style and thus gain greater insight not only into Percy's piece in particular but also into writing more generally.

A sign that tinkering is especially generative occurs when a simple substitution prompts the tinker to invent in excess of the original. This can be seen with Abigail's tinkering exercise, completed in the same semester. Abigail begins by substituting "New York" for "the Grand Canyon" but then generates a number of new thoughts. What follows is the first part of Abigail's paragraph, with her own writing in brackets.

> Why is it nearly impossible to [visit a city like New York and appreciate every aspect of it the way a person might view a town they have lived in all their lives]? It is [nearly] impossible because [of the way cities like New York have been promoted in everything from movies to music]. Seeing the [city] under approved circumstances is seeing the symbolic complex head on. [All the postcards and travel brochures shape the city in the mind of the consumer to be a city of pretty flashing lights, fancy stores, and Broadway shows. However, when you go to New York you are not seeing the postcard version of the city, with the Statue of Liberty a short hike away from central park and the gorgeous Plaza Hotel. Because of the city's advertisement, people go expecting to find a wonderland and are disappointed.]

Just in this excerpt, which is less than half of the paragraph Abigail produced, we can see that tinkering prompted her to develop many of her own ideas beyond substitutions. The length and elaboration suggest the presence of marked amplification, in that one adjustment leads Abigail to make several changes and eventually find her own voice amidst Percy's. This is a sign that tinkering is developing Abigail's creative capacities while also critically linking her experiences with those that Percy imagines. It furthermore suggests that Abigail engaged in invention both to continue her understanding of Percy and to begin her own intervention through personal experience, making amplification not a final stage in composing but an intermediate one.

The term *critical-creative tinkering* sounds akin to Matt Ratto's "critical making." A distinction between the two practices is that the former results in a text and the latter a material object, but an important connection between them is an emphasis upon process and reflection. Ratto states that "while critical making organizes its efforts around the making of material objects, devices themselves are not the ultimate goal," but rather, "a practice-based engagement with pragmatic and theoretical issues" is (253). In my sequence of assignments, the tinkered-with text is not a product to display but a thing to think with. I usually tell students that I am more interested in reading their reflections than their tinkered-with texts, so the latter can be messy or confusing. Rather than deemphasizing the work of tinkering, I mean to stress the powerful cognition and reflection that comes along with tinkering.

In reflection, students consistently noted that tinkering helped them make discoveries about Percy's text and about writing more generally. For instance, Jonathon commented, "This tinkering exercise made me think about changing my writing style a bit. [. . .] A bit more change and diversity between sentence lengths, and rhythms would improve my writing." Importantly, students learned about their ideas and about writing while in the process of tinkering. In other words, tinkering acted as a heuristic promoting invention. Sean, who substituted "computers" for "the Grand Canyon," used his reflection to elaborate that "we sometimes view computers as inadequate even though they are remarkable feats of engineering" and then added, "That idea came to me *as I was tinkering*; I did not start with that claim, only with the word computer and the original paragraph" (emphasis added). Likewise, Jonathon wrote, "*I learned throughout tinkering*; there was a lot more to the writing than what I had gathered during the first pass through" (emphasis added).

I suggest that this heuristic aspect of tinkering led students to generate abundance, or copia. They created more ideas than just the one produced by the initial substitution of "the Grand Canyon" with something else. Sebastian, for instance, initially wrote about a fast food restaurant, but additional ideas came to him, too:

> Tinkering led me to think about pop culture's influence on society's view of things, whether it be music, clothing, etc. I can especially relate to this myself. If a song is on the top charts on Spotify, I automatically save it to my downloads and listen to it. Even if the song isn't that great, the fact that it is liked enough by other people to get onto the top charts list, sits in the back of my mind whenever I listen to it and influences my opinion. In a way, fads can lead to the lack of originality, or the "loss of the creature" as Percy puts it. The preformed complex in Percy's piece could be pop culture, in the sense that it seems to make up peoples' minds for them.

Furthermore, many students discovered a new direction for the sequence of assignments upon completing the tinkering task. Few persisted with their initial substitution in subsequent assignments. This finding is somewhat unsurprising given that as writers we often veer away from first ideas as we continue to write and think, but it also highlights the inventive potential of amplifying a text through tinkering with it. Robert summarized the heuristic experience of writing within a preexisting text: "I actually really liked the experience because it gave me a guide to edit and do what I wanted. I was not forced to put words on a blank page with no help. I see how tinkering can be an effective tool for future pieces of writing that I encounter. Tinkering will allow me to discover relationships between past texts and the modern day." Here, Robert places himself in the web of relations that practices of reuse make visible. He connects tinkering to what Banks proposes is so valuable: forging relationships across history and culture.

Conclusion: A Pedagogy of Amplification

Amplification is a useful tool for inventing new text while learning more about an existing text. But it has its limits: unrestrained, it can grow tedious. Nevin Laib voices a prevailing view when, amidst praise (and demonstration) of amplification, he grants that "It is a sin to be superfluous. Pad, repeat, ramble on too much and risk correction. Redundancy is moral failure. It reveals a proclivity for slackness, inefficiency, and deception, a fondness for listening to oneself, for self-indulgence, a lack of substance and weight. People who say too much (and mean too little) are considered verbose, garrulous, prolix, tedious, unreadable, and irrelevant" (446). Furthermore, not all occasions call for amplification. As Genung acknowledges,

> It is not always necessary to the life and distinction of a thought that it be followed out in detailed, amplified form. Not infrequently the very opposite treatment is more effective. Some ideas, from their

nature or from the part they play in the composition, should be expressed as tersely and sententiously as possible, or should be merely hinted and left to work their way by suggestion. It gives vigor to the work when a considerable proportion of such condensed material is interspersed with the rest . . . (286)

Genung identifies the value of balance and variety. As Laib concludes, "Amplification and conciseness are companion arts" (457).

Recognizing that amplification can serve the needless and even deceptive padding of texts, I do not condone unrestrained amplification in all rhetorical performances. I do, however, promote amplification as an educational experience. I distinguish amplification as a pedagogy from amplification in rhetorical performance. When amplifying in a particular rhetorical performance—an essay or speech, perhaps—a rhetor must be selective. He or she must ask which points require amplification and when to apply tinkering's procedures to elevate and extend a text. Yet even then, amplification is not necessarily mere padding but can serve useful, even graceful, repetition: "Amplification is useful and necessary. Restatement helps readers understand the concept. Those who do not grasp an idea when it is first articulated may understand it better when it is phrased differently or when the subject is described from a different perspective" (Laib 449).

A pedagogy of amplification, in contrast, favors amplification for purposes of invention, development, and learning. As Laib puts it, "Amplification, I would suggest, is not the addition of superfluous material to the text but an essential part of explanation itself, a basic skill of interpretation and inquiry, a means through which we explore and articulate what we perceive and what we mean" (448-9). It is essential to writing-to-learn. This version of amplification promotes "reexamination, reinforcement, reconsideration, and refinement, a *process* of writing and rewriting the thought until it is truly clear, until its nature is completely described and its nuances are revealed" (Laib 449; emphasis added). These, I suggest, are the ends promised by so many rewriting exercises of the nineteenth century. They, like Parker's and Waddy's exercises, promote a version of amplification that encourages learning, clarifying, and realizing—in short, inventing. Yet as Banks reminds us, we must be aware of which cultural and historical traditions we are amplifying, whether such amplification is for performance or pedagogy. Amplification, in fact, offers students and scholars opportunities to acknowledge the many traditions in which their writing is situated because it favors enlargement, expansion, and thus greater connection.

Notes

1. See Carr at al. (17-18) for distinctions among *rhetoric*, *reader*, and *composition book*. I have followed these distinctions, though I sometimes use *rhetoric and composition textbook* to identify a broader class of texts instructing students in rhetorical principles (the province of rhetorics) and in practical exercises (the province of composition books).

2. The bricoleur has figured prominently in multimodal composing theory. K. Shannon Howard, for example, analyzes the composing practices of a character in a recent movie by identifying them with bricolage and explains, "The term *bricolage* has been associated with new media and popular culture for years now [. . .]. Its typical employment connotes the collage-like activity of online users and writers as they take pieces and links from different locations and juxtapose them in a new work" (140). Her description emphasizes the key role of reuse in bricolage, of combining disparate preexisting materials.

3. In both tinkering and remixing, composers combine prior materials in new ways, making both terms widely applicable to multimodal composing. Tinkering, however, emphasizes a process of coming to terms with an existing text by reworking it and building upon it—by amplifying it. In this way, tinkering accords with Arola's revision of remixing and making as process-oriented rather than product-oriented endeavors.

Works Cited

Arola, Kristin L. "Composing as Culturing: An American Indian Approach to Digital Ethics." *Handbook of Writing, Literacies, and Education in Digital Cultures*, edited by Kathy A. Mills, Amy Stornaiuolo, Anna Smith, and Jessica Zacher Pandya, Routledge, 2018, pp. 275-284.

Banks, Adam J. *Digital Griots: African American Rhetoric in a Multimedia Age*. Southern Illinois UP, 2011.

Blakesley, David. "Reconceptualizing Grammar as an Aspect of Rhetorical Invention." *The Place of Grammar in Writing Instruction: Past, Present, and Future*, edited by Susan Hunter and Ray Wallace, Boynton/Cook, 1995, pp. 191-203.

Burton, Gideon O. "Figures of Amplification." *Sylva Rhetoricae*, http://rhetoric.byu.edu/Figures/Groupings/of%20amplification.htm. Accessed 14 Jan. 2021.

Butler, Paul. *Out of Style: Reanimating Stylistic Study in Rhetoric and Composition*. Utah State UP, 2008.

Carr, Jean Ferguson, Stephen L. Carr, and Lucille M. Schultz. *Archives of Instruction: Nineteenth-Century Rhetorics, Readers, and Composition Books in the United States*. Southern Illinois UP, 2005.

Fahnestock, Jeanne. *Rhetorical Style: The Uses of Language in Persuasion*. Oxford UP, 2011.

Garvey, Ellen Gruber. *Writing with Scissors: American Scrapbooks from the Civil War to the Harlem Renaissance*. Oxford UP, 2012.

Genung, John F. *The Practical Elements of Rhetoric with Illustrative Examples*. Boston, Ginn & Company, 1899. *Google Books*, https://books.google.com/. Accessed 22 Jul. 2019.

Harris, Joseph. *Rewriting: How to Do Things with Texts*. 2nd ed., Utah State UP, 2017.

Harvey, Thomas W. *New Language Lessons*. New York, American Book Company, 1900. *Google Books*, https://books.google.com/. Accessed 22 Jul. 2019.

Howard, K. Shannon. "Beca as Bricoleur: How *Pitch Perfect* Embraces the New College Composer." *Studies in Popular Culture*, vol. 38, no. 1, 2015, pp. 139-156.

Kalbfleisch, Elizabeth. "*Imitatio* Reconsidered: Notes toward a Reading Pedagogy for the Writing Classroom." *Pedagogy*, vol. 16, no. 1, 2016, pp. 39-51.

Koupf, Danielle. "Proliferating Textual Possibilities: Toward Pedagogies of Critical-Creative Tinkering." *Composition Forum*, vol. 35, 2017, https://compositionforum.com/issue/35/proliferating.php. Accessed 20 Jul. 2019.

Laib, Nevin. "Conciseness and Amplification." *College Composition and Communication*, vol. 41, no. 4, 1990, pp. 443-459.

Metcalf, Robert C., and Orville T. Bright. *Elementary English*. New York, American Book Company, 1895. *Google Books*, https://books.google.com/. Accessed 22 Jul. 2019.

Michael, Ian. *The Teaching of English: From the Sixteenth Century to 1870*. Cambridge UP, 1987.

Murray, Donald M. "Internal Revision: A Process of Discovery." *The Essential Don Murray: Lessons from America's Greatest Writing Teacher*, edited by Thomas Newkirk and Lisa C. Miller, Boynton/Cook, 2009, pp. 123-145.

Parker, R. G. *Progressive Exercises in English Composition*. Boston, Lincoln and Edmands, 1832. *University of Pittsburgh*, https://digital.library.pitt.edu/collection/19th-century-schoolbooks. Accessed 22 Jul. 2019.

Percy, Walker. "The Loss of the Creature." *Ways of Reading*, 9th ed., edited by David Bartholomae and Anthony Petrosky, Bedford/St. Martin's, 2011, pp. 459-471.

Prins, Kristin. "Crafting New Approaches to Composition." *composing(media) = composing(embodiment): bodies, technologies, writing, the teaching of writing*, edited by Kristin L. Arola and Anne Frances Wysocki, Utah UP, 2012, pp. 145-161.

Ratto, Matt. "Critical Making: Conceptual and Material Studies in Technology and Social Life." *The Information Society*, vol. 27, no. 4, 2011, pp. 252-260.

"Requiescat, *n.*" *Oxford English Dictionary Online*, http://www.oed.com/. Accessed 22 Jul. 2019.

Schultz, Lucille M. *The Young Composers: Composition's Beginnings in Nineteenth-Century Schools*. Southern Illinois UP, 1999.

Shaw, Edward R. *English Composition by Practice*. New York, Henry Holt & Company, 1898. *Google Books*, https://books.google.com/. Accessed 22 Jul. 2019.

Stodola, Denise. "Using Stylistic Imitation in Freshman Writing Classes: The Rhetorical and Meta-Rhetorical Potential of Transitions in Geoffrey of Vinsauf's Medieval Treatises." *The Centrality of Style*, edited by Mike Duncan and Star Medzerian Vanguri, WAC Clearinghouse, 2013, pp. 57-69.

Swinton, William. *A School Manual of English Composition*. New York, Harper & Brothers, 1879. *Google Books*, https://books.google.com/. Accessed 22 Jul. 2019.

Tarbell, Horace S., and Martha Tarbell. *Essentials of English Composition.* Boston, Gunn & Company, 1902. *Google Books,* https://books.google.com/ Accessed 22 Jul. 2019.

Waddy, Virginia. *Elements of Composition and Rhetoric with Copious Exercises in Both Criticism and Construction.* New York, American Book Company, 1889. *Google Books,* https://books.google.com/. Accessed 22 Jul. 2019.

Williams, William. *Composition and Rhetoric by Practice, with Exercises, Adapted for Use in High Schools and Colleges.* Boston, D. C. Heath & Co., 1894. *Google Books,* https://books.google.com/. Accessed 22 Jul. 2019.

Course Design

Constellating Community Engagement in a Cultural Rhetorics Seminar

Maria Novotny, Claire Edwards, Gitte Frandsen, Danielle Koepke, Joni Marcum, Chloe Smith, Angelyn Sommers, and Madison Williams

Course Description

ENG 712: Theories in Public Rhetoric & Community Engagement is a required course for MA and PhD students concentrating in Rhetoric, Writing, and Community Engagement at the University of Wisconsin-Milwaukee (UWM). The topic for this course rotates depending upon the teaching faculty member's area of expertise. In the 2020 rotation, Maria opted to theme the course around cultural rhetorics (CR), as an introduction to the theories and methodologies useful to practicing CR. To familiarize students with these practices, two goals structured the course. The first goal was for students to identify the practices and theories defining the field of CR. The second goal was for students to build a CR methodology in relation to their individual scholarly areas of study. As such, this course asked students to move beyond an orientation centered on 'what is cultural rhetorics?' to a more methodological orientation that invited them to consider 'how does one practice cultural rhetorics?'

Embracing the CR pillar of constellation, this course design offers a constellated, multi-vocal approach by several students (Claire, Gitte, Danielle, Chloe, Madison, Joni, and Angelyn) and the instructor (Maria).[1] In what follows, Maria explains the institutional context and theoretical framing of the course. The students reflect on their experiences in the course, which prompts a dialogue on a surprising outcome: how the course prepared students to engage in a range of community projects. We believe that others may read and build upon this course design to consider how they may embrace CR theories and practices to guide community-engaged work.

Institutional Context

There are four graduate concentrations in the English Department at UWM. ENG 712 is a course offered by the Rhetoric, Writing, and Community Engagement (Plan B) concentration. This is a recently revised plan which is grounded in rhetoric and writing studies but also offers students "opportunities to apply that knowledge in pedagogical, professional, and/or community spaces" ("Graduate Plans: Summaries"). The curriculum is designed to support MA and PhD students who have wide interests in composition pedagogy, rhetorical theory, digital rhetorics, professional writing, and technical communication. Additionally, Plan B aims to support students who wish to apply their graduate education to higher education but also those with an interest in working in community settings.

As a new faculty member joining Plan B, I (Maria) suggested ENG 712 as a CR course for three reasons: one, my own graduate training centered on CR methodology and pedagogy; two, to my knowledge, an explicit course focused on CR had not been taught in the English Department at UWM; three, over the last few years there has been a growing embrace and demand for graduate students on academic job announcements for scholars whose work aligns with CR. For these reasons, my colleagues supported a CR theme for ENG 712.

Theoretical Rationale

The rationale for the course design grew out of my prior graduate experience as a student who took a cultural rhetorics graduate course and as a member of the Cultural Rhetorics Theory Lab.[2] These two experiences underscored an embodied, experiential, and practice-oriented approach to teaching CR. In addition, because I came from a CR graduate program, I developed a series of friendships with my fellow graduate students and mentorship relationships with faculty teaching and researching CR. Therefore, as I designed ENG 712, I consulted some of these colleagues (Phil Bratta, John Gagnon, Les Hutchinson, Katie Manthey) and mentors (Trixie Smith, Ames Hawkins, Julie Lindquist) to talk about the course structure.[3]

I scaffolded the course around a self-proposed final project, which included a proposal where students explained how the project practiced CR. Such an end goal was intentional to allow for flexible interest with how students may position themselves and/or their interests in the course. For instance, some students (especially GTAs) may want to explore pedagogical connections between CR and first year writing. Other students not enrolled in Plan B (taking the course as a student from a different English concentration) may desire using CR as an interdisciplinary lens to think about their dissertation design. Given the multiple entrances with how students may come to engage with CR, the course emphasized the practice and application of CR to students' specific areas of interest over mastery of CR theory. Evidence supporting the need to have students practice their own CR approach to a topic of their choosing is grounded in the "impossibility of simply laying out a 'universal' (or, an 'essential') frame for cultural rhetorics work" (Bratta and Powell). In this way, the course was designed for students to understand that "cultural rhetorics is a *practice*, and more specifically an embodied practice, that demands much from the scholars who engage in it" (Bratta and Powell).

To ground the course's embodied, experiential, and practice-oriented approach, I relied upon the four pillars of CR: (1) story, (2) decolonization, (3) relations, and (4) constellation (Bratta and Powell). While not all four practices must occur or be in operation at the same time to be seen as 'doing cultural rhetorics,' I emphasized the need for at least one of those pillars to be in operation. The decision to emphasize one over all four again emphasized the practice-oriented approach where students could 'try on a pillar' to reflect on the effectiveness of said pillar in relationship to their project. In essence, the pillars then served as a useful framework to discuss questions like, "What makes a rhetoric project a cultural rhetorics project?" and "What is cultural rhetorics pedagogy?"

Structurally, the course was divided into two experiences. The first half of the semester asked students to grapple with foundational CR texts and critical theory. For instance, the first three weeks of class, students read texts that were fundamental to the origins and development of what rhetoric and composition refer to as cultural rhetorics. These readings included a set of origin stories, which date back to the 1990s and early 2000s and feature Victor Villanueva's "On the Rhetoric and Precedents of Racism," Jacqueline Jones Royster's "Disciplinary Landscaping," and Malea Powell's "Dreaming Charles Eastman." These readings offered a glimpse into some of the foundational pieces advocating not for a CR orientation to the discipline but for a different, more culturally-conscious orientation to the discipline. My goal was to help students understand the scholarship and scholars whose work paved the path for CR to emerge. In doing so, students had an opportunity to realize how CR offers a re/orientation to the Westernized and canonized narrative of rhetoric and composition.

With the origins of CR mapped, students then engaged in a series of new readings that offered a critical re/orientation to the discipline (e.g. Ahmed; Maracle; King; Tuck and Yang). Collectively, these readings pushed students to critically reflect on the disciplinary narratives they have been told (i.e., "the canon" and Aristotelean histories privileging a Westernized narrative of rhetoric and composition). With a critical orientation toward the discipline established, the course then pivoted towards theory so students could begin to trace the crossovers and variances between cultural studies (CS) and CR. Students read historiographers (Cruickshank), cultural studies scholars (Hall), postcolonial theorists (Bhabha; Spivak), Indigenous theorists (Kimmerer; Warrior), and decolonial theorists (Mignolo; Tuhiwai Smith). These readings provided a layered orientation to the ideological and global shifts embraced by institutions and disciplines. In this way, the first half of the semester offered students two theoretical narratives: a CR narrative to rhetoric and composition and a narrative about the wider academic theoretical shifts embracing colonial critiques. Both narratives were essential to students understanding (1) what CR is in relation to the discipline and (2) why CR in relation to decolonialization is important.

The second half of the semester was organized around applications of CR in rhetoric and composition. We read works by authors who self-identify as cultural rhetoricians yet also identify with other rhetoric and composition scholarship (such as queer rhetorics, feminist rhetorics, Asian American rhetoric, embodied rhetorics, and even technical and professional writing). Unique to the course was the incorporation of actual authors into the class. Several of the cultural rhetoricians we read joined our class virtually for a portion of time (see syllabus for names of scholars). For instance, one week was themed around methodological ethics of CR. For that week, students read articles by Ames Hawkins, Phil Bratta, and John Gagnon; the authors later joined our class for 45 minutes to talk about the pieces, the methodological issues encountered in doing CR, and how they identify as cultural rhetoricians. Such experiences were essential to pedagogically modeling a constelled approach and fostering relationships through storytelling in rhetoric and composition. Cultural rhetorics, in this way, is its own disciplinary community where scholars are talking with each other and writing a new orientation to the traditional, Westernized canon.

The course projects mirrored much of the two-part structure of the course—reflection and revision—to emphasize the importance of practice over perfect production. There were four main assignments: (1) a cultural, rhetorical orientation statement; (2) a self-proposed seminar project; (3) a co-led student reading facilitation, where two students lead discussion based on the week's theme/focus and offered practice with pedagogical application of CR; and (4) weekly reading responses.

The Cultural Rhetorics Orientation Statement was the first assignment. This statement served as an opportunity for students to begin articulating how CR orients them to their work. In particular, students described their orientation within one of the following genres: (a) a research statement, (b) a teaching statement, or (c) a professional statement. Students submitted a draft of this statement midway into the course and then significantly revised at the end of the semester. Students also submitted a reflection narrating the changes made between their drafts as a method to document student learning. I developed the orientation statement assignment as a way for students to practice talking about their work to an audience that may be unfamiliar with CR.

A main objective of mine was for students to have an embodied experience of doing CR and reaffirming the belief that "it is here, at the space of embodied practices of the scholar—and not simply the scholar's attitude—that cultural rhetorics connects those who study it and those who live it" (Bratta and Powell). As such, I structured the major project for the course as a self-proposed seminar project. This required students to create an initial project proposal that provided a tentative project title and description, a discussion on how the project is situated within CR, the various deliverables that would be connected to the project, a justification of why this project is worthwhile (connects to a student's research, assists with a student's exam, connects to teaching and/or professional aspirations), a list of sources to consult, and any specific questions for me. I acted as a CR mentor by offering suggestions regarding scope and readings and asking students to explain the purpose of the project to ensure there was a reciprocal component to each project.

During the second half of the semester, students submitted a progress report and updated me and their classmates about their projects. This report proved essential to students revising the general scope, objectives, and aims of the project. As I anticipated, many students ultimately changed their project proposals when they learned of and read about the projects of our virtual guests. Here again, the reflective and revisionary components of the self-designed project acted as a tool to reward practice over perfected products.

The assessment of the self-designed project encouraged the process of practicing CR, evaluating the students' abilities to: (a) articulate a cultural-rhetorics-informed project (evident in the proposal); (b) practice that project (evident in the progress report); and (c) demonstrate a developing cultural-rhetorics methodology (evident in the final project). Such assessment coincides with "cultural rhetorics approaches [that] move us beyond plain study and mere critique encouraging relational accountability and active engagement in making and building" (Gagnon 3). Having first understood rhetoric and writing studies as disciplinary narrative history, students then respond by layering critical theory on top of the Westernized canon of rhetoric and writing studies. Their responses to selective narratives become "rhetorical slippages," moments in which narrative gaps and discursive slips emerge and offer space for rhetoricians to respond (Gagnon 7). In this way, students in the course needed to learn the display narratives first, then, along with the critical theory, to begin to identify and practice a CR response.

Pedagogical and Methodological Student Reflections

At the end of the spring 2020 semester, I proposed the idea of collaboratively reflecting and writing about ENG 712. This invitation was open to all students who took the CR course and seven of the eleven students enrolled emailed me to indicate their desire to work together. Collectively, we believe the course was unique for several reasons. One, it was the first time the course was offered to graduate students at UWM and therefore a new experience for all of us. Two, it was a course that occurred during the beginning of COVID-19 and, despite the shift to virtual learning, the class retained a close-knit, communal bond. In many ways, the very pillars of CR became even more relevant in the midst of a pandemic. Three, all of the students opted to create public-facing projects that operated on the principles of CR, which accounted for a more embodied and experiential course outcome. In the section that follows, seven students from ENG 712 reflect on their personal experiences in the course and discuss the two major areas in which CR became relevant: pedagogy and methodology.

Pedagogical Connections

Decolonializing Higher Education – Claire

I returned to graduate school to complete a PhD after several years of working at southern California community colleges as an adjunct professor, tutor, and writing center administrator. Since starting my PhD coursework, I have contemplated how the privileging of figures such as Aristotle, Socrates, and Burke as the forefathers of rhetoric, both ancient and modern, has obscured the rhetorical practices of feminists, Indigenous communities, Black Americans, and so many others. Yet I did not know what to call these problems or what larger system of thought they might be a part of.

It was in this course that I finally came to see decoloniality as a necessary approach to rethinking higher education. For instance, the elements of the course that solidified this realization were readings that both explicitly discuss marginalized cultural and rhetorical practices as well as demonstrated them. These include King's *The Truth about Stories*, which demonstrates conventions of orality, such as returns and repetitions to emphasize the ever-changing nature of reality and experience, and Kimmerer's *Braiding Sweetgrass*, which shows us the possibility of bringing together Western science and indigenous approaches to nature. King and Kimmerer's cultural ways of being, seeing, and writing are often not valued in academia. That was the problem I wanted to interrogate entering the PhD program, and I could see it and name it now as an effect of colonizing thinking about discourses and ways of being. In the community college setting, as well as the four-year university, a decolonial approach can push students not only to learn about a greater variety of communicative practices but also to assert the value of ones they bring with them as they move forward with their professional lives.

Story as Praxis in the FYC Classroom – Gitte

I came back to graduate school after teaching high school and college for fifteen years. What prompted me to return were questions that kept nagging at me about institutional, departmental, and personal socially unjust practices when teaching multilingual students in FYC programs. Early in my teaching career, I took an assimilationist approach that reproduced monolingual ideologies about language and language difference. In graduate school, scholarship in translanguaging, critical race theory, anti-racist teaching, and culturally sustaining pedagogy moved my own thinking forward, but CR offered a comprehensive heuristic and set of concepts to both anchor and transform my understanding and practice.

The theories and research I was reading in class and Maria's modeling of the CR philosophy in her teaching were pivotal in the practical, pedagogical, and assessment decisions I made teaching my FYC course. It was so clear to me that my students were desperate to make sense of how COVID-19 had upended their lives, and in my communications with them we shared stories about how the pandemic had affected our lives, communities, workplaces, and course work. I had students who were working as RNAs at hospitals and nursing homes, or who worked in retail or at restaurants. I had students who suddenly became the breadwinners of their families; students who got ill with COVID-19; and students who witnessed people die from COVID-19. I had students who were struggling with their schoolwork because of the online environment and students whose teachers gave them way more homework than before. There were so many stories. Towards the end of the semester, I gave my students the option of writing a story-based research paper as an alternative to a more traditional paper. The students who chose this option—about three out of four—wrote papers with strong voices, but also with linguistic and rhetorical awareness and careful analysis of sources. They used their stories as an exigence to engage critically with information and stakeholder perspectives in a way that seemed invested and curious.

The Power of Story in Graduate Seminar Pedagogies – Danielle

I was a student in this class during the second semester of my PhD program. As a GTA, I was interested in professors' pedagogical practices, especially at the graduate level. A graduate seminar built on CR pedagogy—particularly story—was something I'd never experienced before. For instance, narrative was how Maria introduced us to CR. She told us stories of how cultural rhetorics came to be, stories of her own CR experiences, and stories of the connections between scholars whose works we were reading. It was important for us to take the time to draw lines of relationality between scholars through citations and for us to understand how CR emerged from other fields such as cultural studies, historiography, postcolonial theories, and rhetoric, which built a web of relationality between people and ideas. Maria embodied the content she taught us. She constellated ideas with us and allowed us to draw our own individual and collective conclusions about what CR encompassed within the larger field of rhetoric. To aid in this collective knowledge-building, we worked collaboratively on digital class notes each week. While Maria scaffolded the general structure of these notes, we added in ideas presented in readings, connections we made between concepts, and how these things fit in—or didn't—with our idea of CR. I appreciated this, as it not only reflected CR pedagogy but also reflected a genuine care for our growth as individual students and as a class community.

Methodological Connections

Finding an Academic Home – Chloe

I am a first-generation college student. I grew up in a small Midwestern city in a working-class family. As far back as I can remember, my parents stressed the importance of education to me, and for years, everything I did was to achieve that goal. Now, as a PhD student, when I visit family over the holidays they tell me how proud they are and call me a "professor," even though I assured them that I'm not one. Their pride in me warms my heart, but I felt a bit like I was on a pedestal, a position that I didn't really feel comfortable occupying. I felt like the more success I had in the world of academia, the more I left part of myself behind. Navigating these tensions between family and academia, I found myself comforted by scholars like Victor Villanueva, Steven Alvarez, and others whose writing styles and research topics seemed to blur the line between academia and "real life" (Powell et al.). Still, I couldn't quite shake the nagging feeling that perhaps the only way to become a "real" scholar was to let go of my old life. If I'm being honest, I didn't expect this CR course to alter that feeling at all. But it did.

In reading "Our Story Begins Here," I came across this line: "We have been taught to separate academia from real life, and that academia is not a cultural community" (Powell et al.). I distinctly remember highlighting that and thinking, *finally*. The fact that such accomplished scholars could make such an explicit acknowledgement in a published piece made me feel that maybe CR was what I had been seeking. CR helps me feel at home because of its emphasis on relationality. It does not place academics on a pedestal; instead, it gives us the tools to stay connected to and serve the communities we come from. For me, CR doesn't just allow me to embrace all sides of myself but encourages it. As Julie Lindquist writes in *A Place to Stand*, "I was driven by my desire to prove that you didn't have to wear a suit—didn't have to leave the neighborhood—to be important" (15). CR has helped me to find an academic "home" without leaving the neighborhood. It's like I can finally settle in, get comfortable, and get to work—leaving a welcome mat by the door so maybe someday, students and scholars like me can know they've finally found their place.

Cultural Rhetorics as a Decolonial Practice – Madison

During the first weeks of the course, Maria asked us to ponder the question: what is cultural rhetorics? As an MA student, I found the readings engaging, but our class discussions left me feeling confused and sometimes frustrated as I struggled to understand CR. What made it different enough to be considered its own subfield? And how is it different from other concepts of rhetoric? These seemed like simple enough questions, but even with the texts we read, I couldn't pinpoint a concise response. It wasn't until we spent time learning about decolonial theory that the jumbled pieces of CR finally began to come together in my mind. Decolonial practices call attention to colonial systems of power, challenge the rhetoric of modernity, and make space for multiple knowledge systems by reclaiming the power to control their own representation. This means that CR views decolonial practices as "an orientation that includes 'both the analytic task of unveiling the logic of coloniality and the prospective task of contributing to build a world in which many worlds will co-exist'" (Powell et al.). In other words, "Critique is not the end of the process of decolonization—it's the beginning" because it goes beyond the postcolonial frameworks and leads to action (Powell et al.). CR moves away from the criticism typical of traditional rhetoric, calling instead for action and works that grow into a more equitable culture. So, what is cultural rhetorics? Here is how I answer that question now: CR is built upon understanding meaning-making as situated in specific cultural contexts and/or communities and then engaging with decolonial methodologies to create space for those multiple knowledges to exist. Although I couldn't pinpoint exactly how or when it happened, CR became a fully embodied aspect of how I have come to view, and intend to practice, rhetoric.

Reorientation in the Final Stretch – Joni

It is never too late to shift positions, to reorient oneself to concepts previously outside of one's field of vision. I am a fifth-year PhD candidate in the Media, Cinema, & Digital Studies track with an emphasis in Writing Pedagogy and Administration. Furthermore, I currently hold a leadership position as a WPA in our first year writing program, which involves mentorship of incoming GTAs. I found delving into CR to be beneficial to me despite, and maybe even because of, my late stage in my program. I view my experience as a student of CR as a re-orientation; though it may be slight, I recognize that the smallest shift in my present trajectory will have a lasting impact. In the moment of extreme change we are in during the COVID-19 pandemic, a flexible leadership style informed by a CR approach has been at the forefront of my mind: I see my work in my WPA role as a constant constellating of ideas from different places. There is now a fresh importance to slowing down, checking in with members of the team when needed, and taking care of the community of teachers and students of which I am a part, because each member of the community has a story to tell that is relevant to their needs from department leadership.

CR concepts have already proven useful as I work completing my dissertation as well. Constellating ideas means drawing knowledge together from different academic and cultural groupings in a way that acknowledges the histories and advantages of each. As I work with the environmental and energy humanities (in addition to film theory and history), engaging with CR in my project has become a guiding force. My aims have shifted to examine how historical film has influenced the discourse surrounding energy use, why these were the historically privileged discourses, and how to address environmental concerns in ways that incorporate broader perspectives to better serve environmental justice in the present. I will continue constellative practices in my scholarly work as I bring climate science and film scholarship together with questions about environmental discourse and public knowledge.

Cultural Rhetorics + Technical Communication – Angelyn

As an MA student studying Professional and Technical Writing, this class reoriented my view of community and expanded my understanding of narrative's role in technical communication. For example, I started to recognize my own positionality and how it affects my view of the world and the choices I make as a technical writer. This realization deeply impacted my views on what it means to write for a community and, more broadly, what constitutes technical communication. As I began to recognize that communities develop their own tactical communication practices, I realized these practices are often based in story (a CR pillar). This was new for me because I had not always considered stories as compatible with the supposedly "objective" field of technical communication. Yet in studying CR, I came to see narrative practices as the key to effective technical writing—stories help us to recognize the constellations of different ideas, build relationships with communities, and understand the structures of power present in our societies.

Angela Haas's essay, "Race, Rhetoric, and Technology," exemplifies this, reminding us that "all our users are not reflections of ourselves" (281). Stories have power. As a technical communicator, I must account for such power. This means I first need to listen to my particular audience's stories if I'm to understand and write for them. Technical communicators need to recognize that our audience is a complicated constellation of human experience, never static or easy to delineate. A CR framework based on story helps technical communicators break away from the belief that we can segment our audience into convenient boxes or speak to them neutrally. Stories allow us to truly see the individuals that make up our users because stories help us to understand their lived experiences and see the world from their point of view. And while stories give us new methods of understanding our audiences, they also give us options for communicating with those audiences in more inclusive ways. To be clear, technical communicators are not just listeners of stories, we are tellers of stories. This class has helped me to reorient my view of technical communication to one that values the practice of storytelling and recognizes the potential narrative has for connecting with communities in more just ways.

Constellating Our Reflections: Cultural Rhetorics as a Tool for Community-Engaged Work

When I (Maria) was designing this course, my main objective was for students to develop an understanding of the concepts, theories, and pillars that define CR. And, even though the course was themed within a Public Rhetorics and Community Engagement seminar, my course design was less concerned with having students find linkages between CR and community engagement (CE). It was surprising to me how connections between CR and CE suddenly emerged in the class. To illustrate how students drew upon CR theories and practices to guide their work within communities, we (the students and myself) follow the tradition of "Our Story Begins Here" and offer a collective dialogue about how CR and CE began to coalesce. Such a structure mirrors CR and CE commitments in collective meaning-making.

***

Us: Collectively reflecting on the course, one of the more surprising moments that emerged was realizing how integral coursework can be to community work. Often, we think about the academy and the various communities we inhabit as separate worlds; yet, there were clear moments where the two intersected.

Danielle: For sure! I saw how stories need to be honored and cared for as we enter into relationships with communities that we may work with. A story is more than words; it is an embodied experience. When a person chooses to share a story, they are trusting the listener with a part of themselves. As a PhD student hoping to engage in meaningful research with my own local community, I now see at a deeper level the need for being a part of a community before engaging in research pursuits with that community. This kind of work is messy. It takes time to build meaningful relationships. I wonder how community-engaged graduate programs can adapt to allow graduate students to build the necessary relations before engaging in research for their dissertations? Incorporating cultural rhetorics pedagogy and methodology into graduate seminars can be a starting place.

Us: Danielle raises an important observation that really "sunk in" for all of us in this class: work within communities is often messy and being a researcher in a community can be fraught with tensions. There were so many of our discussions focused on relationships and, specifically, the cultural rhetorics pillar of relationality. These conversations asked us to consider how CR can alter the very locations of how you define a community and where you find it.

Gitte: Absolutely. This was the case for me. Looking at classrooms as communities is not in itself novel, but the pillars of CR help me both theorize about what community engagement looks like in the classroom and envision a community praxis in the classroom. By defining community as a "place/space where groups organize under a set of shared beliefs and practices," we can see the classroom is not just made up *of* different communities but functions *as* a cultural community (Powell et al.). In this respect, the classroom acts as a contact zone (Pratt 34). There are social, political, and material components that tend to shape hierarchies in the classroom because elements of the macro-structure manifest themselves in the classroom, as everywhere in academia.

Us: Gitte's remark, while situated within the classroom, extends to all of the various relationships we have in our community projects. CR demands that we reflect on our own positionalities in relationship to our projects. Such a practice acts to account for asymmetrical power relationships that on the surface may appear well-intentioned but in actuality cause more harm to a particular community.

Gitte: Yes. Not attending to power dynamics can be an obstacle to building trust in a community. However, I also see the application of CR in first year composition classes as having some particular affordances that can be drawn upon to foster a classroom community. For instance, by incorporating a story-based pedagogy built on CR pillars, we may be able to better sustain and integrate students' cultural and linguistic resources. We can strategically use our power and positionality as instructors to nurture students' relationality, reciprocity, and respect for each other and their cultural histories.

Us: This commitment to relationality, reciprocity, and respect was a thread we found woven throughout many of the self-designed final projects. For students like Angelyn and Joni, who self-identified as belonging to other disciplinary orientations, focusing on response and not just critique led to more community-oriented projects. Creating public-facing deliverables was a first in a graduate seminar for both of them.

Angelyn: Yes, it really was a first, and it took time to figure out how to do more public-facing work. In my final project, I looked at an online healthcare community. I was particularly interested in how the members of this online community jointly navigated their conditions through the telling of stories and the sharing of experiences and knowledge. As a student of technical communication, I was beginning to see a major disconnect between the information given to these patients by their medical professionals and the types of information the patients shared with each other. The information these community members received from their doctors was often incomplete and, at times, even inaccurate. Furthermore, the official medical information available on the condition did little to prepare people for what it was like to live with the condition. I soon noticed that these community members had taken the task of technical communication upon themselves by creating informational documents, infographics, blog posts, and videos that blended personal experience and advice with medical facts and knowledge. CR helped me to see that including community input into the technical communication process is not only valuable, but essential. Without listening to the needs of the community—as expressed by the voices of those within the community—information shared through official channels can fall short of its goals and fail to benefit its community audience.

Joni: For me, the thought of reaching an audience outside of academic journals with community-engaged work was very exciting but didn't seem possible before taking this course. My areas of interest within the environmental humanities are discard studies and theories of waste. My final project sought to visualize my personal experience learning about waste processes and trending cultural discourse on consuming, curating, and discarding objects based on specific criteria such as minimalism, usefulness, thrift, and even whether items elicit joy (as Japanese organizing expert Marie Kondo recommends). Dominant public discourse about consumption and waste strongly influence these decisions, and I see the potential to design a variety of community-engaged projects based on this line of inquiry.

Us: While Angelyn and Joni's projects applied many of the CR pillars to help them do more community-engaged discipline work, Madison's final project took a slightly different approach: using CR tools to reimagine and redesign community maps. For her, CR provides affordances to change community issues, not just disciplinary ones.

Madison: My final project for the class focused on decolonizing maps of Milwaukee, one of the most common things with which visitors and newcomers to the city engage. Maps are created as a communicative text to help people understand the world around them, but the rhetorical nature of their construction means that those with the power to produce maps have the ability to decide what particular view of the world is being represented. Given this, I had two goals for my decolonized map. The first was to reveal the power dynamics beneath the myth of cartographic objectivity, creating a space for decolonial options and reconstruction to materialize. The second was to move toward reconstruction and make space for decolonial options using the emergent mapping of trails as representations of the performative function of knowledge-making and the constellating of relationships through space. My intention, given how the project was situated within a common, everyday text, was to help the public reimagine the embedded connections between cartography and colonialism. Doing so, I wanted to illustrate a critical reorientation to the everyday person how maps symbolically represent a particular way of knowing and an understanding of maps as social constructions.

Us: And Madison's reimagining work was not the only project that embedded community-engagement experiences; Chloe and Claire share moments of using CR—not in the classroom or in their graduate education—but in very real and messy community work.

Chloe: During this course, I was also an intern for Vote Yes for MPS, a campaign to pass a referendum that would increase funding for Milwaukee Public Schools. Participating in the campaign while taking the CR course was pure luck. One of the things I love most about CR is how much it values story and the personal experience of vulnerable individuals and communities. I saw these ideas and values in action every day that I was at my internship. My responsibilities ended up going beyond the expected writing: I helped curate brief interviews with parents, students, and community leaders at schools around the city, completed data entry for voters and volunteers, and canvassed an entire territory by myself. My abilities as a writer certainly helped me in this position, but looking back now, I don't think that I would call them my main contribution to this campaign, and furthering my writing experience is definitely not my main takeaway. What I really took from this position were the connections I made with people, the pride that came from working for a group so driven by the idea that students deserve an equitable education no matter what their zip code is, and the knowledge that I played a small role in something that will hopefully have a huge impact on students' lives. Experiencing all of this while simultaneously learning about an academic field that makes space for and values these ideas has left me invigorated. I want to take the experience I gained in my internship and the knowledge I gained in our CR course and incorporate the notion of connections, equity, and vulnerability into my work as a scholar and teacher.

Claire: While in our CR course, I was also receiving credit as a writing and editing intern for UWM's School of Freshwater Sciences. Working with this research team was a great way to see how academic research can have immediate impacts on a community. Learning more about science writing, though, has also shown me some of the barriers to communication and understanding that exist between academics (in the sciences and otherwise) and the communities in which they live. When writing public-facing documents, I often struggled to wade through the existing scholarship on subjects such as wastewater contamination. The CR course allowed me to think about the work I was doing in my internship in a different way, and the internship brought a sense of immediacy to some of the works we read in class. I have become much more attuned to the rhetorical nature of science communication as well as the deep importance of it, which enabled me to really take in works like Kimmerer's *Braiding Sweetgrass* and sense an urgency in the discussion of Indigenous ways of knowing vis a vis typical Western scientific forms of communicating and understanding. As I continue to gain experience in science rhetoric, I plan to continue to look for ways to better communicate with the communities affected by research initiatives and to continue to interrogate the assumptions made by Western scientific paradigms so we might find room in those discussions for different ways of knowing and understanding the natural environment.

Us: We have all come away from this course changed, though in different ways. The theory and practice of CR have had a profound effect on how we view and conduct ourselves in the various roles we occupy both in and outside of academia. CR is often messy. It's rooted in stories, community, and the idea that we can rebuild academia and the world around us into something better. We hope to take these stories, this knowledge, and these experiences to do just that.

Notes

1. This approach mirrors what cultural rhetoricians modeled in "Our Story Begins Here" and acknowledges the necessity in cultural rhetorics to represent the multiple bodies that influenced the course.

2. Lab members acted as collective authors of "Our Story Begins Here: Constellating Cultural Rhetorics Practice," a pinnacle essay in defining "cultural rhetorics."

3. While talking through a course design with past cohort colleagues and mentors may not be unique to CR and could be practices commonly found in other graduate course prep, they are essential to what it means to practice CR as it demands an unwavering commitment to relationships, more specifically 'relationality,' vis-à-vis CR work.

Works Cited

Bratta, Phil, and Malea Powell. "Introduction to the Special Issue: Entering the Cultural Rhetorics Conversations." *Enculturation*, April 2016, enculturation.net/entering-the-cultural-rhetorics-conversations

Gagnon, John. "How Cultural Rhetorics Can Change the Conversation: Towards New Communication Spaces to Address Human Trafficking." *Poroi*, vol. 12, no. 2, Feb. 2017, pp. 1-21.

"Graduate Plans: Summaries." *College of Letters & Science: English*, University of Wisconsin–Milwaukee, uwm.edu/english/graduate/graduate-plans/.

Haas, Angela M. "Race, Rhetoric, and Technology: A Case Study of Decolonial Technical Communication Theory, Methodology, and Pedagogy." *Journal of Business and Technical Communication*, vol. 26, no. 3, 2012, pp. 277-310.

Lindquist, Julie. *A Place to Stand: Politics and Persuasion in a Working-Class Bar*. Oxford UP, 2002.

Powell, Malea, Daisy Levy, Andrea Riley-Mukavetz, Marliee Brooks-Gillies, Maria Novotny, and Jennifer Fisch-Ferguson. "Our Story Begins Here: Constellating Cultural Rhetorics." *Enculturation*, Oct. 2014, enculturation.net/our-story-begins-here.

Pratt, Mary Louise. *Imperial Eyes: Travel Writing and Transculturation*. Routledge, 1992.

Where We Are: Intergenerational Exchanges

Intergenerational Exchange in Rhetoric and Composition: Some Views from Here

John Brereton and Cinthia Gannett

"We all got history. Some of us just don't know it."

—Ellen Hazard

"It's a funny kind of history that only looks backwards."

—Lewis Carroll

Let us be clear. We feel humbled in the face of the invitation to write about intergenerational dialogue and collaboration in this moment of deep cultural and educational change, even as we continue our long, slow improvisational journey away from active teaching, department meetings, and the pressures to publish or perish (Actually, perishing is no longer a metaphor as we look ahead). Using our own experiences across nearly fifty years of work-life in literacy studies and teaching, we want to explore some forms of intentional intergenerational work and think out loud about why it is so critical to undertake intergenerational work mindfully.

Of course, intergenerational exchange is always happening. Faculty study with and learn from earlier generations of scholars, formally and informally, and they in turn teach many generations of students across the academic lifecycle, some of whom they mentor as future professionals. And the cycle continues. But we may not always recognize the cycle's potential; worse, we may see it as simply inconvenient or even a burden, especially when it is easy to see insights of earlier generations as obsolete or out of touch. Indeed, in some respects, it may be easier to speak to the power of intergenerational work when you have lived through multiple generational shifts and can reflect on the kinds of intergenerational exchanges you have had to have with yourself across your own life.

In this active stage of our retirement, we also have the luxury of pausing to consider all the *multidirectional* forms of professional exchange that have made our lives so rich, looking back to teachers, older scholars, and mentors, and looking forward to our students and younger colleagues, all of whom have supported, stimulated, and provoked us at every turn. We understand that the field—broadly construed—and American higher education undergo constant change, sometimes continuous and incremental, sometimes discontinuous, and that we all enter and are formed by distinct temporal intellectual and social forces. While those differences are significant and can—and do—cause gaps and tensions, we offer the metaphor of *accompaniment*[1] as a means of respecting critical differences in view, while sharing some portion of our lifelong journeys as literacy educators.

We entered the field as graduate students and beginning teachers/scholars almost by accident, as so many did across the late 1960s and 70s. It was a turbulent time with odd resonances to this one—the terrible bloody fight for civil rights, the assassinations of John F. Kennedy and Martin Luther King Jr., the early feminist movement with its fight for equal rights and control over women's bodies, an untrustworthy government, a corrupt megalomaniac for a president, and an unjust international war that killed thousands of poor white, Brown, and Black young Americans, as well as countless Southeast Asians. We were witnessing the opening of a huge fissure in the social and political fabric of our society—a time when one could not look away. These moments revealed deep conflicts over the "present schemes of wealth and power" a apt phrase coined by Jonathan Swift in his well-known essay "Argument Against Abolishing Christianity."

It was during this time of discontinuity and rupture that multidirectional intergenerational exchange—what we have come to think of as *accompaniment*—was necessary for the survival of students and higher education itself, especially over the question of empowerment through literacy. The CUNY Open Admissions movement of the early 1970s, which John participated in as a brand-new teacher in New York, was a direct response to students' (often poor, minority, and/or immigrant students) demands for access to higher education. He and several of his colleagues realized they needed to listen to their students, question much of their own training and education, develop radically different resources and approaches cobbled together from many developing areas of applied research, and attempt to meet the needs of these new generations of students. Teachers committed to Open Admissions did so in the face of immense resistance from many of their fellow faculty, administrators, and purveyors of academic culture writ large who implicitly believed that white male standards were being "compromised."

CUNY administrators attempted to initiate an intergenerational dialogue among English faculty, with mixed results. A series of annual CUNY Conferences were organized, but these one-day affairs could not build a true community of scholars all committed to the same project. Instead, what emerged over time was what John has called "an invisible college," teachers teaching each other what they were learning about—and from—their students. It was a rich intergenerational dialogue. This accompaniment started spontaneously but over time became the CUNY Association of Writing Supervisors (or CAWS), the direct forebear of today's CWPA. And there were also other less obvious, but enduring, positive legacies. For example, one early CAWS president, Ken Bruffee, focused his research on how student dialogue within group settings can lead to enhanced learning and into a mode of collaborative intergenerational teaching/learning, which can also be seen as a kind of facilitated accompaniment. Bruffee's notions of peer collaboration in learning have been taken up in many classrooms to increase student agency and empowerment and have been central to the development of peer tutoring and writing center programs (1972, *Collaborative* 1984, *Peer Tutoring*, 1984).

We know our efforts to make change were provisional, incomplete, and riddled with imperfect efforts, but we tried throughout the decades both to understand our antecedents better and to be open to the work that newer generations of scholars and scholarship would bring to bear (Gannett and Brereton, 2020).

Fifty years later, we find ourselves collectively in another period of great and discontinuous change, a paradigm shift, or rather, several simultaneously. We are now engaged in a wild new world of virtual communication networks, which have radically reshaped the forms, formats, and nature of human discourse, enabling mass instant transmission of information, making online educational, social, political, and cultural work possible. This new digital universe is also complicated and compounded by the nature of false information and virulent social media, where public communication, niched to create "alternate facts" (and "alternate worlds" to live in), fosters radical social division. There are clear similarities to the era of our own entrance into the field: an uncertain democracy, the devastating consequences of a corrupted government, and a president who has encouraged the public acceptance of serious racial and gender bias and violence yet again—both within the US and across its borders. And sitting on top of it all: a global pandemic.

So what might it mean to meet the moment through accompaniment? There are many responses to this question, and sadly little space to do more than touch on one or two.

Archival Work

One way we can practice intergenerational work as accompaniment is through the joint undertaking of archival work. While it is common to think of "the archive" as a repository of old, privileged artifacts of high culture, newer notions of archiving as intergenerational, democratized literacy work is reinvigorating composition studies. When John and I created the Robert J. Connors Writing Center/WAC Archive at the University of New Hampshire some years ago, we invited graduate students Kate Tirabassi and Amy Zenger to collaborate as full partners with us and bring their own perspectives on what should be preserved and why (Gannett et al.). And if we want to ensure that our histories reflect and honor our diverse literacy histories, we need to support (that is, accompany) new, diverse generations of scholars to undertake this critical recovery work. Indeed, intergenerational work that draws on archival materials or the production of archival materials themselves is becoming increasingly popular in undergraduate and graduate courses in rhetoric and composition, as seen in Graban and Hayden's forthcoming collection (2021).

Boston Writing and Rhetoric Network (BRAWN)

Regional and local associations or groups can be one means of continuing valuable, meaningful accompaniment work outside of institution-specific structures. As one example, the Boston Area Rhetoric and Writing Network is a space that affords retired faculty productive, mutual, cross-generational engagement. BRAWN began over ten years ago as a collective effort by a small group of college and university WPAs to pool and share professional resources for local teachers of composition and rhetoric without traditional rank or status (graduate students, instructors, lecturers, adjuncts) who teach the vast majority of writing courses in the larger Boston area, often without regular access to useful professional development.[1]

While many of these faculty are pre-and early career, the group includes instructors of all ages and serves all institutional types (community colleges, specialized technical schools, liberal arts, and research colleges and universities). Anchor schools—such Boston College, Boston University, MIT, Northeastern, UMass Boston, and others—provide modest financial resources and organizational infrastructure, thereby receiving ongoing supplemental professional support for their own graduate students and contingent faculty.

Importantly, BRAWN is overseen by a Board that is deliberately diverse in terms of role, status, and life-stage. For example, even as a retired professor without institutional status, Cindy was welcomed to the Board (and, in fact, became its President). Intergenerational collaboration is therefore both necessary to fuel the initiative and intentionally cultivated; the operating principle is that everyone is always both expert and novice in different contexts. Said differently: we are all learners as well as teachers and scholars. Organizational leaders and workshop leaders provide their work voluntarily; we accompany each other along the way. We share our labor and our curiosities.

BRAWN undertakes many initiatives (a list-serv, book receptions, reading groups, writing retreats), but most importantly, it sponsors a free annual Summer Institute for up to a hundred contingent faculty. In keeping with our commitment to mutual mentoring, the workshops are facilitated by pre-, early, mid, and late-career professionals, and workshop leaders are expected to attend other workshops as *learners* like anyone else—that is, we accompany each other here, too. We have also instituted a Microhistories Session at the end of the conference, inviting local senior rhet-comp scholars to share their own (often messy) academic journeys, with a view to creating rich, complex, panhistoriographic faculty and field perspectives, and to invite all participants to situate themselves in—and across—embodied individual and collective pasts, presents, and futures.

Through BRAWN, intergenerational exchange is fostered for all participants: newcomers are supported beyond their own institutions as they enter the field and contribute their fresh pedagogical and scholarly insights to a larger community of practice. Non-tenure faculty with varying identities, allegiances, and support systems can find (and create) a community to sustain their ongoing development, value their labor, and engage in networking, while they contribute their own insights, lived experience, and research interests. Retired faculty offer their time, expertise, experience, and sometimes a meal (precious commodities!) to nourish present and future generations, while being continuously renewed and refreshed as members of our broad, collective, vital enterprise.

Accompanying each other forward: How might we deliberately sponsor rich cross-generational, cross-role associations and relationships *adjacent to* (or even temporarily unmoored from) the hierarchies of academic structures of specific institutions? What are the challenges to fostering these kinds of activities? What could we gain collectively, individually?

Notes:

1. BRAWN is most publicly accessible through its website, which is at https://bostonrhetoricwriting.org/

Works Cited

Bruffee, Kenneth. *A Short Course in Writing*. Winthrop, 1972.
---. "Collaborative Learning and the 'Conversation of Mankind'." *College English*, vol. 46, no. 7, 1984, pp. 635-652.
---. "Peer Tutoring and the "Conversation of Mankind'." *Writing Centers: Theory and Administration*, edited by G.A. Olson, NCTE, 1984, pp. 3-15.
Gannett, Cinthia, and John C. Brereton. "Framing and Facing Histories of Rhetoric and Composition." *Talking Back: Senior Scholars and their Colleagues Deliberate the Past, Present and Future of Writing Studies,* edited by Norbert Eliot and Alice S. Horning, Utah State UP, 2020, pp. 139-152.
Gannett, Cinthia, Elizabeth Slomba, Kate Tirabassi, Amy Zenger, and John C. Brereton. "It Might Come in Handy: Composing a Writing Archive at the University

of New Hampshire." *Centers for Learning: Writing Centers and Libraries in Collaboration,* edited by James K. Elmborg and Sheril Hook, American Library Association, 2005.

Graban, Tarez Samra and Wendy Hayden, eds. *Teaching through the Archives*. Southern Illinois UP (forthcoming, 2021).

The Intergenerational Blunder of Elitism as Fun(k)tionality, aka An Open Letter on Choices When "Keepin' It Real Goes Wrong …"

Todd Craig

Hey CompRhet World,

When asked about my perspective on intergenerationality in the field, I immediately think of J. Cole's "Middle Child." In 2019, Cole defined his "Middle Child" positioning, spitting "I'm dead in the middle of two generations, I'm little bro and big bro all at once," as he leaves a studio session with rapper 21 Savage for a lunch meeting with billionaire Jay-Z. In this song, Cole depicts the tightrope walk required by being in the middle: too young for inclusion with peers who've come prior, yet too old to run with those who've come after. However, Cole sees this moment as a bridge and uses this positionality as beneficial to his maneuverings.

I, too, have seen these moments. There were times I was shunned by both the older guard and my peers, considered too "non-conformist" for the respectability politics needed to blend into the traditionalist sentiments of the field. My jeans sagged a little too low, my sneakers weren't "shoes" enough, and my Queens-based slang just way too much. Sheesh, I was almost penalized in a teaching observation for using the word "y'all" too frequently (the observer had the count around seventeen). Throughout this #PumpkinSpiceLatte brand of academic hazing, with theft starring as "love" and the ecstasy of influence, I slowly realized it was *never* about the work; it was *always* about the choices I made, the scholar I decided to be. I realize now, on the other side of tenure, they were probably envious they didn't choose to walk in their true selves.

Who we are within intergenerational contexts can be complex; it's an action-packed question given our geopolitical location within the "twin pandemics" of racial injustice and COVID-19. And I put one before the other because one's been bubbling waaaaaaaay longer. Funny how things work around race, huh?

Does the new climate of higher education post-pandemic ever allow us back to the "normal" that once was? In the past year (which will probably total out to two years), colleges have closed. Public institutions and universities alike have consolidated, taking Ginsu knives to prior budgets, slicing and dicing "fiscal fat;" so if you thought there weren't enough jobs *before*, what'chu think's about to go down *now*, my G? A quick look at RhetMap.org's market comparison visuals tells you all you need to know. I assert we return to a place where a younger generation of scholar/researcher/educators *must* take heed, as there will be a premium placed on teaching like never before. The plush R1 gigs with that 1-1 or 2-1 teaching load – even more slim (and it was already crackhead skinny to begin with, but alas, I digress...). Thus, this new iteration of academia will require people who can teach *well*, in public *and* diverse settings, and in locations where your whole classroom might NOT look like you at all.

This hasn't been an issue for me; I've cut my teeth teaching and conferencing, researching and publishing in CUNY – one of the biggest and possibly most underfunded public universities nationally. We've been teaching under that "austerity funding" umbrella for at least two decades. My CUNY school is particularly known for its perpetual debt, so I've *always* taught under the hip-hop mantra of "making something outta nufin!" But many schools don't see that value; in fact, one R1 institution "recruiting" me presented a salary cut so severe that it's overt racism was simply white and blinding. Sure, they're thinking "we're *saving* you from malnourished conditions." However, I teach more than anyone on their faculty. The 2-1 load capped at 20 yields 60 students a year, *if* those classes are full.... My 3-2 load, with skyball caps of 42 in Fall 2020 (a different story for my next selection, "The Miseducation OF and BY..."), yielded about 90 ZoomRoom students. So I saw roughly 1.5 years' worth of your teaching load in one semester. The irony is said R1 doesn't even recognize none of their faculty can train graduate students (especially BIPOC students) to navigate *that* work. Did I mention I traditionally do this level of teaching while doing three conferences, one to two keynotes, and publishing one to two articles and/or book chapters a year?

The upcoming generation of CompRhet scholars must understand how to navigate *and* thrive in such overload scenarios.

CompRhet's GenNext scholars must also tackle the remaining twin of the pandemics once the health crisis eases its way on down the road. For decades, academia has not dealt with diversity and racial complexities in ways that honor our elders and forefolx' freedom struggles of the 1950s and 60s. Instead, the current field at large has duplicated older racialized attacks in less futuristic – and actually more elementary – ways. You think the field would get more savvy with racism ... but why? Why get savvy when you can continue to slap people in the face with ignorance, offering Flint water to BIPOC and marginalized CompRhet scholars while swearing it's spring water straight from some Icelandic glacier?

Again, I think back to that R1 institution's "courting"; in that salary cut, said administrator stated I'd be paid "as much as the white guy...and I think that's just fine." When I explained it was clear there was a powder-keg-problem on campus called racism, the response was "well, you'll be tenured. So you can choose when you decide to engage or not engage in the racism here." This false equivalent is yet another episode of "When Keepin' It Real Goes Wrong": in this moment, said administrator "kept it real" – quadrupling down on the campus' nationally-televised racist climate by comparing the worth of my Black body/teaching/mentorship/research to said white male colleague. But also, this administrator needed to be told "I'm a Black man in America – I can't step out of my skin and not address racism!"

So with the upcoming intergenerational struggle, I see the need to push towards what I'm calling "Comp3.0." I'm coining this phrase now, but be clear, you'll see this laid out thoroughly in *K for the Way* (spoiler alert – new CompRhet book on hip-hop and DJ rhetoric coming) …

Comp3.0 requires we meet this overt racism, discrimination, and respectability politics head on, pushing innovative research and scholarship that simply doesn't ask the field for permission. For generations, we've witnessed many of our elders navigate this field. Sometimes successfully, and oftentimes not. We've seen colleagues denied tenure, denied promotion, rejected for awards, and gatekept in peer review processes at journals and academic presses. We've watched quietly as some scholars usurp creative consciousness from younger folx, snatch up research, go on Award Tours, and dishonestly claim the work as their own (oh yeah, we *see* y'all … see *Get Rich* track 18). We've even seen budding scholar/researcher/educators of color excluded from the patchwork fabric we call doctoral programs. I contend Comp3.0 should rail against this cycle, pushing back in a way that *requires* the field to change.

I'm super lucky to sit with J. Cole-like positionality. I'm cool with many respectable CompRhet OGs: elders and forefolx in the field who have come before me. So like Cole, I want to shout out those OGs, elders, and forefolx who excavated the foundation for part of this field, blazing some fierce scholarly trails for me and others to run. I'm also cool with some younger folx on the come-up, those CompRhet GenNext scholars, cutting they teeth, getting bumps and bruises along the way. Fortunately, I can get slightly brolic with knowledge, and share a lil game based on my own travels, bumps, and bruises. Shouts to April and AD, Aja and Regina, Laquana and Shereen, Khirsten and Lou, Victor and Sherita, Sara and Vani, Yanira and Bene. I see y'all moving out here – salute! Continue to push the field forward by droppin' that CompRhet crack! And keep supporting each other, while making your way through this treachery called "the field."

I remember watching my mentor levitating through hallways of academe – strong, fearless and vocal, calling folx out for their Tom Foolery immediately!

But *how*, Sway?

Simply by outpacing *ery'body*! While in my doctoral program, she had more publications and conference presentations than the other three racist directors combined. Yes … *combined*! And tenure wasn't easier for her … nah, they were clear about making it hard, evidenced when her materials came up "lost" for one full year (ironically, this happened to me, too – my chair at the time told me the following: "suck it up, get over it and reproduce your documents").

My most valuable mentor-lesson defines my intergenerational message: know it's all about your choices. The choices you make dictate your path; so no matter what, make sure those choices are ethical, equitable, and just. They will be the litmus test for how you are judged. And know the more ethical, equitable, and just your choices are, the more the field's treachery will come for you! I've been in spaces where the prior generation hated me simply because I set my own pace and did the work. And sometimes, the generation after me was like, "Bruh … can you slow down, please?" You must understand the impact of your choices.

I *chose* to work in CUNY at a PBI knowing full-well the institution's reputation wasn't the greatest, according to "the university" or the "negative press." I could've made other choices then, and would love to make even more choices in the future, as I grow and expand as a scholar/educator/researcher. But in April 2014, I made a calculated choice to hopefully serve as a beacon amongst a younger generation of Black and Brown scholars. Kermit the Frog once said "it ain't easy being green." So you already *know* what my Black ass is going through …

Finally, when you make those choices, stand by them. Be humble enough to move off a square if you realize you're standing in the wrong spot. But to be very clear – and I mean Crystal like Billy – stand firm when you know you're standing on a square that's just.

And keep pushin' – cuz ain't nobody gon' make it easy for you.

So who I am, you ask? I'm that MiddleChildDude, sitting between two generations, hoping with all I have that I'm making the right difference for my forefolx' legacies, building upon the legacy of my mentor and making it easier for those on the come-up. As long as I'm hitting those marks, I'm Gucci, and that's word to Big Bird.

I hope this letter hits different for you each time you read it as you move through this field.

And with that, I ain't even tryna hold you …

Peace and Love,
T O Double D

Works Cited

50 Cent. "U Not Like Me." *Git Rich or Die Tryin'*. Shady/Aftermath/Interscope Records, 2003.
A Tribe Called Quest. "Award Tour." *Midnight Marauders*. Jive Records, 1993.
Alvarez, Sara P., and Amy J. Wan. "Global Citizenship as Literacy: A Critical Reflection for Teaching Multilingual Writers." *Journal of Adolescent & Adult Literacy*, vol. 63, no. 2, 2019, pp. 213-216.

Baker-Bell, April. *Linguistic Justice: Black Language, Literacy, Identity, and Pedagogy*. Routledge, 2020.

Carson, A. D. *I Used to Love to Dream*. University of Michigan Press, 2020.

Cole, J. "Middle Child." *Revenge of the Dreamers III*. Dreamville/Interscope Records, 2019.

Cooke, Laquana, et al. "Culturally Responsive Computing: Supporting Diverse Justice Projects In/As Computer Science Education." *2019 Research on Equity and Sustained Participation in Engineering, Computing, and Technology (RESPECT)*. IEEE, 2019.

Diana Ross and Michael Jackson. "Ease on Down the Road." *The Wiz: Original Motion Picture Soundtrack*. MCA Records, 1978.

Duthely, Regina. "Black Feminist Hip-Hop Rhetorics and the Digital Public Sphere." *Changing English: Studies in Culture and Education*, vol. 24, no. 2, 2017, pp. 202-212.

Echols, Khirsten. "Composing with Black Noise." *Kairos: A Journal of Rhetoric, Technology, and Pedagogy*, vol. 21, no. 2, 2017.

Hierro, Victor Del. "DJs, Playlists, and Community: Imagining Communication Design Through Hip Hop." *Communication Design Quarterly Review*, vol. 7, no. 2, 2019, pp. 28-39.

Inayatulla, Shereen and Michael T. MacDonald. "Sans Papiers: Humanizing Documentation." *Literacy and Pedagogy in an Age of Misinformation and Disinformation*, edited by Tara Lockhart et al., Parlor Press, 2021, pp. 225-241.

Kannan, Vani. "Taking a Lead from Student Movements in a 'Political Turn.'" *Writing Democracy: The Political Turn in and Beyond the Trump Era*, edited by Shannon Carter, Deborah Mutnick, Stephen Parks, and Jessica Pauszek, Routledge, 2019, pp. 130-137.

Kermit the Frog. "It's Not Easy Bein' Green." Written by Joe Raposo. 1970.

Maraj, Louis M. *Black or Right: Anti/Racist Campus Rhetorics*. University Press of Colorado, 2020.

Martinez, Aja Y. *Counterstory: The Rhetoric and Writing of Critical Race Theory*. National Council of Teachers of English, 2020.

Nas. "Ether." *Stillmatic*. Ill Will/Columbia Records, 2001.

Ridolfo, Jim. "Rhet Map Market Comparison." *Rhet Map: Mapping Rhetoric and Composition*, 2021, www.rhetmap.org/market-comparison/.

Roundtree, Sherita V. and Michael Shirzadian. "Third Space: A Keyword Essay." *Community Literacy Journal*, vol. 14, no. 2, 2020, pp. 173–184.

Slick Rick. "Hey Young World." *The Great Adventures of Slick Rick*. Def Jam/Columbia Records, 1988.

Simmons, Benesemon, Vani Kannan, Sherita Roundtree, B. López and Yanira Rodríguez. "We Read Your Letter." *Writers: Craft and Context* vol 1, no. 1, 2020, pp. 6-14.

Sway's Universe. "Kanye West and Sway Talk Without Boundaries: Raw and Real on Sway in the Morning." *YouTube*, uploaded by Sway's Universe, 26 November 2013, https://www.youtube.com/watch?v=S78tT_YxF_c

On Podcasting, Program Development, and Intergenerational Thinking

Eric Detweiler

I spent my first year of college as a music business major, a wannabe audio engineer. Thanks to two main factors, that major didn't take. First, I learned audio engineering wasn't just being present while cool music happened. Second, I took first year writing, which convinced me to become an English major (more on that in a bit).

Despite the major switch, my audio experience proved an unexpected asset when I began pursuing a PhD in English at The University of Texas at Austin in 2011. While at UT-Austin, I worked in the Digital Writing and Research Lab, collaborating with other graduate students on projects at the intersection of digital media and rhetoric and writing studies. At the time, podcasts were attracting more and more academic attention, and, given my background with digital audio, I ended up leading a team that created a rhetoric podcast called *Zeugma*. When my work on that project ended, I started my own podcast: *Rhetoricity*.

Even though I washed out of that music business program, I enjoy recording, editing, and producing podcasts. But, to be frank, I didn't just start *Rhetoricity* for the love of the medium. It was also an excuse to engage in some intergenerational networking. Having a podcast gave me a pretext to reach out to established scholars without the anxiety-ridden experience of walking up to them at a conference and introducing myself out of the blue. Instead, I could email them to tell them I appreciated one of their recent publications, then ask if they'd be interested in a podcast interview at an upcoming event.

As a result, I've spent the past decade interviewing scholars across disciplinary generations.[1] And, because podcast interviews tend to be more personal and free-wheeling than academic publications, I've often learned not just about interviewees' research interests and teaching philosophies, but about their on-the-ground career experiences—the departments, programs, collaborators, and day-to-day obstructions that shaped their professional lives. Before I started conducting and coordinating podcast interviews, I had read scholarship like Sharon Crowley's *Composition in the University* and Lisa L. Coleman and Lorien Goodman's "Rhetoric/Composition: Intersections/Impasses/Differends," which gave me a sense of where, when, why, and how rhetoric and writing studies coalesced in US higher education. But reading such scholarship is different than hearing firsthand about Crowley's experiences in her PhD program, or how Andrea Lunsford first found out about the Conference on College Composition and Communication, or how Tarez Samra Graban navigates the specific terrain of her program's undergraduate curriculum.

There's a risk that the preceding sentence will sound like I'm exalting myself and my interviewees—the academic equivalent of placing myself proximate to power in the proverbial room where it happens. But while I have great respect for those three interviewees, my point is that those interviews gave me a clearer impression of how prosaic, local, and material—how pointedly *un*exalted—teaching and studying rhetoric and writing can be. My experiences coordinating other intergenerational audio projects, most notably the Rhetoric Society of America's 2018 Oral History Initiative, have reinforced that impression (Detweiler and Williams).

In particular, intergenerational interviews have taught me to appreciate the influence that mundane institutional, departmental, and programmatic structures have on interviewees' careers. It made a big difference whether they were the lone rhetorician in a literature department or working alongside faculty with similar disciplinary backgrounds; whether there were networks of colleagues at other local institutions with whom they could correspond or meet up; whether they found themselves collaborating or competing with potential allies in communication studies or colleges of education.[2] I learned that things like what department they were in, what that department's curriculum looked like, and what administrative positions they held (e.g., working as WPAs or writing center directors) affected their careers at least as much as their research and teaching interests.

But the kinds of intergenerational networks common in rhetoric and writing studies tend to emphasize research and teaching more than the everyday planning and development that shapes programs, departments, and institutions. That's not to say the latter isn't addressed at conferences and in published work (consider Johnson, Simmons, and Sullivan; Peeples, Rosinski, and Strickland; Shelton 20), especially when it comes to the general-education writing programs that have long played central roles in the field's scholarship and teacher training. But the intergenerational work graduate students do with their thesis and dissertation advisors and the training they receive in teaching practicums prioritize particular kinds of thinking that can take broader institutions and programs for granted.

So let me rewind for a moment to trace out my own after-the-fact programmatic genealogy. The Belmont University first-year writing course that convinced me to become an English major was taught by a rhetoric and writing studies specialist whose class gave me a radically different sense of what English studies could be than the literature-centered courses I took in high school. That continued throughout my undergraduate career: because I chose the English major's writing concentration, I took a number of courses (e.g., Theories of

Writing, Advanced Composition, Book Editing in Context) that I only later learned to identify as rhetoric and writing courses. Like most undergraduates, I was largely unaware of the field's existence as such and completely clueless that getting a de facto undergraduate degree in rhetoric and writing studies was a remarkably rare opportunity. I did not and probably could not have grasped the work that went into developing such a curriculum.

From there, I landed in the English MA program at the University of Louisville, mostly because it offered a decent stipend in my hometown and not because I had any sense of the scope and quality of its rhetoric and writing faculty, much less Kentucky's state-level restrictions on redundant graduate programs at public universities, which meant Louisville offered the commonwealth's only PhD in Rhetoric and Composition. And so, almost by accident (but also, in retrospect, through the careful guidance of undergraduate mentors), I ended up in an MA program that fostered an explicit interest in rhetoric and writing studies.

And then, after a few years teaching writing at two- and four-year institutions around Nashville, Tennessee, I was accepted into a PhD program at UT-Austin, aware of but still not fully recognizing the rarity of its standalone Department of Rhetoric and Writing as well as the affiliated (and aforementioned) Digital Writing and Research Lab. While I was technically an English PhD student, almost all my assistantships and the faculty members with whom I worked operated under the auspices of that department.

But where did these things come from? How did such majors and graduate programs and departments happen? Why, as I later learned, were they relatively few? Even five years after finishing my PhD, and a couple of years into the work of starting a Public Writing and Rhetoric degree program at my current institution, I am still putting such things together. But/and/thus, I would wager, rhetoric and writing-centered program development is a particularly important site of local and cross-institutional intergenerational thinking. What do our undergraduate and graduate degree programs look like? What are their histories, politics, and futures? What is the obscure state policy, institutional exigence, or forgotten argument that prevented or gave rise to this or that rhetoric and writing course, concentration, major? Precisely because they can become so workaday—as overlooked as the asbestos in a Brutalist humanities building—broader programmatic structures, rationales, and elisions can be challenging for newcomers to both the field and specific institutions to apprehend. Such things pop up in podcast interviews and passing conversations, but are often not baked into intergenerational mentorship in the ways research and teaching are. Even as rhetoric and writing programs pop up with increasing frequency (Giberson, Nugent, and Ostergaard), they can still fly under the intergenerational radar.

Yet as I have realized (often accidentally and anecdotally), because effective program development can require the breadth and depth of institutional knowhow possessed by more established generations, but also the flexibility and awareness of the field's burgeoning corners possessed by relative newcomers, I would position it as a key site for intergenerational thinking and a significant ongoing concern as we map out where we are and where we're going in rhetoric and writing studies. That's not to say intergenerational thinking is a panacea. After all, a network that is intergenerational but otherwise homogeneous can perpetuate inequities in hiring and other programmatic practices that have long pervaded rhetoric and writing programs. This has been a lingering issue in my podcasting work as well: given that my professional network is disproportionately white, what can I do to invite scholars of color into the conversation ("Rhetorical Juxtapositions")? But intergenerational thinking provides one way to broaden perspectives in institutional conversations that can span years if not decades. Does that mean making programmatic matters more central to graduate training or (though I can't imagine "more podcasts!" is anyone's idea of a solution in 2021) conducting and recording more intergenerational conversations? Of that I'm not yet sure. We'd have to think about that together.

Notes

1. To clarify, I'm using "generation" here less as a marker of age and more as a marker of how long people have been in the field. For the purposes of this piece, a thirty year old who started their first faculty position in 2021 would be the same "generation" as a fifty year old starting a similar position at the same time.

2. For examples of such factors' effects, consult Detweiler and Williams 569.

Works Consulted

Crowley, Sharon. *Composition in the University: Historical and Polemical Essays*. U of Pittsburgh P, 1998.

---. "The Exemplary Sharon Crowley." *Rhetoricity*, interviewed by Kendall Gerdes, produced by Eric Detweiler, 9 Apr. 2015, https://rhetoricity.libsyn.com/the-exemplary-sharon-crowley.

Coleman, Lisa L., and Lorien Goodman. "Rhetoric/Composition: Intersections/Impasses/Differends." *enculturation*, vol. 5, no. 1, 2003, http://enculturation.net/5_1/index51.html.

Detweiler, Eric, and Elizabeth McGhee Williams. "A Living Rhetorical Enterprise: The RSA Oral History Initiative." *Rhetoric Society Quarterly*, vol. 49, no. 5, pp. 566-582.

Giberson, Greg, Jim Nugent, and Lori Ostergaard, editors. *Writing Majors: Eighteen Program Profiles*. Utah State UP, 2015.

Graban, Tarez Samra. "Unflattening Global Rhetorics and Archival Pedagogies: An Interview with Tarez Samra Graban." *Rhetoricity*, produced by Eric Detweiler,

23 Feb. 2021, https://rhetoricity.libsyn.com/unflattening-global-rhetorics-and-archival-pedagogies-an-interview-with-tarez-samra-graban.

Johnson, Meredith A., W. Michele Simmons, and Patricia Sullivan. *Lean Technical Communication: Toward Sustainable Program Innovation*. Routledge, 2018.

Lunsford, Andrea. "Rhetoric, She Wrote: Andrea Lunsford on the Discipline and its Histories." *Rhetoricity*, interviewed by Ben Harley, produced by Eric Detweiler, 2 Dec. 2019, https://rhetoricity.libsyn.com/rhetoric-she-wrote-andrea-lunsford-on-the-discipline-and-its-histories.

Peeples, Timothy, Paula Rosinski, and Michael Strickland. "*Chronos* and *Kairos*, Strategies and Tactics: The Case of Constructing Elon University's Professional Writing and Rhetoric Concentration." *Composition Studies*, 2007, vol. 35, no. 1, pp. 57–76.

"Rhetorical Juxtapositions." *Rhetoricity*, 14 Jul. 2020, https://rhetoricity.libsyn.com/rhetorical-juxtapositions.

Shelton, Cecilia. "Shifting Out of Neutral: Centering Difference, Bias, and Social Justice in a Business Writing Course." *Technical Communication Quarterly*, vol. 29, no. 1, 2020, pp. 18–32.

Intergenerational Knowledge, Social Media, and the Composition Community: Insights and Inquiries

Amanda M. May

Social media has been a cornerstone of my professional life since before I formally entered my doctoral studies, but I never rushed to sign up for new platforms. I didn't use Facebook until 2007, when I joined because a friend encouraged me to. I took even longer to create a Twitter account; in March 2016, I joined, once again because a professional peer highlighted its networking and informal professional development uses. I still maintain both accounts: Twitter as a mostly professional online space, Facebook as a hybrid space showing professional and personal interests. During my doctoral studies, my interest in social media deepened: such media became something I both researched and practiced in multiple contexts and capacities. In considering where we are in terms of intergenerational exchange, I want to use social media as a lens to read some of composition's current fieldwide issues (as well as how those concerns might be intergenerational) by exploring four insights. I hope that, in doing so, we begin to determine what knowledge and pedagogies we hope to carry forward about these media and their place in the composition classroom.

Insight 1: Interest in and Perceptions of Social Media are Generational

Social media is commonly—but not always—an interest of younger generations. We are rapidly approaching a time when the eighteen-year-olds in our classrooms will be younger than Facebook's earliest iteration. These individuals will enter our classrooms having grown up with digital renditions of social media, and their experiences with such media will likely be different than our own. They may even have parents who were avid social media users when platforms like Facebook and MySpace first emerged.

Interest in social media doesn't develop purely because such platforms exist; it instead emerges from what these platforms can do. My own experiences with Facebook and Twitter reflect this point: I initially didn't see a use for Facebook or Twitter, but my perceptions changed when I learned both could serve what I considered meaningful purposes. I adopted Twitter, specifically for reasons similar to those David Coad identifies in his study of graduate student Twitter use at a writing conference: not at the encouragement of instructors, but because of peers. Likewise, my decision to use Twitter in the classroom emerged from interactions with outgoing graduate students. My peers played a large role, but so did my instructors, who provided me with opportunities to explore my research interests related to social media.

I've had interactions with individuals from previous generations outside of academia who claim social media is "ruining writing." I suspect that, were my peers of a similar generational mindset, my interests and perceptions would be much different. One thing we should work to carry forward is how to gauge interest in and perceptions of social media in the classroom.

Insight 2: Differences in Social Media Knowledge and Literacies are Generational

Intersecting with intergenerational interests and perceptions are knowledge and literacy differences regarding social media, a fact which applies to both students and instructors of writing.

As a university student fresh out of high school, I wrote traditional MLA papers with no chance for revision for both of my composition classes back in 2005. In my first semester of teaching composition, over a decade after taking my university's first year writing sequence, my major assignments looked very different, and I used social media for low-stakes purposes. In doing so, I assumed most of my students were interested in—or at least familiar with—social media. And most were, but they understood social media differently than I did. Similarly, Heather Fielding implemented Twitter to increase classroom engagement but found that some students were not familiar enough with Twitter to implement it effectively (110). Moving forward, we should work to preserve the knowledge that not all incoming students are as familiar with social media as we might first assume.

Likewise, we cannot assume all incoming graduate students or composition instructors will be literate in these technologies (even if they are familiar with them), either due to limited personal use or because they use such platforms purely for personal reasons. Stephanie Vie encourages instructors to include technologies familiar to students, including blogs and social networking sites, but she also underscores a need for instructors to familiarize themselves with these technologies before their implementation (10). Graduate students, much like undergraduate students, may be from different social generations and backgrounds. Their knowledge and perceptions of social media, as well as their literacies, may be radically different than what we assume.

Insight 3: Social Media Contexts Vary, but Generational Differences may Obscure such Differences

My own social media use started as purely personal. In fact, looking back at my experiences with teaching first year writing, I suspect many of my students had limited views of how social media could function as writing. It's possible that they understood personal and professional purposes, but their understanding of such implementations varied. Further, they were largely unfamiliar with using social media in an academic context to portray their identities as first year writing and/or university students.

In many cases, composition scholars frame social media in fairly intergenerational terms: our pedagogies, frequently centered around a single platform, serve as new means with which to carry forward old(er) concepts central to the composition classroom and to help students understand these concepts. As several examples, Elisabeth Buck discusses audience awareness and Facebook or MySpace profiles, Lindsay Sabatino describes teaching visual cues with the Facebook game *Mafia Wars*, and Samuel Head argues that because of how much text exists on platforms like Facebook and Twitter, "these sites can be used as a bridge to rhetorical analysis, particularly with audience awareness and appeal" (28).

The students in our classrooms, however, may not automatically understand the links between these contexts, a point worth remembering. Ryan Shepherd exemplifies this issue through a survey of 474 students in which he found that many considered Facebook writing as informal and, therefore, did not see the connection between social media and first-year composition (90-92). As teachers, we should work to make these connections and disconnections between contexts clearer for incoming students who may not understand how they utilize concepts taught in the composition classroom—audience awareness and the rhetorical situation, for instance—relative to social media.

I pose the same consideration for graduate students and teachers, as they may need to understand how to use social media in varying capacities: as a networking tool (Coad) and by choice as part of their first year writing pedagogy (Vie).

Insight 4: Pedagogies for Teaching Social Media Should be Specific but Adaptable

The question of how to teach composition effectively has been an ongoing theme in our discipline for as long as its existence. In the first volume of *The English Journal* in 1912, Edwin M. Hopkins questioned whether good teaching of composition was possible in then-current conditions. His answer was simple: "No" (8).

Social media has offered us new ways to teach students and has, as my examples highlight, served as texts for analysis (Buck) and as writing itself (Fielding). Composition scholars like Pamela Takayoshi and Stacey Pigg both provide research toward specific pedagogies for newer forms of writing, including social media. To continue to develop such pedagogies, we might look backward at the knowledge we have inherited from previous generations of composition teachers and scholars and determine how we carry it forward. One intergenerational approach, as I have suggested, is to integrate social media with existing concepts and frameworks to help students understand the differences between genres and processes. Buck used Facebook and MySpace to teach students about audience, for instance, by asking them to complete tasks that included analyzing their own—or a family member's—social media profiles.

A cautionary addendum is in order: as a field, we tend to engage in single-platform studies of social media. However, while pedagogies might emerge out of single platforms, they should be adaptable enough to be transferred to others, if only because social media changes so quickly. MySpace and *Mafia Wars* are both good examples of social media, or elements of it, that have faded from use or that have been discontinued. By attending to specific pedagogies applicable to different platforms, we can better support students and teachers with different backgrounds and levels of interest in social media. Further, we can begin to help students better connect social media contexts and make the most of their learning.

Conclusion: Where Are We Going?

Social media has taken a back seat since I entered my tenure-track position, partly because I'm cognizant that our largely nontraditional student body may have limited interest in using it. It is still very much present as an option in my two current writing classrooms, technical writing and a junior-level course on writing as advocacy, but mostly as an optional form of writing or as a form of writing that we study. I'm still invested in social media research and practice, and I'm also interested to see what new pedagogies emerge as the students we teach, and social media platforms we use, continue to change.

Works Consulted

Buck, Elisabeth H. "Facebook, Instagram, and Twitter -- oh my!: Assessing the efficacy of the rhetorical composing situation with FYC students as advanced social media practitioners." *Kairos: A Journal of Rhetoric, Technology, and Pedagogy*, vol. 19, no. 3, 2016, https://kairos.technorhetoric.net/19.3/praxis/buck/. Accessed 23 Mar. 2018.

Fielding, Heather. "'Any Time, Any Place': The Myth of Universal Access and the Semiprivate Space of Online Education." *Computers and Composition*, vol. 40, June 2016, pp. 103-114, https://doi.org/10.1016/j.compcom.2016.03.002.

Geerats, Kendra, Jan Vanhoof, and Piet Van den Bossche. "Teachers' Perceptions of Intergenerational Knowledge Flows." *Teaching and Teacher Education*, vol. 56 2016, pp. 150-161, https://doi.org/10.1016/j.tate.2016.01.024.

Head, Samuel L. "Teaching Grounded Audiences: Burke's Identification in Facebook and Composition." *Computers and Composition*, vol. 39, Mar. 2016, pp. 27-40. https://doi.org/10.1016/j.compcom.2015.11.006

Hopkins, Edwin M. "Can Good Composition Teaching be Done under Present Conditions?" *The English Journal*, vol. 1, no. 1, 1912, pp. 1-8.

Pigg, Stacey. *Transient Literacies in Action: Composing with the Mobile Surround*. WAC Clearinghouse, 2020.

Sabatino, Lindsay. "Improving Writing Literacies through Digital Gaming Literacies: Facebook Gaming in the Composition Classroom." *Computers and Composition*, vol. 32, Jun. 2014, pp. 41-53, https://doi.org/10.1016/j.compcom.2014.04.005.

Shepherd, Ryan P. "FB in FYC: Facebook Use Among First-Year Composition Students." *Computers and Composition*, vol. 35, Mar. 2015, pp. 86-107, https://doi.org/10.1016/j.compcom.2014.12.

Swartz, Jennifer. "MySpace, Facebook, and Multimodal Literacy in the Writing Classroom." *Kairos: A Journal of Rhetoric, Technology, and Pedagogy*, vol. 14, no. 2, 2010, https://praxis.technorhetoric.net/tiki-index.php?page=Multimodal_Literacy. Accessed 14 Mar. 2021.

Takayoshi, Pamela. "Short-form writing: Studying process in the context of contemporary composing technologies." *Computers and Composition*, vol. 37, Sept. 2015, pp. 1-13, https://doi.org/10.1016/j.compcom.2015.04.006.

Vie, Stephanie. "Digital Divide 2.0: 'Generation M' and Online Social Networking Sites in the Composition Classroom." *Computers and Composition*, vol. 25, no. 1, 2008, pp. 9-23, https://doi.org/10.1016/j.compcom.2007.09.004.

When the Family Tree Metaphor Breaks Down, What Grows?

Benjamin Miller

When I think about generations, I often think about more-or-less discrete cohorts: siblings and cousins lining up neatly across a family tree, never minding small differences in age, with their parents' generation doing the same a little further up, and their children spreading out across their own horizontal row a little further down. As a metaphor for understanding disciplinary history, the traditional family tree suggests a similar kind of coherence: we might speak of the generation that founded composition studies; the generation that founded composition graduate programs; the generation of undergraduate writing studies. Or choose a less institutional and more intellectual way of marking time: the leaders of the process movement; the drivers of the ethical turn; the social constructivists. There are many resting places or dividing lines to choose. Regardless, the language of *generations*, and the family tree it invokes, suggests a movement from one group to another – the passing of seasons, of wisdom, of a torch.

That sense of intergenerational exchange was certainly on my mind when I and my colleagues at CUNY started the Writing Studies Tree as graduate students nearly a decade ago.[1] As we framed it in an early grant proposal, the primary audiences for the "genealogies of mentor/student relations" that the WST would store were "newcomers to a field" and "well-established members," imagined as more or less cleanly separable groups; several of our proposed benefits were framed in family-tree terms, such as a "lineage" newcomers could take pride in, or "successors" as a measure of success:

> Genealogies of mentor/student relations have a long history in academia, stretching back at least as far as the links tying Alexander to Aristotle and back through Plato to Socrates. For newcomers to a field, such genealogies offer many benefits: tracing lines of influence and resistance can aid in reconstructing the logic behind the field's commonplaces; locating sub-communities of scholars can suggest new authors to read or programs to apply to; and locating oneself or one's colleagues within such a lineage or network can engender a sense of prestige or belonging that enhances professional development. For well-established members of academic fields, a genealogy offers a way to pay public tribute to early influences, and another way to measure one's own success, in terms of successors and collaborations. Finally, for those studying the dynamics of networks or

disciplines, an academic genealogy offers a record of the formation and evolution of communities-by-choice – a record which, because it is rarely captured by publications alone, runs the risk of remaining local knowledge, disaggregated from other comparable histories and patterns, or becoming lost entirely.

We envisioned the WST as a kind of hyperlinked family scrapbook, a place for stories to be made more discoverable by tying them to structured data, and for data to be made more accessible by tying them to human stories and personal connections. Or maybe a digital community quilt, built from patchwork by many hands, showing the threads that bind each of us, through others close by, to those a little further away. An intergenerational repository.

At the same time, we made some choices early on that would begin to unravel some of the assumptions in the metaphor of genealogy and clear generational alignment. Traditional academic genealogies, such as the Mathematics Genealogy Project or NeuroTree, tend to assume that the essential relationship to track is dissertation advisement: each person has one, or maybe two, direct advisors; in STEM fields, students tend to work in one lab at a time, with a primary investigator directing the research. In such cases, it's clear where you draw the lines. But as we thought about our own influences, it became ever clearer that that wouldn't be enough. Non-chair members of the dissertation committee, at a minimum, felt important to accommodate within the database, to acknowledge and thank; Writing Program Administrators played an important role in my own introduction to the field, and into the database design they went. And what about the professors whose framings and lessons stuck with us, even when they weren't directly advising us beyond their courses? Or what about the people down the hall or across the desk in the shared office? Weren't they, too, part of our mentoring network? In fact, what about each other? As we worked alongside each other on this and other projects, as we drafted conference presentations and, eventually, articles, we learned from and taught each other laterally, and lifted each other up. Rather than keep the traditional data fields, then, we invited contributors to the WST to document more multifaceted lines of descent and affiliation, prepopulating the data entry forms with a wide range of both mentoring relationships and collaborative relationships, such as co-authorship, that we see as a form of co-mentoring.

Because the database has been almost entirely crowdsourced, we've been able to see how these invitations are taken up: the choices people make in what they contribute, and thus on some level the relationships that contributors find especially compelling, worth recording and sharing. One thing that strikes me is just how often the mentoring relationships entered do go beyond the dissertation. As of this writing, there are 1,962 distinct people named in the WST database and 551 institutions, with 5,589 relations recorded among them. Of those relationships, 1,968 (a little over a third) are directed, *mentored/mentored by* relationships, but only 622 are dissertation chairing, the old marker of a generational baton-pass for academic genealogies; nearly the same number of graduate professors outside the dissertation committee (616) have also been posted as mentors. Another 643 people are linked by virtue of having *worked alongside* each other.

These connections sometimes do, but often do not, bear out expectations of generational cohorts. People don't have unique locations in the tree: for one thing, dissertation advisors can, and do, coauthor with their students or former students, such that the same person can appear both as mentor/mentee and as collaborator. For another, within a couple of years of graduating as a PhD student, you can become a PhD advisor, or committee member, or certainly professor; you can, in a sense, become part of the prior generation, even relative to those in school at the same time as you.

So when we try to use the family tree layout to map the mentoring relationships in the WST, some strange things happen. Even within the same basic relation type, more than one path can lead to the same person. In my own local network, Sondra Perl appears both one "generation" up (because she advised my dissertation) and two (because she advised the dissertation of Mark McBeth, another member of my committee); as a result, they are simultaneously of the same and of adjacent "generations." Amanda Licastro appears in my co-mentoring branches no fewer than six times, reflecting that she and I have worked together not only on several projects (including the WST itself), but also in combination with various other groups of people, making the collaborative relationships not easily reducible.

At first, we felt a little concern about these quirks in rendering the network, but over time I've come to accept and even embrace them. It makes sense that there is no single line that explains our relationships; the multiplicity, reciprocity, and sometimes, yes, the surprise of where we encounter a mentor's influence are all part of what makes them influential, part of our fabric.

Or maybe it's time I stopped being surprised. *Generation* has the same root as *generate*, after all: it's not just groups, and it's not just genres, it's what we make of (and by) what we share. As we remix across age groups and stages of career, we re-imagine what it means to be "of a generation" with someone. Recent initiatives like DBLAC and NextGen have given us new lenses on the received hierarchies of composition studies, new ways of drawing networks together and of seeing the roles we play within them. Revisiting our early WST proposal now, I cringe a little at the mention of "prestige," which I see is more a problem than a positive – but I also want to reaffirm the value of "communities-by-choice," of finding and celebrating those communities and making them visible. I do still want the database to help new scholars locate themselves and their potential allies and mentors.

In closing, I want to acknowledge something that has maybe been obvious all along: the Writing Studies Tree affords only a glimpse of only some of writing studies. When I said above that I interpret what it shows as a reflection of "the relationships that contributors find especially compelling, worth recording and sharing," it's only the *contributed* relationships we're able to see there – and that's not even all of those the contributors value, as some add only names, and not their networks. But I still believe there's something here, as tangled or paradoxical and un-tree-like as it may be, that is worth cultivating and growing. And so I'll end with an invitation: that if you also see that potential, you'll help us make it not only a fuller database, but a newer one; a *re*-generation that your insights will make possible. And we can iterate forward, together, from there.

Notes:

1. Amanda Licastro and Jill Belli have been my closest co-designers and co-maintainers of the project; see http://writingstudiestree.org/live/about#support for other essential team members.

Where Would We Be?: Legacies, Roll Calls, and the Teaching of Writing in HBCUs

Beverly J. Moss

In their article "We are Family: I Got All My (HBCU) Sisters with Me" in the 2016 "Where We Are: Historically Black Colleges and Universities and Writing Programs" section of *Composition Studies,* Hope Jackson and Karen Keaton Jackson state, "It is our hope that the HBCU experience will one day be fully integrated in composition studies . . . without the designation of 'special issue'" (157). While their article focused on writing center studies, their call echoes that of Jacqueline Jones Royster and Jean C. Williams in "History in the Spaces Left: African American Presence and Narratives of Composition Studies." Royster and Williams call out composition and rhetoric's sanctioned historical narratives that ignored the role of African American contributions to the field, especially those from HBCUs (572). Keith Gilyard, in the same 1999 issue of *CCC* that the Royster and Williams article appears, ends his essay by suggesting "...there never was a time when we failed to contribute to the field in some way. We may not have always been in the house of mainstream composition studies, but we were always knocking on the door" (642). Royster and Williams and Gilyard do the work of documenting intergenerational exchanges of African Americans in composition studies in their 1999 articles, providing evidence of Gilyard's assertion that, yes, we have always been contributing to the field even when it has gone unnoticed.

A major move that took place recently points to HBCU writing program scholars charting a new path, creating spaces for intergenerational conversations that take place in their home spaces: Symposia on the Teaching of Writing and Rhetoric at HBCUs. Hosted by North Carolina A&T in 2014 and Howard University in 2018, these symposia brought together people in the field who converged around issues defined by HBCU writing program administrators, teachers, and scholars. As Karen Keaton Jackson, Hope Jackson, and Dawn N. Hicks Tafari wrote in their *CCC* article, "We Belong in the Discussion: Including HBCUs in Conversations About Race and Writing,", the first symposium led to more spaces dedicated to such conversations. One such space is Collin Craig and Staci Perryman-Clark's collection *Black Perspectives in Writing Program Administration: From the Margins to the Center* that features primarily Black writing program administrators (WPAs) extending scholarly conversations in writing program administration to include the voices of HBCU WPAs. And while we celebrate the necessary conversations these spaces provide, Jackson, Jackson, and Hicks remind us that there is more work to do. They offer a set of recommendations and initiatives to eradicate the consistent erasure of HBCU voices in central conversations in the field, especially conversations about Black students and Black community rhetorical and literacy practices. Those recommendations highlight the actions that our national organizations, publishers, and scholars at PWIs should take to ensure that HBCU voices are visible and central in the field's ongoing scholarly and pedagogical conversations.

As I reflect upon the intergenerational terrain of HBCUs, I ask this question:

> where would we, in composition studies, be without writing and rhetoric faculty who have taught or currently teach at HBCUs and/or scholars in the field who are alumni of HBCUs?

I see this topic of intergenerational exchanges as another moment to point out that HBCU contributions are part of the foundation upon which composition studies is built. I argue that there is no mainstream house without HBCU contributions.

My story. As someone much closer to the end of my career—that gives me pause—than the middle, I take this moment, as a proud HBCU graduate of Spelman College, to point out a few important parts of the foundation. I had the great fortune to be introduced to the field of rhetoric and composition when I was an undergraduate at Spelman College by my first year writing and advanced composition professor and Spelman alumna Dr. Jacqueline Jones (before she became Jones Royster). While serving as Freshmen Dean, she hired me as the first tutor in the Spelman Writing Center. This was my first experience as a practitioner in composition studies. As a doctoral student at the University of Illinois at Chicago, I attended my first CCCC conferences in New York, then Minneapolis, and Cincinnati, where Dr. Royster (it took years before I could call her "Jackie") introduced me to her friends -- remarkable Black women like Jerrie Cobb-Scott, who was a faculty member at HBCU Central State University, Dolores Straker, and eventually Shirley Wilson Logan, an alumna of Johnson C. Smith University, my hometown HBCU. These women introduced me to the NCTE/CCCC Black Caucus and to the scholarship produced by Black scholars in the field who I was not reading in any of my graduate courses. Members of the Caucus, many of whom were faculty at HBCUs or alumni, modeled for me how intergenerational exchanges take place. It was in these conversations that I came to understand who Jackie Royster was in the field. So I ask, what would composition studies be as a field without the groundbreaking work done by these HBCU faculty and/or alumni? Where would the field be, for example, without caucus member Melvin Butler's (Southern University) leadership in composing and publishing *Students' Rights to Their Own Language*?

The Legacy. Let's look even further back. We can put Anna Julia Cooper in conversation with Royster and Logan. Cooper attended and then taught rhetoric, among many other subjects, at Saint Augustine's (NC) in 1885 until she left to attend Oberlin. This line of intergenerational exchanges must include also Hallie Quinn Brown, former dean at Allen University and Tuskegee University, who was an alumna and a professor of elocution at Wilberforce in the nineteenth century and published several books on elocution. Let us not forget poet and professor Melvin B. Tolson who attended Fisk and Lincoln (PA) universities, and who built the Wiley Forensic Society that gave birth to the award-winning Wiley College debate team (made famous in the 2007 movie *The Great Debaters*) that defeated the national champion University of Southern California debate team in 1935. Racism kept them from being named national champions (Stone and Stewart remind us that Tillotson College, an HBCU in Austin, Texas, was closed because of the success of their declamation teams in defeating local white colleges). This focus on rhetorical delivery and oratory at HBCUs was not an exception (Kates, Royster and Williams, Gold).

Black rhetorical excellence has thrived at HBCUs. Pedagogical and scholarly creativity in the teaching of writing has excelled. Intergenerational exchanges (that is, mentoring, introducing younger scholars to the field, encouraging each other, and teaching Black students like Vice-President Kamala Harris, activist Stacey Abrams, and the late congressman John Lewis, to name a few) consistently take place. It was Royster, Logan, James Hill (Albany State faculty), and Teresa Redd (Howard faculty), along with scholars like Smitherman, who inspired my generation and the ones to follow, including Faye Spencer Maor (FAMU alumna and North Carolina A&T faculty), Eric Darnell Pritchard (Lincoln alumnus), Valerie Kinloch (Johnson C. Smith alumna), Karen Keaton Jackson (Hampton alumna and North Carolina Central University faculty), Hope Jackson (North Carolina A&T alumna and faculty), Dawn Hicks Tafari (Winston-Salem State University faculty), and too many more to name.

And a new generation of scholars teaching at or having been educated at HBCUs have continued to literally and figuratively author and embody the history of writing and rhetoric at HBCUs. These scholars—David Green (Hampton alumnus; Howard faculty), Brandon Erby (Tougaloo alumnus), Kendra Mitchell (Florida A&M University alumna and current faculty), Khirsten Scott (Tougaloo alumna and co-founder of DBLAC), Brittany Hull (Lincoln alumna), Mudiwa Pettus (Claflin alumna, Medgar Evers faculty), Cecilia Shelton (Winston Salem State University alumna; former HBCU faculty),

Temptaous Mckoy (Elizabeth City State alumna; Bowie State faculty), and Laura Allen (Spelman College alumna), among so many more—also continue to push the field forward engaging in critical conversations, making waves in areas within the field where people don't expect us to be (for example, digital media, technical communication), and creating a path for others to follow. Mckoy and Shelton, whose dissertations were awarded CCCC Outstanding Dissertation Awards in Technical and Scientific Communication in consecutive years (2020 and 2021), along with Natasha Jones and others, established a Black presence and excellence in technical communication. Where would the field be without their work—work that is changing the conversation to examine Black spaces in technical communication? And let me take this moment to make this point: From North Carolina A&T's technical communication concentration (directed by Professor Kimberly Harper, a NC AT&T alumna) to Bowie State's three-course sequence in technical writing, HBCUs are preparing students to enter into professional and technical communication as scholars and practitioners.

This roll call is by no means exhaustive. It is not meant to be. It is meant to suggest, as Gilyard reminded us earlier, that we have been here all along, we are still here, and will continue to be. This incomplete roll call is my way of suggesting that HBCU intergenerational exchanges are about how the very existence of those who teach at HBCUs and/or attended HBCUs (along with those like Kynard and Kynard and Eddy whose scholarly agendas include HBCUs) enter into a long-standing, dynamic conversation that not only strengthens the foundation of composition but also reimagines it.

Works Consulted

Craig, Collin Lamont and Staci M. Perryman-Clark, editors. *Black Perspectives in Writing Program Administration: From the Margins to the Center.* NCTE, 2019.

Gilyard, Keith. "African-American Contributions to Composition Studies." *College Composition and Communication*, vol. 50, no. 4, 1999, pp. 626-44.

Gold, David. *Rhetoric on the Margins: Revising the History of Writing Instruction in American Colleges, 1873-1947,* Southern Illinois UP.

Jackson, Hope, and Karen Keaton Jackson. "We Are Family: I Got All My (HBCU) Sisters With Me." *Composition Studies*, vol. 44, no. 2, 2016, pp. 153-157.

Jackson, Karen Keaton, Hope Jackson, and Dawn N. Hicks Tafari. "We Belong in the Discussion: Including HBCUs in Conversations about Race and Writing." *College Composition and Communication,* vol. 71, no. 2, 2019, pp. 184-214.

Kates, Susan. *Activist Rhetorics and American Higher Education, 1885-1937.* Southern Illinois UP, 2001.

Kynard, Carmen and Robert Eddy. "Toward a New Critical Framework: Color-Conscious Political Morality and Pedagogy at Historically Black Colleges and Universities." *College Composition and Communication,* vol. 61, no. 1, 2009, pp. 24-44.

Kynard, Carmen. *Vernacular Insurrections: Race, Black Protest, and the New Century in Composition-Literacies Studies.* SUNY Press, 2013.

Royster, Jacqueline Jones and Jean C. Williams. "History in the Spaces Left: African American Presence and Narratives of Composition Studies." *College Composition and Communication*, vol. 50, no.4, 1999, pp. 563-584.

Stone, Brian J., and Shawanda Stewart. "HBCUs and Writing Programs: Critical Hip Hop Language Pedagogy and First-Year Student Success." *Composition Studies*, vol. 44, no. 2, 2016, pp. 183-186.

Intergenerational Exchange as a Practice of Negotiation

Juli Parrish and Wendy Chen

Juli Parrish: As a doctoral student at the University of Pittsburgh in the late 1990s, I learned to write—and to assign—the difficulty paper. Mariolina Salavatori asked me and my peers to do the same work that we graduate students asked of our own students: to articulate our efforts to understand texts in writing, leaning in to moments of confusion or frustration and describing our processes, coming to "act[s] of interpretation and understanding" (85). Throughout my own graduate education, I was engaged in one long difficulty paper. Whether I was learning about rhetoric or literacy or pedagogy, I was writing myself through difficulty. That is a practice that I have worked to sustain throughout my career so far: to give voice to my own difficulty as a way of beginning to move through it. If the field of composition studies has a canon passed from one generation to the next, I want to say it is a canon of practices more than of texts: a canon of the ways we and the students we teach negotiate meaning, ask questions, unpack and figure out texts, speculate, theorize, and analyze; the ways we reflect on our own literacies; the ways we come through difficulty to understanding.

Wendy Chen: Currently, I am a first year PhD candidate in English at the University of Denver. Before that, I was a master's student. Before that, I was a college student. For most of my life, I've largely been in the position of a student in intergenerational exchanges with faculty within academia. The power dynamics and structures that shape exchanges with those with greater authority are always present and pressing upon me. Moreover, I am always aware of my position as a woman of color within academic institutions that were designed to exclude people like me. It is alienating. The relationship a student of color has to the concept of difficulty within academia may be just as alienating. We seem to take for granted the idea that the more one is challenged by a class, extracurricular, or experience, the more one can learn and grow. But when and where does difficulty and challenge become less an opportunity for personal growth and learning and more a barrier toward those that society and academia view as "unworthy"? Indeed, is difficulty something that should be prized within academia at all?

Juli: I've been interested in seeing how others have written about the difficulty paper. Meghan A. Sweeney and Maureen McBride, for instance, found that teaching the difficulty paper can make visible "cultural disconnects" (609) that some students encounter in their reading of some texts; Jonathan Cisco has explored the value of the "difficulty paper as a formative assessment for disciplinary literacy instruction" (83). I also consider the ways I have centered difficulty in WAC workshops, especially with graduate students, as a way to help them to articulate and share their knowledge about writing in their fields.

As a white, cis-gendered teaching professor, writing center director, and journal editor, I continue to value grappling with difficulty as a useful and even potentially transformative practice, but I also increasingly see that I embrace difficulty from a position of privilege. Barriers to access, exclusion from knowledge-making, and demands to whitewash experience are real and concrete difficulties faced by many of my own students, the consultants in my writing center, the students and faculty with whom we work, and the scholars who submit work to the journal I co-edit, *Literacy in Composition Studies*. My relationship to difficulty is not the same as theirs, and perhaps I should not ask them to make their difficulty visible to me, to voice all of their silences.

Wendy: What does silence mean within the classroom? How does a white professor interpret a silent student? How does a professor of color interpret a silent student? Is a silent student of color judged differently than a silent white student? How is difficulty interpreted and valued differently by a white professor vs. a professor of color, or by a white student vs. a student of color? As dialogues inside and outside of academia begin to grapple, more and more, with questions of marginalization and inclusion, concepts like silence and difficulty are being reexamined, redefined, and reclaimed by scholars across fields. In my current work on the role of silence within the writing center, I have been informed by Kendra L. Mitchell's recontextualization of rhetorical choices and responses—including silence—culturally; by Suzan E. Aiken's assertions of silence as a strategic, intentional, and rhetorical choice; and by Martina Ferrari's recent explorations of the "coloniality of silence" (Ferrari, qtd. in Ferrari 326), to name a few.

Juli: I mentioned the canon of practices that I see as a link among generations of scholars and teachers and writers in our field(s). I want—and we need—to do more to recognize that this is a canon full of difficulties and silences that our students sometimes see and understand more clearly than we do. Jamila Kareem, in a recent issue of *Literacy in Composition Studies*, reminds us that our pedagogies and our histories often enact "yet another erasure of lived experiences." That is, the practices we rely on, as much as the texts we celebrate and use to establish new paradigms, may silence some of my students and prevent me from hearing, in that silence, their contributions. I ask myself a version of the question that writing center consultant and doctoral student Lucien Darjeun Meadows asks: how can I "co-create" with students, writers, and the generations that come after me a "liminal zone" for "issues of power and privilege, voice and silence, enactment and negotiation?"

Wendy: The ways in which silence, difficulty, and other concepts are interpreted and negotiated within the classroom will inevitably echo the greater social tensions outside of academia. Take silence, for example. In *Black Bodies, White Gazes: The Continuing Significance of Race in America*, George Yancy observes that "[w]hen Blacks speak or do not speak, such behavior is codified in the white imaginary. To be silent 'confirms' passivity and docility" (69). Thus, to a white gaze, the silence of people of color can be passive, empty, or even threatening. Moreover, people of color cannot take silence for granted. Rather, they are often asked to identify or explain themselves and pressured to comply out of fear for their own safety. For people of color, silence, therefore, is a fraught privilege, rather than a right. Silence can often be a matter of life and death.

As Dalia Rodriguez explains, how a student of color uses silence—or has silence used against them—within academia can be an incredibly different experience from that of a white student. A student of color might be judged more harshly for their silence, which may signify to the white gaze blankness, unproductivity, or uncooperativeness. Kazim Ali's chapter in *Resident Alien: On Border-crossing and the Undocumented Divine* argues that "[w]ithin the silent spaces is an immensity of energetic activity of various emotional tonalities. . . . The body that knows its sounds and silences increases its power and ability to speak in the face of the growing injustice and technology that works to supplant the functions of the body" (185).

* * *

Juli: When I think about intergenerational exchange, I think first of the individuals with varying degrees of agency who set the terms for not just what is exchanged but how: the professors and administrators and journal editors who make specific decisions about whom to allow a voice and whom to silence, about whose difficulty to seize on as evidence of learning and whose difficulty to dismiss as irrelevant or disqualifying.

I want less to pass on the more static roles of teacher/student and editor/writer, and more to understand and think hopefully about the process of exchange itself: in which assumptions are surfaced about histories and legacies and canons and their relationship to our current practice, about the pathways that are available and how we make them visible to one another. In processes of exchange that invite all parties to collaborate, we have the chance to negotiate and navigate silence and difficulty differently.

Wendy: The question of how intergenerational exchanges should themselves be navigated today is fraught with questions of power and oppression. What does intergenerational exchange look like in American academia where students, more and more, do not have the same racial identities, gender expressions, and so on as their teachers? Do intergenerational exchanges that aim to provide answers or guidance based on past experiences only end up passing down and further entrenching the power dynamics of the past?

Wendy and Juli: We hope, in offering one intergenerational exchange, that negotiating questions and acknowledging difficulty and silences can stand in as one generative way to continue the work of interrogating or dismantling power structures that so many others before us—and the field more broadly in our current moment—have done and are doing.

Works Cited

Aiken, Suzan. "Silence as a Rhetor's Tool: Rhetorical Choices for and Uses of Silence." Electronic Thesis or Dissertation. Bowling Green State University, 2011. *OhioLINK Electronic Theses and Dissertations Center.* Accessed 17 Mar 2021.

Ali, Kazim. "Ode to Silence: Lecture Notes." *Resident Alien: On Border-Crossing and the Undocumented Divine,* U of Michigan P, 2015, pp. 179-86. *JSTOR,* www.jstor.org/stable/10.3998/mpub.8252696.21. Accessed 18 Feb. 2021.

Cisco, Jonathan. "Embracing Difficulty Across the Disciplines: The Difficulty Paper as a Tool for Building Disciplinary Literacy." *Teaching and Learning Inquiry,* vol. 8, no. 2, 2020, pp. 73-89, https://doi.org/10.20343/teachlearninqu.8.2.6. Accessed 24 Mar. 2021.

Ferrari, Martina. "Gloria Anzaldúa's Decolonizing Aesthetics: On Silence and Bearing Witness." *The Journal of Speculative Philosophy,* vol. 34, no. 3, 2020, pp. 323-38, https://doi.org/10.5325/jspecphil.34.3.0323. Accessed 24 Mar. 2021.

Kareem, Jamila M. "Independent Black Institutions and Rhetorical Literacy Education: A Unique Voice of Color." *Literacy in Composition Studies,* vol. 8, no. 1, July 2020, https://licsjournal.org/index.php/LiCS/article/view/704. Accessed 11 Mar. 2021.

Meadows, Lucien Darjeun. "Power and Passing as a Native 'Native' Speaker in the Writing Center." *Power, Access, and Privilege*, special issue of *The Dangling Modifier*, vol. 25, no. 1, 2018, https://sites.psu.edu/thedanglingmodifier/?page_id=3825. Accessed 11 Mar. 2021.

Mitchell, Kendra L., and Robert E. Randolph. "A Page from Our Book: Social Justice Lessons from the HBCU Writing Center." *The Writing Center Journal*, vol. 37, no. 2, 2019, pp. 21-42. *JSTOR*, www.jstor.org/stable/26922016. Accessed 17 Mar. 2021.

Rodriguez, Dalia. "Silence as Speech: Meanings of Silence for Students of Color in Predominantly White Classrooms." *International Review of Qualitative Research*, vol. 4, no. 1, 2011, pp. 111-44. *JSTOR*, www.jstor.org/stable/10.1525/irqr.2011.4.1.111. Accessed 17 Mar. 2021.

Salavatori, Mariolina Rizzi. "Difficulty: The Great Educational Divide." *Opening Lines: Approaches to the Scholarship of Teaching and Learning*, edited by Pat Hutchings, Carnegie Foundation for the Advancement of Teaching, 2000, pp. 81-93.

Sweeney, Meghan A., and Maureen McBride. "Difficulty Paper (Dis)Connections Understanding the Threads Students Weave Between Their Reading and Writing." *College Composition and Communication*, vol. 66, no. 4, pp. 591-614, https://www.jstor.org/stable/43491902. Accessed 24 Mar. 2021.

Yancy, George. *Black Bodies, White Gazes: The Continuing Significance of Race in America*. Rowman & Littlefield Publishers, 2008.

A Form of Phronesis

Diane Quaglia Beltran

Transgenerational and intergenerational memory relies on the voices of those who precede us. I crave the insights and wisdom of those voices.

***

I remember a professor in my MA who was fluent in German and read the Greek of Plato and Aristotle. He studied with scholarly luminaries at the University of Chicago; he understood classical rhetorics in a way I may never. In his archiving course, he discussed composition studies evolving into its own discipline and the composition-literature and composition-communications separation; he asked whether we thought the splits were a good idea. Interestingly, I can't remember his answer. He taught writing courses through models of expression that tried on new outfits every 10 years or so: expressivism, cognitivism, socio-cognitivism, social-epistemic, the linguistic turn, right to one's own language, code mixing, code-meshing, digital materialism. His articles were few, but important.

Sitting in his office/storage area on the top floor of an old drafty campus building and looking at his bookshelves was a delight. Anyone who was anyone of note was on those shelves. Crammed shelves that spilled onto the floor: rhetorical history, theory, and criticism, composition theory, writing with computers, WAC, WID, WIC, primers, readers, style guides from the 1800s to 2014. And so many literary works in translation. Whenever we talked outside of class and I thanked him for the conversation, he'd say, "I'm always teaching."

One day his graduate assistant was cleaning out the boxes of books that were stacked at odd angles in his office. Getting rid of duplicates, she said, as she handed a stack to me. On the top was Robert Conners' *Composition-Rhetoric: Background, Theory, & Pedagogy*. Someday, I'd like to have a class of grad students spend part of a semester creating an annotated digital timeline using that book. Someone probably already has. Or at least now they will.

***

In 2019, I met a composition scholar of note at a retirement gathering. Star-struck PhD student that I was, I thanked him for writing his work on heuristics. He couldn't believe anyone still reads it. People still read Aristotle, or James Berlin, I responded. They're both dead, he responded.

At the retirement gathering, I looked around the room. An endowed professor, a program chair, a publisher/professor. Generations of scholars whose work in rhetoric and composition was foundational to the field. Soon, they'll retire. Two of them have.

***

Collectively—as an affiliated group who socially perpetuates and carries forward memories and practices—what do we bring forward with to future generations teaching composition? Culturally—as the practiced values, beliefs, artifacts, and technology (yes, writing)—what are we advancing as culturally important? And who are the *we* in either?

Databases with articles become our memory storage, a digital mind palace that we cannot readily navigate without the correct search terms. And whose terms are those? Cultural memory strangely morphs into collective wisdom that never really tastes the phronesis it's supposed to be. The practical wisdom many of us crave as composition instructors comes over time and over years of inquiry and study. I wonder whether that wisdom would be sooner reached through the requested response of pedagogues and scholars like the one in my MA program. Encouraging inter- and transgenerational conversations with mentors, professors, and colleagues through blogs, websites (please, no discussion forums…ok, maybe), podcasts, videos to archive the conversations between generations. We could ask. *We*, the mentees, students, and colleagues.

We all could benefit from their memories of teaching in our field of study and praxis. In the age of digital communications and multiple paths of circulation, *we*, the composition students, teachers, scholars, researchers, have opportunities to include the voices of other generations, older and younger, in a dialogue that could be made widely accessible. I would like to do that during a semester while teaching graduate students. Maybe someone already has.

Maybe I should.

Tradition and Change

Victor Villanueva

1981. The one comment on a paper I submitted on something by Wordsworth (we were all lit majors then, allowed to dabble in rhetoric and comp, but the emphasis was on the literary periods):

"Nonsense."

That didn't raise my confidence. I could quit (and in fact I did, but only for that quarter; recovered, and then I returned) or I could speak with the professor (and in fact I did). After some chit chat about the politics of the time, he told me (1) that I have to learn to survey the forest and look for the daylight. Got it: see what's been written and find what's missing. And (2) that I must stop attempting novelty. That professor had committed—twice—what the New Criticism of the 1940s would call the "intentional fallacy": that he knew Wordsworth's intentions in the poem and that he knew *my intentions*. Reader-response criticism wasn't yet in the discussion (Jane Tompkin's book would come out within a year or two). Had reader response been legit, my response as a reader couldn't have been nonsense. He might have disagreed, or I might not have been persuasive, but not nonsense. What's more, I had not intended to be novel in my reading of the poem. I did not even know my reading was unconventional.

Over the most recent decade or two, I have met more students like I was: of color, first generation, from poverty, new to the culture of the university, the veteran who wasn't a commissioned officer, a high-school dropout. Add to that, I have come to meet the occasional recipient of an online undergraduate degree, disallowing for the kind of learning to be had in classrooms. And the university, to some extent, has responded: students' right to their own rhetorics (to their own language has been theoretically accepted but rarely truly enacted, it seems), translingualism, counterstory. But the traditions also remain. Some of us, however, try to look at traditions differently, and in so doing, change the traditions, perhaps.

The professor had assumed a kind of incompetence rather than difference in my writing. Unconscious of my rhetorical "difference" in those days, I hadn't prepared the reader that what I was describing were *my* views, hadn't explained how I had arrived at that reading in some general sense. I simply asserted my reading but hadn't set it up. Today, despite a rising consciousness about diversity among students and professionals, the deficit presumption far too often remains in assessing students. It's a tradition in need of change. But since the tradition remains, we can't afford to forget the forest, even when looking less for an opening but looking for a way out of the woods.

Recognizing that the master's tools can have alternative uses is important, a matter of thinking and writing in terms of the totality rather than binaries. There is a Same to the Othered that has to be recognized, less an assimilation or an accommodation—and certainly not a compliance—than a recognition, that identification begins with the commonalities no less than the differences, the overlap between identification and division that Kenneth Burke sees as place where rhetoric takes place.

And this gives rise to another concern—another memory. There was an article published in *CCC* back in 1983 by someone in the position that I'm in now: a former leader of Cs, retired, contemplating the trends back then: Robert Gorrell's "How to Make Mulligan Stew" (vol. 34, no. 3, 1983, pp. 272-277). He argued that though it's true that one can't know much about writing through the product alone, one also can't know much through the process alone, that the processes and the products come out different every time, like a Mulligan stew. The change in focus to the process still requires some attention to the tradition of assessing the product. That line of thinking would be taken up by others and reappear as "post-process." Now, I'm not so concerned about process and product here. I am more concerned with Mulligan stew and theoretical binaries. Having been told to do my homework back then, to survey the forest, I went out of my way to review the lit for whatever I was writing. I was thorough, every source till the sources started looping back. And I've seen that same kind of thoroughness in countless dissertations and first attempts at publishing monographs during my stint as editor. But thoroughness in and of itself can be a problem. It can lead to contradictory sources. A Mulligan stew.

Or let me put it this way. One of my professors in rhetoric, William Irmscher (also a former Cs chair), responded to a paper of mine that included a very dense forest. He handed me the paper and asked me if I didn't think eclecticism was a cop out ("cop out"). I didn't have an answer, mainly because I knew it really wasn't a question. Still, I had to wonder why he would suggest that, given that it was Irmscher who had introduced us to Kenneth Burke in graduate school, a Burkean acknowledged in *CCC* by Burke himself about Irmscher's use of the pentad in teaching comp ("Questions and Answers about the Pentad," vol. 29, no. 4, 1978, pp. 330-335). Can one get more eclectic than Burke? Well, William Rueckert in *Kenneth Burke and the Drama of Human Relations* writes that Burke is *syncretic*. Tomatoes, to-mah-toes. Or is it? Eclecticism doesn't necessarily assume an overarching order. Mulligan stew. Pot luck. Syncretism can be consistent, even when dense. Bouillabaisse (or zarzuela, the Spanish stew, *¡Que rico!*). There is an overarching set of principles to Burke, characterized, perhaps (and I'm being necessarily simplistic here) as symbology.

So what am I getting at? I am suggesting, even urging, that as one begins as an academic in rhetoric and writing that one must work to create one's consistent, underlying conceptual framework or foundation. Now, when Irmscher prompted me to find my own conceptual framework, my first impulse was apostolic. What I mean is that I tried to decide which philosopher or theorist I would follow, like a disciple. I began with Burke, of course, since graduate students can tend to continue the work of mentors, at least at first. But to follow Burke I had to follow Marx or Nietzsche or Schopenhauer or Aristotle or so many others. And then, early in my career, I discovered Gramsci. That's it! I will follow Gramsci. His concepts seemed to me to fit well with rhetoric, and my need to try to flesh out how racism is maintained when race is so clearly a myth, smoke and mirrors. But that started to fall apart, or rather, to grow: to Marx (again) and Althusser and Lukacs and Chantal Mouffe and Erik Olin Wright and Manning Marable and Castro and el Che, Fanon, Paulo Freire, and on and on. And each discovery connected to some other scholar, philosopher, thinker. Lost in the woods again. Now what?

And then came the realization that I did not want to be thought of as a "Marxist." When someone would identify me as one, I'd say "No; I'm a Catholic." It was a quick way to get a laugh. But it wasn't merely a joke. The term, Marxist, runs the risk of invoking a dogmatism, an absolute Truth (even, ironically, as that truth counters idealism).

One more story. I had published on Gramsci and on Freire and some of those I just mentioned. About that same time, a colleague where I was a young assistant professor died. Someone who had been something of a mentor to me in those days had been the colleague's close friend. She suggested I go to his funeral service, saying "Don't worry; it'll be nonsectarian." Her assumption was that since I was a Marxist, I would be agnostic, at best, if not an atheist (which is a misinterpretation, I'd say, of Marx's "opium of the people" comment). We had been to each other's homes, had a reading group, been friends. But she nevertheless saw me a certain way. And it wasn't a way that felt comfortable to me. Do I tend toward the materialist thinkers? Yes, I do.

For me, there is no other way to work through racism as rhetorical, and if rhetorical, ideological, and if ideological, then hegemonic, with real political economic consequences, despite race being smoke and mirrors. But I cannot accept materialism to the exclusion of the spiritual. No spiritual equals no faith (even faith in humanity is spiritual). At bottom, I'm a teacher. A teacher has to have faith, faith in the possibility of something better. So, even though the term is no longer heard, my philosophical framework is a material Catholicism, a personal, Americanized Liberation Theology.

I'm trying to demonstrate here the differences among three terms: philosophy, theory, concept. A philosophical framework is simply a set of beliefs. That set of beliefs, once one becomes conscious of them, becomes a part of how one arrives at particular theoretical frameworks. A theoretical framework provides the set of theories that inform empirical research, calling on theories that already exist. A conceptual framework, however, is a consistency we formulate for ourselves.

In all of this that I'm saying here I'm suggesting that it is important to know something of one's philosophical framework in order to act—in scholarship, research, teaching, in all one does—within the consistence of a conceptual framework. The problem with eclecticism is that it's flexible to a fault. The problem with eclecticism is that it leaves open the possibility of a reactionary response when challenged. Reactionary. Not simply reactive. When pushed and shoved, it's way too easy for an eclectic to respond by calling on known assumptions, conservative, even dogmatic. So think through your tendency, discover the overarching principles that can lay a foundation. Often, I'll ask graduate students or young professionals to create a personal phrase, brief, even absurdly short, but one they can test themselves with. Mine has been "Tradition and change for changes in tradition." I still ask myself if that's what I'm doing.

Too Green to Talk Disciplinarity

Zhaozhe Wang

We weathered the winter of division, disconnection, and distance; we march into the spring longing for togetherness in difference. We witnessed spectacle: words dehumanize and dispossess; we reaffirm why our work revitalizes and reunites. As the material consequences of our symbolic acts and discursive practices are increasingly seen and felt in a disoriented public, composition studies has yet to reassert the core values it upholds and the cultural capital it preserves upon entering its septuagenarian years. Reading on, you may notice that composition studies is and has been conceptualized liberally in myriad, sometimes-conflicting metaphors. Maybe that's part of why I feel too green to talk disciplinarity?

As a disciplinary community, we fought—and we fought hard—to get where we are today within our respective institutions and out in the marketplace of disciplines. Still, we continue to reflect on and rewrite who we are in response to rapidly changing political and institutional realities. Yet I often wonder, as a junior scholar, who we have in mind when we matter-of-factly insert the inclusive pronoun *we* in the grand disciplinary narrative. I know for certain that I did not attempt to put myself in the narrative when typing the first *we* of this paragraph. I did, however, picture an assembly of pathfinders, pioneers, and prominent scholars (many of whom also contributed to this issue) that we—here I mean the next generation—look up to and cite in our papers. Aren't we too green to talk disciplinarity anyway?

A discipline is constitutive: in a similar fashion as we (re)shape the identity of the discipline, the discipline molds our professional identity. I attended CCCC for the first time in 2015 as a master's student seeking my way into the field. I fondly recall walking into the Newcomers' Coffee Hour early in the morning, anxiously looking around the room filled with excitement and not knowing where to place my body or emotions. As I was hesitating to stay, Professor Cindy Selfe approached, handed me a cup of coffee, and introduced herself with a welcoming smile. Her air of modesty instantly put me at ease. For a moment, I was in disbelief: one of the pathfinders whom I read in the literature was greeting me in person and opening the door to the professional community I now call home. That initial cross-generational contact set the tenor for the growth of my sense of belonging.

But not every door is wide open. Some doors are closed but unlocked. Some doors are closed and locked. A discipline disciplines. It "sets boundaries and demarcates hierarchies of experts and amateurs" (Lenoir 72). The more consolidated the disciplinary identity, the more disciplined we need to be to "make it." And the longer it takes to be professionalized, the more regimented generational hierarchies become, and vice versa. Borrowing Bronwyn Williams's metaphor, as the disciplinary solar system expands and grows more diverse, we are "out of contact with nearby solar systems," despite the powerful centripetal force the core enterprise of composition exerts (128). The traditional monolithic notion of "composition" has now become a meta-discipline that encompasses a multi-center landscape of subfields, each with its distinctive norms and agendas. The job market is a barometer of this trend: in an advertisement, the term *compositionist* used to denote a specialist, but now marks a new kind of generalist. We, especially the young, the new, and the green, are defined less by what we do and more by where we belong. Our paths to the promised land have become narrower. Generation after generation, we push the boundaries, chart new territories, and make new connections; yet, we seem to be losing interest in our neighbors. We are too busy making sure we are on the "right" track.

To be sure, under the auspices of the strong disciplinary identity and the infrastructures and superstructures that have been laid out, numerous channels have been established to facilitate communication and push back against scholarly and generational silos. For example, CCCC maintains the long tradition of the Newcomers' Orientation at its annual convention and provides various awards/grants and editorial assistantships for junior scholars; we benefit from mentoring programs such as the CCCC Committee on the Status of Graduate Students and the WPA-GO co-sponsored mentoring program; there are also evolving grassroots advocacy groups that serve to connect and support graduate students, such as nextGEN. Other forms of institutionalized or informal mentorship abound in different professional spaces. It's a truly wonderful time to mature as a junior scholar in composition studies, thanks to all the nurture and care.

Suffice to say, the field has been pushing hard for trans-generational communication, mentorship, and allyship. Yet I do not think we as a disciplinary community have done enough to frame our trans-generational exchanges around the notion of "partnership" and foster trans-generational collegiality. The idea of trans-generational partnership rejects (although perhaps only nominally) the rigid hierarchical structures and domination/oppression framework inherent in different forms of mentorship and allyship. It highlights collaboration and shared responsibility in trans-generational activities on equal terms. It invites the young, the new, the shy, and the marginalized to not only work together with the established, but also to unsettle the field, make some noise, and break some walls. While, as Goggin reminds us, stability should remain our priority, given where we are today I wonder if we are confident enough to embrace a little bit of instability by transcending the generational boundaries and co-constructing the knowledge/practice enterprise upon partnerships. I wonder if we are confident enough to make the young and new front and center in our partnerships, at least every now and then.

Although I received extensive systematic training in composition studies during my master's studies, I did not enter my doctoral program as an "official" composition student, as I was affiliated with the second language studies program in the same department. Thanks to the inclusivity of the rhetoric and composition program at Purdue University and the discipline at large, I managed to grab anything I could eat like a hungry kid—taking courses, attending conferences, conducting and sharing research, seeking mentorship—to stay relevant. In retrospect, I wonder if it was my "peripheral" status and lack of an institutionally structured pathway that allowed me to take an eclectic approach and chart my path to finding my professional identity. Every one of us, especially the young and new, inhabits rhetorical and scholarly spaces meaningfully differently. We may well make bold and sometimes unorthodox claims that sound facile, skewed, jarring, even rude. Perhaps the wise and experienced could let us speak before eagerly lending a hand in the name of mentorship. Perhaps think along the lines of a partnership.

As a normative discipline, composition studies takes official stances on what we should be doing. For example, the various position statements that CCCC actively produces, updates, and promotes provide useful guidelines for our professional practices. Invoking a "franchise" metaphor, Gregory G. Colomb cautions that these standards-setting documents, though they strengthen our disciplinary standing, may inevitably lead to uniformity at the cost of local variance. A trans-generational partnership framework would invite us to question whose norms we are validating or denying. It would also invite us to co-author our norms as a means of assessing the grand narrative of what "is" and "ought to be," as we all dwell in drastically different sociopolitical and institutional ecologies.

Infrastructures are emerging to undergird trans-generational communication. A pioneering project is the journal *Young Scholars in Writing* (*YSW*) that exclusively publishes articles written by undergraduate researchers/scholars in rhetoric and writing. For decades, we have been disciplined to approach undergraduate students as research subjects or those needing help and to treat their writing as research data. *YSW*, and events like the Naylor Workshop, are demonstrations of a meaningful stride toward trans-generational partnership in that it urges us to read student writing as scholarship and invites us to converse with the next generation as peers (see the founding editors' introduction by Grobman and Spigelman, and also Johnson and Rifenburg's *Composition Studies* piece).

But could we do more? Our scholarly citation practices may have betrayed our scruples (for a full account of disciplinary citation practices, see Amy E.

Robillard's *College English* article). A neoliberal attention economy finds its manifestation in our scholarly activities and gives rise to attention inequality. Our attention is unevenly distributed: most of our limited attention is given to a relatively small number of established scholars and publication venues. Concentrated attention turns into citations, which then translate to professional currency that represents legitimacy and authority. The new voices, if not being listened for, often end up getting dismissed and becoming irrelevant. A transgenerational partnership framework demands that we not only critically reflect on our scholarly practices that may inadvertently reinforce the generational hierarchy, but also proactively dialogue with scholars across generations and circulate scholarship produced by the young and new. As the undergraduate scholars Courtney Buck, Emily Nolan, and Jamie Spallino aptly put it, "inexperience can foster innovation" (123).

A few weeks into my first semester at the University of Maine as a master's student, I had a meeting with my graduate teaching assistant mentor, Dylan Dryer. As a fresh college-graduate, non-native English-speaking instructor teaching writing for the first time in a culturally unfamiliar classroom, I found the incredibly daunting task of teaching much less formidable than familiarizing myself with and positioning myself within the voluminous bodies of composition scholarship. Sensing my frustration, Dylan, with his intense gaze, said to me, "Remember, as a scholar in the field, you need to...." Years later, I forgot what the exact advice was, but the characterization of me as a fellow "scholar" has empowered me to engage and to give. I still feel the weight of the title and the responsibility to guard it.

Am I too green to talk disciplinarity? Perhaps. But despite my broad-stroke generalizations (or ungrounded mischaracterizations) in this piece, I did. And I appreciate this very space that sponsored a trans-generational partnership. We wish for more.

Works Cited

Buck, Courtney, et al. "Inexperience and Innovation." *Composition Studies*, vol. 48, no. 1, 2020, pp. 121-23.

Colomb, Gregory G. "Franchising the Future." *College Composition and Communication*, vol. 62, no. 1, 2010, pp. 11-30.

Goggin, Maureen Daly. "The Disciplinary Instability of Composition." *Reconceiving Writing, Rethinking Writing Instruction*, edited by Joseph Petraglia, Lawrence Erlbaum Associates, Inc., 1995, pp. 27-48.

Lenoir, Timothy. "The Discipline of Nature and the Nature of Disciplines." *Knowledges: Historical and Critical Studies in Disciplinarity*, edited by Ellen Messer-Davidow et al., University of Virginia Press, 1993, pp. 70-102.

Williams, Bronwyn T. "Seeking New Worlds: The Study of Writing beyond Our Classrooms." *College Composition and Communication*, vol. 62, no. 1, 2010, pp. 127-46.

Notes on Intergenerational Exchange: The View from Here

Kathleen Blake Yancey

Intergenerational is such an interesting term, and given my childhood, for me something of an abstraction. My extended family—the four grandparents, the two aunts, the two uncles (until the very unhappy divorce), the seven cousins—lived in the Bay area, we in metro DC (then more DC than metro), before moving even farther east, to West Germany, for four years. We were distant. When I was 10, we traveled to California to visit the entire family for a full month, and I remember being envious of my cousins' relationships with my maternal grandmother especially. Not that she loved us any less, I thought, but that she knew my cousins in ways she did not know us, that they preferred sugar cookies to oatmeal raisin, spent every Wednesday afternoon at the swimming pool, caught fireflies before watching TV together on Saturday evenings. By the time I next saw my grandmother, when I was 18, my grandfather, who genuinely wasn't always sure who I was, referred to me simply, as that girl.

The abstraction began to take form as I began teaching, or perhaps it's more accurate to say that through my teaching I began to understand what intergenerational could mean, or perhaps that I began to define it, and refine it, through my own experience. My first year teaching, as a TA, and before that, even my student teaching, was unremarkable: pretty much, students liked me; pretty much, the classes went well. I taught, they learned, and we all walked happily out of the door. All that changed when I began teaching 8th grade. It wasn't just that one student literally could not read, although he could not. And for him, it wasn't a matter of smarts, of course, since he arrived in 8th grade not because he could read, but rather in spite of *not* being able to read. Still, how could I help him? Worse in its own way: although most of his classmates could read, they could not read the class textbook—and we had only one set of textbooks for the five classes I taught—so students weren't going to be supported by that textbook very well. Not only could they not take the book home, but they also couldn't highlight, underline, annotate, or even doodle in it: they could not make it, or the reading of it, their own. Almost desperate—such a teaching/learning situation was precisely *not* what my teaching credential prepared me for--I adopted an adage I'd heard from elementary school teachers: follow the child. What that adage meant, a colleague explained, was that the teacher takes her cue from the child in order to understand what he or she is ready for so as to plan learning opportunities, materials, and support. So it was with those 8th graders: they signaled what they were ready for—reading shorter texts, writing about them, mapping them, illustrating them, making posters of them, sharing their re-texts—and I drew on that readiness as a design principle for the curriculum. In other words, while the school district supplied a curriculum, the children and I worked intergenerationally to remix it with what they knew and could do so that it was usable for *their* learning. As important, this intergenerational dialogue then became the way I thought of all classroom teaching: as a site for *our* learning.

If differently, I found something of the same thing when I directed a testing center at Purdue University. The center, the Office of Writing Review (OWR), administered a writing test that specific populations of students, including all graduate students and selected undergrads, in education and engineering, needed to pass. When students failed the test, I met with them, ostensibly to help them by reviewing the test results and then recommending a better approach to help them pass the re-test. We met those goals, but not in the way that I had originally imagined. As a teacher and as the OWR director, I had thought that after looking at the student text and its accompanying score, I'd pretty much point them in the right direction. But the texts didn't tell me what I had thought they would. One student's text, for instance, displayed fairly serious organizational difficulties, so the recommendation seemed to be something like "plan before composing." When we talked, however, the student explained that he hadn't engaged in any invention activities: he'd just jumped into writing, and the writing got away from him. "Is that the way you usually write?" I asked. "Well, not really," he replied, "but it's a test, you know?" With this explanation as a point of departure, the student described how he usually wrote, the inventional strategies he ordinarily employed, and how he considered ways to meet a purpose and engage the audience. With his description as a foundation, we outlined an approach, based on his outside-of-testing writing practices, that could be adapted to a testing situation. (And he passed the test!) Put more generally, I'm not sure how one can be a writing teacher *without* working intergenerationally.[1]

I might make the same kind of observation about much of the kind of research I do, particularly research directly involving students. I like lenses and frameworks, but I don't want those to overwhelm what students say, so I tend to work inductively, which means that I count on student accounts to help me see what I hadn't seen before. Such work is inherently intergenerational: I bring context and questions; students bring experiences and articulations; we learn from each other.[2] Of course, this approach can also mean that my learning lands other than intended. One student I interviewed several times was interning at Florida State University's Museum of Everyday Writing (MoEW); I had hoped she would tell me about how her writing had changed as a function of the MoEW internship, but what had changed was not so much her writing, but rather her *conception* of writing. Of course; that makes perfect sense and raises other kinds of questions. In a different study, when I interviewed a graduating senior about her writing development in hopes of learning from her about transfer, I learned instead about how her visual writing practices had *not* transferred and about how a critical incident in high school had exerted a profound influence on her writing ever since: all good, but not as expected.

In other situations, it's not a choice or a question of disposition, but rather one of need: because I can't play one or more of the roles a research project requires, I engage with others, thus incorporating other layers into what is already a layered practice. In one case, I was asked to contribute a chapter to a book on reflection; what I wanted to talk about was how smart some of my students' ePortfolios were, so I asked them, please, to co-author. In another situation, I wanted to write about undergraduate ePortfolios, but I wasn't teaching undergrads, so I invited some TAs to join me. Since they all drew from the same class, a junior-level class in writing with a succinct but clear set of outcomes, I learned how they interpreted those outcomes and then enacted them variations-on-a-theme-like in the different iterations of the course. And for more than a decade now, my research has taken transfer of writing knowledge and practice as the focus. Once again, because of my own teaching responsibilities, I couldn't teach the first year composition (FYC) classes that provided the original focus for the inquiry into writing transfer. Luckily for me, Kara Taczak and Liane Robertson were teaching FYC, and together we began a line of research on the efficacy of a given curriculum, the Teaching for Transfer curriculum, that was only possible because of intergenerational exchange. As interesting, over the decade, this intergenerational exchange has widened to include six other researchers from across the US, collectively including boomers, generation X, and millennials. It's probably worth noting that in this project, instead of emphasizing our intergenerational exchange, we highlight its inter-institutional nature. That's important, of course, but I wonder what we'd see if we thought about the project in terms of intergenerational exchange.

As I came into rhetoric and composition in the 1970s, intergenerational exchange was another kind of abstraction. Although the field included people of different generations, it didn't have many generations of its own. Put another way, the field was too young to boast many generations—unless, of course, you count Aristotle,[3] and you might: one form of intergenerational change, an important one, is surely textual. Still, when I thought of the field-now-becoming-if-not-already-a-discipline, I always took my first CCCC, in Kansas City in 1977, as a touchstone: a large tent with many people figuring out somewhat on the fly how to teach better, how to study writing, how to create the spaces, traditions, journals, and books that would constitute a field, people in rhetorical history, FYC, technical communication, writing centers.

Later generations—since we now have generations—entering the field see it much differently. I remember one graduate student who patiently explained this to me. I had asked her why she seemed to identify more with computers and composition, which I saw as an important subfield, rather than with the field at large. Her reply: "Dr. Yancey, when you came into the field, it was smaller, easier to navigate. Now it's so large that we need another way into it; that's what a subfield does, provide a way in." Clearly, I was reading the field out of my context, my history; she from her context, her history. I was better at capturing the history I'd lived; she was better at articulating the current moment. Through this kind of intergenerational exchange, we create meaning of both past and present as we also, concurrently, set the stage for the future.[4]

Since early pandemic times, I have written weekly letters for our three grandchildren.

```
                                    (circle one): February  5  6  7

Dear Grandad and Nana~~
      How are you? Today I thought I would tell you about my school. This is the thing I like
doing best at school: _____ My favorite teacher is
_____. One of my favorite friends is _____.

On the other side of this letter is a picture I made for you. Please write back soon!

Love (write your name),


____  ____  ____  ____  ____  ____

          Circle the indoor rhymes (two rhymes in each column):

Rug     Bed      Chair    Bath     Sheet    Refrigerator
Hug     Pillow   Stove    Math     Sleet    Sink
Table   Said     Clove    Toilet   Blanket  Wink


Find the mistakes: what 3 numbers are missing? ____ ____ ____
37 39 40 41 42 43 44 46 47 48 49 50 51 52 53 54 55 57 58 59 60 61 62 63 64
```

Each letter also includes a templated letter for each grandchild to "write" to us, with fill-in-the-blank sentences, spaces for the letters of their names, rhyming words to circle, numbers to identify. The grands complete them, draw a picture on the back, and mail these letters to us: we've exchanged weekly letters now for over nine months. About two weeks ago, an additional letter from our 5-year-old grandson Calder was tucked into the envelope. He'd created this letter for me to complete: it includes spaces for my name, just as I create for him; numbers for me to identify, just as I create for him; and a picture that he drew--so he drew a picture for me rather than asking me to draw one for him. I knew that in our weekly exchange he was learning a lot and variously—about forming letters of the alphabet, about being creative, about writing letters to people at a distance, about writing to loved ones--but in this letter, he took the lead, playing back to me what I had shared with him and making it anew. Here, too, I think, is (yet) another form of intergenerational exchange, in this case of a grandmother writing letters as a form of affection to a five-year-old grandson returning that affection and demonstrating what that letter writing means to him, all as he learns to write in the middle of a pandemic.

One way or another, we all live intergenerational exchange; it's how we live it, and what we learn from it, that matter.

Notes

1. Often students are the same age as the teacher, but they are generationally different in what they know about writing.

2. As a testament to that, I often hear from students I've worked with, even years later; it's quite rewarding to learn from them about what they are doing now.

3. As Victor Villanueva explains in this issue.

4. The field now has structures to foster intergenerational exchange: see, for example, the CCCC Standing Group for Senior, Late-Career, and Retired Professionals in RCWS, which has been explicitly designed to foster such exchange.

Book Reviews

Dismantling Anti-Blackness and Uplifting African American Rhetoric: A Review Essay

Rhetorical Crossover: The Black Presence in White Culture, by Cedric D. Burrows. U of Pittsburgh P, 2020. 171 pp.

Linguistic Justice: Black Language, Literacy, Identity, and Pedagogy, by April Baker-Bell. Routledge, 2020. 129 pp.

Reviewed by Chloe J. Robertson, Virginia Tech

> "If y'all actually believe that using 'standard English' will dismantle white supremacy, then you not paying attention!" (Baker-Bell 20)

It would not be an exaggeration to claim that academia has disproportionately privileged white language for decades, contributing to the idea that students who use dialects, other languages, and colloquialisms must conform to a standardized white eurocentric value system that oppresses other modes of speaking. At best, students and scholars have felt devalued as they learned how to code-switch in certain spaces. At worst, this practice has damaged people's sense of self and has contributed to dangerous, and oftentimes life-threatening, racial injustices in America. *Linguistic Justice: Blank Language, Literacy, Identity, and Pedagogy* by April Baker-Bell and *Rhetorical Crossover: The Black Presence in White Culture* by Cedric D. Burrows build on the work of scholars such as Geneva Smitherman (2006) and bell hooks (2003) to present a much-needed voice advocating for linguistic equity in our school systems. Baker-Bell received the 2020 NCTE George Orwell award for *Linguistic Justice*, and with the book's unapologetic demand for Black linguistic justice, it isn't hard to see why. With Baker-Bell showcasing how Anti-Black pedagogy is still propagated in school systems, and Burrows emphasizing the societal impacts of whitescripting, whitescaping, and whitesplaining, these books demand a critical eye be turned to the way scholars and educators frame and analyze oppressive linguistic structures.

In reviewing these texts side-by-side, it is important to avoid a deficit mindset that would see us studying the works of Baker-Bell and Burrows without considering how they are responding to the way African American rhetoric has been structured into a "secondary" margin against white eurocentric rhetoric. As a white immigrant in America, I have often found myself taking a seat while listening to my students; they often know things I do not. It is with this mindset, one of openness and listening to different experiences and expertise, that these texts should be read. Instead of seeing African American rhetoric as marginalized, we must recognize the assets of the form and, after reading these two texts, seek ways to undo the structures that strive to keep Black folks in the margins.

We are introduced to the idea of "mainstream" rhetoric early in both texts. Chapter one of *Rhetorical Crossover* introduces readers to the stages of crossover as seen by Burrows. Using the history of Black music after World War II, Burrows outlines five stages of crossover that showcase how speakers learn to adapt their rhetoric to mainstream audiences (23-39). The effect of these crossovers is a dilution of the original rhetorical history which, in Burrow's writing, is African American rhetoric. In opening her book, Baker-Bell discusses the notion of the term "social justice" being used as a thin veneer to cover work that, at its heart, does not seek to promote equitable change. This "check box" method of applying the term social justice also permeates through *Linguistic Justice* in regard to the way Black language has been appropriated by mainstream media, despite racist linguistic structures remaining in place (Baker-Bell 26-28). Therefore, we can see how Black folks learn to dilute their rhetoric in order to appeal to mainstream audiences, while simultaneously their rhetoric is being appropriated by mainstream audiences. This exemplifies the way African American rhetoric is only acceptable when it is molded by mainstream thinking—undiluted African American rhetoric is only allowed in white spaces when those using it aren't Black.

In chapter two of *Linguistic Justice*, Baker-Bell discusses critical race theory (CRT) and tackles the contentious notion of code-switching and the effectiveness of this pedagogical strategy. In a powerful passage, we are reminded that students may be able to switch their language, but they "cannot switch the color of their skin" (42). To further emphasize how code-switching is an ineffective tool at best, and a racist one at worst, Baker-Bell points to the murder of Eric Garner, who repeated the words "I cannot breathe" as police held him in a chokehold. She also names Renisha McBride's words, "I just need to go home," and John Crawford's "It is not real." Attatiana Jefferson, Aiyana Stanley-Jones, and Tamir Rice are also named as Baker-Bell notes that switching to White Mainstream English did not prevent their murders, even as we tell our students that code-switching is the only way they can excel in the world (42). Naming victims murdered for their skin color emphasizes how Baker-Bell puts the "human" back into the numbers that often desensitize Americans as they watch news channels that reduce murders to race and poll numbers on a screen.

Similarly, in the second chapter of *Rhetorical Crossover*, Burrows introduces the idea of "whitescripting," a method of racially coding language that says who can, and can't, talk on a topic (45-46). Whitescripting privileges white eurocentric rhetoric while underplaying how this enforcement marginalizes rhetoric(s) then deemed other. Tactics such as whitescripting create a space in which code-switching becomes expected, as folks who don't predominantly adhere to using white eurocentric rhetoric are then either made to adapt their speech, or have it adapted for them. Burrows explains that many accounts of Martin Luther King Jr.'s rhetoric are whitescripted, privileging white eurocentric values instead of acknowledging all his influencers and where they came from. We can then see how whitescripting is apparent before a student even steps foot in a classroom, or before a scholar enters a conversation.

The use of CRT in Baker-Bell's work is elaborated in chapter four, "Scoff No More," where readers are given Black Language Artifacts to view, along with a contextual note that situates the artifacts. The participants in Baker-Bell's work then respond to those artifacts. In the recorded classroom discussions, readers are introduced to a linguistic teaching style that centers CRT at its heart and both respects and privileges student input. By turning the spotlight onto student-led discussion, readers are shown an oft-forgotten crucial aspect of pedagogical design: the students' opinions. By uplifting student-led research practices, Baker-Bell furthers our understanding of CRT as a strong pedagogical and social paradigmatic lens, and also showcases her reflexive research ethic. In Burrow's prologue, we are introduced to their personal experiences with cultural literacy and what they define as Truth and Reconciliation narratives (14). These narratives focus on seeing past injustices and acknowledging them as damaging. Burrows' uses his own experiences alongside historical accounts to show how certain narratives are woven and how communities push (counter)narratives that seek to ameliorate power inequities while striving for social justice.

However, Burrows notes that Neo-Lost Cause/Racial Nadir narratives are consistently pushing back against Truth and Reconciliation narratives (15). Neo-Lost Cause/Racial Nadir narratives try to undermine the work of affirming Black voices by painting halcyon pre-civil rights stories. These creations inherently push a false narrative of equal rights, as they ignore or demean the struggles faced by those pushed to the margins of society. To combat these false narratives, Burrows suggests cultroscripting. Cultroscripting uses a lens that privileges all cultural influences in an equitable light, without raising any one above the other (55). With these two works, side-by-side, we can see how listening to student voices in the classroom can work against the surge of Neo-Lost Cause/Racial Nadir narratives, as we can choose to privilege the lived experiences of our students over false stories perpetuated in social spaces. The real question, then, is how we recognize, and proactively work against, the stories and structures that seek to keep certain communities in the marginalia of society and the academy.

In this vein, in chapter three, Burrows uses Afroscaping as a way to tackle whitescaping, the visual reinforcement of whitescripting (71). Whitescaping mandates how bodies should appear in certain spaces, and this visual affects the way we see those bodies move in spaces. Burrows lists "character tropes" that have become the single-story of the Black body in white spaces: the altruistic negro (77-78); the one Black friend (78-80); and the angry Black person (80-82). These tropes can be traced back to historical ones that acknowledged racially charged names such as the "Uncle Tom" character. With these tropes mapped onto Black bodies and propagated in mainstream film and media, we can see how those not proactively attending to social justice methodologies begin to insidiously consume the notion of Black folks as fitting certain stereotypes only. Baker-Bell offers a classroom solution to this issue with the use of composite counter storytelling, which she uses as a methodological tool in her work. This method allows researchers to graft data and creative practices together in a way that counters notions of single stories and speaks against the unnamed white narratives that set a bar for "normative" experience. Constellating Aja Martinez (2014) and Victor Villanueva's (2004) assertions that counterstories speak against racial privileges, Baker-Bell uplifts the voices of not only her participants in Detroit, but also the voices of students everywhere who have been told that their narratives should always be judged against the "normative" white stories permeating our culture. Moreover, by presenting data as stories, alongside images of students' work and the class work, Baker-Bell engages audience members with not only thick description, but emotive appeals that humanize the participants of the study. In addition, framing this work through a CRT lens makes an important turn in regard to raising critical consciousness of race. CRT, essentially, places an academic name on work already being done in communities across America. In this way, CRT legitimizes all stories, instead of privileging stories that only occur in the realm of academe. Burrows offers his own methodology to combat whitescaping in the form of Afroscaping. Afroscaping privileges each African American person as being at the forefront of their own narrative and honors the African American rhetorical tradition of community knowledge(s) (82). We can see, then, how a path toward rebutting whitescaping appears through the use of collaborative stories and knowledge(s), where each speaker is exemplified by the composite knowledge they have accrued from all cultural influences. By combatting the singular tropes scripted onto Black bodies in certain spaces, we can work toward social justice goals both in the classroom and in society.

Highlighting her commitment to reflexive design and social justice goals, Baker-Bell makes a point to note that an assemblage of multimodal artifacts was curated when creating her book (22). This method, paired with interviewing students in Detroit, showcases a commitment to community and engagement that has come to be associated with feminist and cultural scholars. Moving away from a traditionalist notion of objectivity and sidelined approaches, Baker-Bell instead embraces and uplifts others' voices in her work, situating them as participants as opposed to the researched. In applying collaborative methods, Baker-Bell names CRT and the resulting BlackCrit framework as the lens through which she approached her research (31-32). By centering race as the lens through which she studied, we can begin to see a counternarrative forming that speaks against the appropriation, oppression, and marginalization of Black voices and language in both the academy and society. In service to this goal, Baker-Bell asks readers to consider, "What stories do Black students tell about their experiences with the language education they are offered in school? how are Black students impacted by Anti-Black Linguistic Racism?..." (50). This centering of student lived experience through a lens of race exemplifies a care and attention to the voices of students, instead of centering pedagogical theories and applying them in a cookie-cutter paradigm to different student bodies.

Centering the experiences of Black folks is a strong goal in both Burrows and Baker-Bell's works. Chapter four of *Rhetorical Crossover* is strongly titled, "Whose Lives Matter?" This title becomes ever more poignant given that the book was published in 2020, a year that saw #BlackLivesMatter movements swell in response to racism and police brutality against African Americans. With this title, we can see that Burrows is situating whitescripting, whitescaping, and whitesplaining in an American landscape that continues to discount the lives of African Americans. Truly, when looking at societal structures in America over the years, and to this day, the answer to the question, "whose lives matter?" is a chilling one. Burrows explicates on the title to this chapter by naming whitesplaining as the practice of white people telling Black folks how social justice issues are affecting them (99). This undergirds the notion of the white savior and casts African Americans in the role of needing help from said saviors. Burrows offers Afroplaining as a restorative measure to whitesplaining, naming Afroplaining as rhetoric that forms a counternarrative to the idea of the white savior and instead affirms African Americans as needing no help from the white people who are in fact impeding progress towards equity (112). However, these Afroplained narratives are often met with more whitesplaining. Burrows offers the #BlackLivesMatter and #BlueLivesMatter movements as an example of these combative ways of explaining the world. The #BlackLivesMatter movement works under the assumption that all lives matter, which then means Black Lives matter. However, the #BlueLivesMatter hashtag was formed in response to #BlackLivesMatter, arguing they were using the same logic. However, as Burrows notes, this is illogical as the "Blue" in the #BlueLivesMatter slogan is in fact referring to an institution, which would be the police force, and not those born into their bodies (124). Given that whitesplaining is the dominant narrative, more pressure is placed on African Americans to carve out a space for themselves in a society that places less value on their bodies.

With the values of white supremacy so apparent in whitescripting, whitescaping, and whitesplaining, how can we, as educators, move to tackle this oppressive ideology in our classrooms? How can we affirm and amplify the voices of all our students? Despite a lens being turned on the lived experience of students, or perhaps because of it, *Linguistic Justice* provides educators with examples for how to teach against White Language Supremacy in the classroom. By providing readers with examples from her own classes, Baker-Bell showcases methods of teaching that can raise critical consciousness of CRT. In chapters four and five, readers are walked through steps to take in the classroom, with examples of students responding well to the learning being shown. Baker-Bell states that the aim of the book is to offer "ALL students and their teachers a critical linguistic awareness of Black Language and windows into broader conversations about anti-Blackness" (101). However, educators should be aware that this does not mean that the pedagogy used in *Linguistic Justice* offers a "one and done" solution to the endemic racism in the academy. Instead, it offers us examples of how to teach Antiracist Black Language Pedagogy. Chapter six, the last in the book, highlights Baker-Bell's commitment to sharing antiracist practices, as she details a classroom design that focuses on Angie Thomas' (2017) *The Hate U Give*. For educators looking to introduce Antiracist Black Language Pedagogy, this chapter walks us through a complete lesson plan with readings and activities. It is a wonderful way to round off a book that, at its core, is trying to help educators better teach their students.

In closing *Rhetorical Crossover*, Burrows reminds readers of the "Black tax" imposed on every African American that, by his definition, is the "societal charges and the communal toil (emotional, economic, etc.) placed on African Americans who wish to enter and participate in white spaces…" (127). Burrows provides a personal example of this tax, recalling when he overheard a hiring committee cutting him from a hiring pool after an interview, deeming him too "hostile" for white students (138-139). Because he did not crossover his rhetoric as much as was expected, he was refused entry into a predominantly white academic institution. This example reminds us that it is not only the role of teachers, but of institutions, to create spaces that uplift the voices of all students, not only those adhering to a white eurocentric rhetorical narrative. So, where does that leave us? While institutions may operate using oppressive structures, we, the educators and scholars, can work toward creating those spaces for our students. We can be vocal in our admonishment of systems that seek to undermine their worth and place taxes on their bodies and ways of knowing. We can, in short, continue the work of scholars such as Baker-Bell and Burrows, pushing toward a future that is equitable for all.

Drawing from a rich collection of sources and lived experiences, *Linguistic Justice* and *Rhetorical Crossover* sit well on the bookshelf alongside H. Samy

Alim, John Rickford, and Arnetha Ball's *Raciolinguistics* (2016), hooks' (1994) *Teaching to Transgress*, and Vershawn Ashanti Young and Michelle Bachelor Robinson's (2018) *Routledge Reader of African American Rhetoric*. These books will serve readers who want to increase their knowledge(s) of racialized language practices that continue to permeate through society in oppressive ways. In truth, *Linguistic Justice* book series editors Valerie Kinloch and Susi Long put it best when they describe the book as a love story that speaks against Anti-Blackness (Baker-Bell 8). In contrast to the love shining through *Linguistic Justice*, Burrows' *Rhetorical Crossover* read, to me, as a book powerfully arguing against a system that has repeatedly refused to affirm the assets of African American rhetoric. In crossing over, African American rhetoric is shown to be frequently diluted even as it's appropriated. This, coupled with the rules imposed on Black bodies, creates exclusionary spaces and practices where barriers should not exist. However, both Baker-Bell and Burrows' love for their culture shines through in every page of these works, despite the differing tones, and their work is stronger for it. *Linguistic Justice* and *Rhetorical Crossover*, then, will likely affirm readers who have felt oppressed by Anti-Blackness in their own lives. Moreover, Baker-Bell and Burrows' clear writing style makes these books accessible not only for scholars, instructors, and teacher-researchers, but also for students. Not only do we see these scholars uplifting the voices of Black folks, but they also provide us with enough explanation of various racialized schemas that readers unfamiliar with the field will be able to dive into the books with little issue. This accessibility allows readers to clearly engage with these books and their call to action for us to be, and do, better.

Blacksburg, Virginia

Works Cited

Alim, H. Samy, et al., editors. *Raciolinguistics: How Language Shapes Our Ideas About Race*. Oxford UP, 2016.

hooks, bell. *Teaching Community: A Pedagogy of Hope*. Routledge, 2003.

---. *Teaching to Transgress: Education as the Practice of Freedom*. Routledge, 1994.

Martinez, Aja. "A Plea for Critical Race Theory Counterstory: Stock Story vs. Counterstory Dialogues Concerning Alejandra's 'Fit' in the Academy." *Composition Studies*, vol. 42, no. 2, 2014, pp. 33–55.

Smitherman, Geneva. *Word from the Mother: Language and African Americans*. Routledge, 2006.

Thomas, Angie. *The Hate U Give*. Balzer & Bray, 2017.

Villanueva, Victor. "*Memoria* is a Friend of Ours: On the Discourse of Color." *College English*, vol. 67, no. 1, 2004, pp. 9–19.

Young, Vershawn Ashanti and Michelle Bachelor Robinson, editors. *The Routledge Reader of African American Rhetoric: The Longue Durée of Black Voices*. Routledge, 2018.

Graduate Student Writing Is Graduate Student Work: A Review Essay

Conceptions of Literacy: Graduate Instructors and the Teaching of First-Year Composition, by Meaghan Brewer. Utah State U P, 2020. 210 pp.

Graduate Writing Across the Disciplines: Identifying, Teaching, and Supporting, edited by Marilee Brooks-Gillies, Elena G. Garcia, Soo Hyon Kim, Katie Manthey, and Trixie G. Smith. WAC Clearinghouse / UP of Colorado, and CSU Open Press, 2020. 372 pp.

Learning from the Lived Experiences of Graduate Student Writers, edited by Shannon Madden, Michele Eodice, Kirsten T. Edwards, and Alexandria Lockett. Utah State UP, 2020. 302 pp.

Reviewed by Turnip Van Dyke, University of Texas at El Paso

Composition studies has increasingly displayed an interest in graduate student writing. Writing may be the most unifying experience of graduate students across programs, disciplines, and institutions, since writing is perhaps the most fundamental action of scholarship. Composition studies' growing interest in this writing is timely, as the guiding question of "what affects graduate student writing" that drives this interest overlaps with other trends in composition such as writing across the curriculum (graduate students write in all disciplines), translingualism (graduate students write with a wide range of linguistic backgrounds and resources), and mentorship (graduate students often work closely with faculty mentors or seek other supportive relationships). Graduate students are also undergoing the significant challenges of enculturation in their chosen field(s), which has prompted increasing social critique and personal reflection on what is at stake in a graduate education.

I am also at an opportune moment in my own life to review the three books selected for this essay. I am a PhD student in a Rhetoric and Writing Studies program, I taught my first semester of first year composition while preparing this review essay, and I am working with a team on the inaugural year of a multidisciplinary peer writing groups initiative for graduate students at my institution. This points to the differing needs for research of graduate student writing. I read scholarship on graduate student writing to figure out how to write larger projects like my looming dissertation, to understand how my writing practices influence my pedagogy, and to make considered administrative choices about writing-related initiatives for graduate students. These are all practical, pressing concerns. I believe these books are written for those faculty and administrators who may also grapple with these concerns, especially composition studies faculty, but my perspective as a current graduate student informs how I took in these authors' insights.

All three of the books I consider in this review essay share an interest in how graduate students are developing as writers, scholars, and teachers. I hope to expand the conversation with this review essay by encouraging us to also recognize graduate students as workers. What I mean by "worker" in contrast to those other titles is that composition scholars have not acknowledged the graduate student experience as a set of labor issues. Here it must be noted that I am writing in a United States academic context. In the US, graduate students are frequently employed by the same people who are researching how to support us, which should pose obvious ethical issues. Our pay is insufficient to live from, and our status in the academy is precarious. This economic precarity is exacerbated for graduate students who hold marginalized identities. Composition studies' growing interest in graduate student writing, then, must come with a growing interest in graduate student work and living conditions.

Meaghan Brewer's *Conceptions of Literacy: Graduate Instructors and the Teaching of First-Year Composition* follows a cohort of new graduate instructors through their first semester of teaching composition. This project is similar in spirit to Jessica Restaino's 2012 book, *First Semester: Graduate Students, Teaching Writing, and the Challenge of Middle Ground*; both Brewer and Restaino work to apply an analytical lens to their qualitative research of graduate instructors in their first semester teaching. In *Conceptions of Literacy*, Brewer makes use of Peter Goggin's scholarship on literacy views to analyze how graduate student instructors' prior conceptions of literacy influence their initial pedagogies in the writing classroom. "Literacy views" refers to the theoretical frame that there are differing operative definitions of literacy that influence literacy cultures. Brewer diagnoses the guiding literacy view each research participant holds prior to their work as a graduate student. She uses these literacy views to explain the graduate students' teaching approaches and challenges. For example, Brewer discusses how three instructors' cultural literacy emphasis on engaging with and understanding assigned readings affected the time spent on students' writing in their classes. She explains that "although [the instructors] wanted to incorporate more writing, because they thought that texts were important and because their own past instruction had focused more on discussing literature, they felt unprepared for the differing curricular goals of the composition classroom" (80-81). Brewer's work offers a pedagogical model for graduate instructor preparation that honors students' prior knowledge and values through the lens of literacy views. Student instructors can better weather the storm of the first semester teaching with a clearer connection between their own educational experiences and their pedagogies.

Finding connections to one's own educational experiences as a learner is critical to communicating writing as an ongoing practice. A book I thought of frequently while reading through these three is the 2018 collection *Out in the Center: Public Controversies and Private Struggles*, edited by Denny, et al. The collection features reflections from scholars about their experiences working in writing centers and how their identities, such as race, language status, and gender, shaped that work. Because of many writing centers' reliance on student staffing, most of the contributors reflect on their work as graduate students in writing centers, and thus their broader experiences in graduate school. Identity, "fit," and vulnerability swirl as topics of concern for graduate students navigating their institutional roles.

The aim of *Out in the Center* to feature personal narratives as a means to explore concerns in writing studies parallels the focus of Shannon Madden, Michele Eodice, Kirsten T. Edwards, and Alexandria Lockett's edited collection *Learning from the Lived Experiences of Graduate Student Writers*. Personal narratives constitute the first of two major sections of *Learning*. I was particularly drawn to the co-written chapter, "Paying It Forward by Looking Back: Six HBCU Professionals Reflect on Their Mentoring Experiences as Black Women in Academia," by Karen Keaton Jackson, Hope Jackson, Kendra L. Mitchell, Pamela Strong Simmons, Cecilia D. Shelton, and LaKela Atkinson. The chapter is an exemplar of the dialogic reflection the *Learning* editors sought to encourage. Together, Jackson and others successfully blend small, individual reflections with a broader discussion of the need to create more support and mentorship of Black women. They highlight the successes of historically Black colleges and universities (HBCUs) in creating mentoring networks Black women scholars can thrive in. This is crucial to learn from because, as the authors explain,

> there are so few African American PhDs in any academic field, finding one in a particular discipline at any institution can be rather difficult if not impossible… it is often necessary for students to go outside their institutions to connect with a mentor of color who resembles them. (119)

Questions of mentorship go beyond concerns of availability or engagement with students. Mentorship will determine who the next generation of composition scholars is. Jackson and others argue that mentorship, especially of marginalized groups, is a responsibility not to a particular program or institution, but to the field and to the graduate students within it.

There are also cross-cultural considerations to make for mentoring. *Learning* has two major sections, bridged by two "Interlude" entries, written by Alexandria Lockett and Amanda E. Cuellar. Cuellar writes about the Anzaldúan notion of "atravesando," crossing (borders), in her experiences moving from a Hispanic serving institution (HSI) in West Texas for her undergraduate studies to a predominantly white institution (PWI) for her graduate work. Cuellar describes how "the borders between my professors and me are so wide it is difficult, oftentimes nearly impossible, to cross them. Usually, I feel I am the one who constantly must do the atravesando" (133). Cuellar and other scholars in *Learning* argue that graduate students are often tasked with moving from the margin to center, rather than their instructors and mentors working to center the marginalized. This is another instance where the ability of students to connect with mentors outside of their department can be crucial.

Learning's second major section, titled "Approaches," features articles that profile extracurricular efforts to support graduate student writing. Extracurricular support of graduate students is crucial, especially as writing instruction is not a part of all graduate programs' coursework. I am currently involved with establishing a peer writing groups initiative for graduate students at my institution. The lack of writing instruction, especially for many graduate programs in the sciences, is a primary motivation for us to create multidisciplinary spaces where students can connect to each other for peer support and engagement with their writing.

Contributors to both *Learning* and *Graduate Writing Across the Disciplines* highlight a number of different extracurricular approaches to supporting graduate student writing. Some of these are tailored for specific demographics, such as international and/or English-language learner graduate students, or students in the sciences. The most common approaches at the moment, judging by these collections, are focused on supporting students currently working on large writing projects like a thesis or dissertation. Short time-intensive writing camps or retreats are common, where graduate students are invited to convene for a predetermined length of time (e.g., an afternoon, a weekend, a week) to create a scheduled space to write in. Longer approaches include developing courses that focus on academic writing expectations and genre familiarization, and establishing a peer writing group initiative where students are able to meet regularly, often with a facilitator.

Anne Zanzucchi and Amy Fernstermaker describe a hybrid of these two approaches (a writing class and a writing group) in their *Learning* chapter, "Not Just Nuts and Bolts: Building a Peer Review Framework for Academic Socialization." In the chapter, they outline the creation of an academic course that focused on developing graduate students' peer feedback skills in a writing workshop atmosphere that emphasized genre awareness. Zanzucchi and Fernstermaker argue that "peer review is a powerful professional activity that can be leveraged as an authentic practice with development and refinement over time—particularly by providing feedback to a variety of writers" (221).

Many of the approaches described in these books seek to put graduate students in conversation with one another. I encourage these peer conversations as it allows us as graduate students to make closer connections with each other, and also to practice the kinds of interdisciplinary scholarly conversations that are important to academic work.

Peer support is of course only one of many pedagogical strategies for graduate student writing. Marilee Brooks-Gillies, Elena G. Garcia, Soo Hyon Kim, Katie Manthey, and Trixie G. Smith's edited collection, *Graduate Writing Across the Disciplines: Identifying, Teaching, and Supporting*, has a sustained focus on approaches that faculty and administrators can consider for supporting graduate students with writing. The book divides these into four sections: first, coursework for graduate writing; second, professionalization and enculturation efforts to help graduate students better understand academic expectations; third, extracurricular graduate writing support; and fourth, genre familiarization. True to the spirit of writing across the disciplines, the contributors have diverse disciplinary backgrounds. This contributes to the variety of research methods used to analyze a writing initiative's effectiveness, making *Graduate Writing* a particularly valuable volume for anyone considering assessment options for a writing initiative. I personally benefited from Gretchen Busl, Kara Lee Donnelly, and Matthew Capdevielle's chapter, "Camping in the Disciplines: Assessing the Effect of Writing Camps on Graduate Student Writers," to develop a pre-/post-survey for participants in a peer writing groups initiative.

Jennifer Douglas' chapter, "Developing an English for Academic Purposes Course for L2 Graduate Students in the Sciences," serves as an excellent example of *Graduate Writing*'s initiative overviews. Douglas discusses the pedagogic thinking underlying her development of a course in the sciences that sought to enculturate international graduate students to expectations for academic writing in English in their respective disciplines. Douglas sought to connect this writing work to graduate students' research interests to better illustrate how writing processes are a crucial and active part of developing scholarship. Douglas makes use of John M. Swales and Christine B. Feaks' *Academic Writing for Graduate Students* textbook to frame writing's value this way for students. Douglas' class focuses on genre familiarization through close article analysis, and "by introducing [this] model early [to frame] specific writing tasks throughout the course within the larger goals of the research paper" (85). This approach resonates with my own experiences as a master's student in a higher education studies program, where our research methods course also served as a process of repeated genre familiarization through analyzing the structure of articles to better understand what graduate students would need to plan for in their own research projects later in the degree.

The editors of *Graduate Writing* also include contributions in the reflective mode from the first section of *Learning*. In "Crossing Divides: Engaging Extracurricular Writing Practices in Graduate Education and Professionalization," Laural L. Adams, Megan Adams, Pauline Baird, Estee Beck, Kristine L. Blair, April Conway, Lee Nickoson, and Martha Schaffer present a series of brief reflections discussing their efforts to transfer skills to the new challenges of academic writing for graduate students. Adams states this succinctly when she writes that "our pasts serve as extracurricular writing spaces and the ground from which—through care and passion—we bridge into new communities" (275). I parallel Adams' insight about our past educational experiences with Brewer's efforts to understand how graduate student instructors used their prior efforts as students in *Conceptions of Literacy*. All three of these books are interested in what knowledge students bring with them to graduate programs and how that knowledge is (not) valued in their graduate experiences. The focus here often remains on how to work with students to acquire new skills or acculturate to graduate expectations. With the risk of making an already-daunting task (preparing graduate students to succeed at writing) all the more difficult, I echo the fear of Janine Morris, Hannah J. Rule, and Christina M. LaVecchia in a recent *Peitho* article that "much of the graduate-level writing support we see increasing across disciplines emphasizes rhetorical features and scholarly genres—approaches that, while useful, can nonetheless atomize and contain writing, cleaving it from its dizzying affective, embodied, and material dynamics." We can turn from the question of "what affects graduate student writing" to "what animates it?"

This animated turn would require a shift from the research priorities represented by these three books. Addressing writing as skill acquisition often obscures any social critique of how graduate schools operate, a kind of critique that is necessary to make sense of how our higher education institutions are failing to support half of graduate students to complete their degrees (*Learning* 4). The oppression of people becomes an abstracted concern when our eye is only on enculturation and genre familiarization. Graduate students are a diverse group of workers with different levels of access to power, even as we are flattened (temporarily and unevenly) by the precarity of our status in academia. We must imagine through practice how to mentor and support each other as such. The nextGEN group, dedicated to graduate student support and advocacy for justice and equity, is an example of a newer model in composition studies. In a conversation in *Composition Studies* in 2019, nextGEN contributing startup members Sweta Baniya, Sara Doan, Gavin P. Johnson, Ashanka Kumari, Kyle Larson, and Virginia M. Schwarz wrote how "justice work is often compartmentalized, and collaboration can be contingent upon having overlapping members… we need to be attentive to the whole of our communities" (209). Practicing writing and scholarship in more nontraditional horizontal support structures can aid graduate students with the work ahead of us. We should understand graduate students as workers with a unique set of labor needs. Recognizing what we are experiencing as labor issues can connect us to the rich history of labor struggles—and yes, that needs to include serious conversations about graduate students unionizing. We can exercise collective governance as graduate workers to improve well-being, pay, and workplace conditions. We can dream of the self-destructive work that K. Wayne Yang (writing as la paperson) burns into us through his *A Third University Is Possible*—we can dare to re-animate our institutions for the work of undoing the white capitalist settler-colonial patriarchy that sustains them. Composition studies must be a part of this, both to exercise writing as a decolonizing force, and because graduate student writing risks becoming a matter of assimilation and acculturation otherwise. Reflect for a moment on the title *Learning from the Lived Experiences of Graduate Student Writers*. We have so much more to learn from each other than the university, as it exists, can bear. There is work ahead for all of us.

If you are currently a graduate student: we need to find each other. Supporting each other through this process will lead to greater success for all of us. If you are currently a faculty member mentoring graduate students: work with us to value the knowledge we bring to the table, and structure programs in ways that leverage our existing knowledge. What these three books offer are perspectives on what the field of composition is attempting toward these ends. What I hope they spark is the ambition to create new spaces and relationships for graduate students to work equitably and thrive in.

El Paso, Texas

Works Cited

Baniya, Sweta, et al. "Where We Are: Dialogue and Disciplinary Space." *Composition Studies*, vol. 47, no. 2, 2019, pp. 203-210.

Denny, Harry C., et al., editors. *Out in the Center: Public Controversies and Private Struggles*. Utah State UP, 2018.

Goggin, Peter. *Professing Literacy in Composition Studies*. Hampton Press, 2008.

Morris, Janine, et al. "Writing Groups as Feminist Practice." *Peitho*, vol. 22, no. 3, 2020, cfshrc.org/article/writing-groups-as-feminist-practice/.

paperson, la. *A Third University is Possible*. U of Minnesota P, 2017.

Restaino, Jessica. *First Semester: Graduate Students, Teaching Writing, and the Challenge of Middle Ground*. Southern Illinois UP, 2012.

Swales, John M., and Christine B. Feak. *Academic Writing for Graduate Students*. 3rd ed., U of Michigan P, 2012.

On African-American Rhetoric, by Keith Gilyard and Adam J. Banks. New York, NY: Routledge, 2018. 146 pp.

Reviewed by Mikayla Beaudrie, University of North Florida

In 1974, the Conference on College Composition and Communication (CCCC) adopted the Students' Right to Their Own Language resolution (full statement published in *College English* the following year). This landmark resolution acknowledged that differences in language production vary according to individual and group non-negotiable differences. While Students' Right helped to reinforce and legitimize the ways historically marginalized speakers make meaning out of language, scholarship in the field of alternative literacies was already underway long before CCCC formally recognized deviations from standardized English. Entire ecologies of meaning-making, such as African-American literacies, African-American rhetoric, Black English, and Black discourse had been (and continue to be) ripe for investigation.

Keith Gilyard and Adam J. Banks' research into African-American rhetoric studies in *On African-American Rhetoric* uncovers the various complex and critical rhetorical methods employed by African-American artists, authors, and orators. The authors unearth a representative sampling of textual, oral, and performative artifacts from a long line of African-American cultural productions. In doing so, Gilyard and Banks locate strategic language use by African Americans in various rhetorical forms, such as slave narratives, poetry, folklore, music, and memes (6). The analysis therein draws from the growing body of contemporary scholarship concerning African-American rhetoric, thereby arming educators, scholars, and students with a critical framework for analyzing the ever-growing field of African-American rhetoric and its rhetorical productions.

Chapter one draws on Deborah Atwater's scholarship to highlight the elasticity of African-American rhetoric. This elasticity is present in the authors' definition of African-American rhetoric as: "the art of persuasion fused with African-American ways of knowing in attempts to achieve in public realms personhood, dignity, and respect . . . for African-American people" (3). In short, African-American rhetoric is about strategy and the way such strategy is communicated. Such communication occurs in private, interpersonal spaces and broader, public spheres, therefore requiring an elastic definition that encompasses a range of epistemologies. Establishing a non-exhaustive definition serves the whole text well by making it easier to access the codes informing the African-American experience.

Having established a working definition, the authors investigate the history of African-American rhetoric in chapter two. They argue there is "no straight line from the ruminations of Aristotle to modern Black thought and verbal output" (10). To come to this conclusion, the authors uncover the origins of the African-American rhetorical tradition from both African and Western influences. Of particular importance is the uncovering of the historic rhetorical methods of African-American literature, agentic self-identification, and public outcries for personhood. Through thematic analysis, composition scholars may identify a unique application of pathos in African-American rhetorical productions: the usage of the oppressor's language as means to seek freedom. Black speakers have historically utilized a pliable and flexible English language for making public their private plights towards freedom, personhood, and humanity.

The major theme in chapter three considers the integrationist and separatist strains of African-American rhetoric. The integrationist strain is identified in the African-American jeremiad (wherein Blacks self-identify as the chosen people whose purpose is to redeem liberty for all). The separatist strain argues for the individual choice to separate Blacks from the rest of the United States to preserve the African elements of Black culture. Gilyard and Banks recognize that both strains are historic but continue to thrive in modern discourses. Their analysis of Black-nationalist thought (e.g., Black Power) charts how separatists and integrationists alike strategically accepted and rejected discourse for specific purposes.

Chapter four traces the history of African-American rhetorical theory. Here, Gilyard and Banks outline three specific theories that continue to frame the way African-American rhetoric is studied and taught in the academy: Molefi Kete Asante's comprehensive scholarship on Afrocentrism; Henry Louis Gates, Jr.'s literary theory of the Signifying Monkey; and broadly, Black feminism. It is made clear that the three ideologies are not alone in college classrooms but prove especially generative (46). In short, ignoring Afrocentric ideals would make the scholarly study of African-American rhetoric impossible, "for it would lack an object of study" (47). Because Afrocentrism acknowledges the African sources of African-American culture in the United States, it is central to the study of African-American rhetoric. Likewise, Gilyard and Banks recognize Henry Louis Gates, Jr.'s significant contribution to literary theory (especially as it pertains to African-American literature) with the Signifying Monkey. It is worth noting that this theory is particularly useful when African-American literature is viewed as a conscious act of language production. Gilyard and Banks broadly identify the final theory as "Black feminism," defined as "identity formation and initiatives for social change fueled by the experiences and perspectives of Black women" (60). Black feminism, the authors argue, is integral to the study of African-American rhetoric because it acknowledges non-negotiable differences outside of nationality and race. Incorporating womanness into the study of African-American texts helps locate the lost voices of Black women and their contributions to the African-American rhetorical legacy. Black feminism also provides various frameworks for understanding and contextualizing Black women's writing when analyzed through the lenses of womanism, wreck, and misogynoir.

An extension of existing academic discourse, chapters five and six expand on Banks' 2011 monograph, *Digital Griots: African American Rhetoric in a Multimedia Age*. Chapter five continues Banks' work into Black digital studies by asking how African-American rhetoric has responded to, adopted, and utilized technology. Technology is found across much African-American literature and is primarily embedded in tropes and motifs. For instance, separatism, escapism, the mothership, and flight are mobilized by means of technological advancement. But it is in the following chapter, "Rhetoric and Black Twitter," where readers see the possibilities and limitations of Black rhetorical productions in the age of social media. Chapter six specifically focuses on Black Twitter and how its users bring Black discourse and perspectives to a technologically proficient yet largely White space. Gilyard and Banks point to specific examples to show how Black Twitter allows users to generate messages of the Black experience beyond the platform itself and into the public sphere, thereby making Black Twitter essential to African American rhetoric. Much of chapter six analyzes different practices seen on Black Twitter, such as "dragging," "clapbacks", and "THIS!!!!!"– each expressing core tenets of African American rhetoric: affirmation, signifyin', and resistance.

In tradition with scholarship in composition and rhetorical studies, chapter seven discusses African-American rhetoric in the college classroom by identifying historic Black voices in rhetoric/composition studies and how those voices have influenced the teaching of literacy and language. The chapter reviews pedagogical scholarship by the authors, in addition to that of Hallie Quinn Brown, Karmen Kynard, Geneva Smitherman, and Carter G. Woodson. Their analysis of useful teaching methods that manifest those core tenets of African-American rhetoric (especially that of legitimacy in a largely White, capitalist, Eurocentric industry) helps us better understand transgressive practices for teaching African-American students *and* teaching Black discourse in academic settings. So, tactics like gospel literacy, rap-imbued writing, Black Queer literacies, code meshing, pluralism, Students' Right, and critical language awareness are possible and work because contemporary rhetoric/composition studies typically advocate for *Black* discourse to be viewed as *academic* discourse. Scholars can use these tactics to validate the epistemological value of Black discursive power within academe.

On African-American Rhetoric serves multifaceted purposes for readers. For instance, composition educators may adopt *On African-American Rhetoric* in their graduate courses concerning writing theory to highlight the contributions of Black and African-American scholars and expose students to emerging subfields. Said graduate students will find chapters four and seven to be particularly useful in developing transgressive pedagogies and for teaching diverse student bodies. But it is in the conclusion where Gilyard and Banks address scholars explicitly. *On African-American Rhetoric* commences with a poignant discussion regarding the possibilities and limits of rhetoric, especially for African Americans. In short, the conclusion asks what rhetoric/composition scholars do now and where they ought to go next as African-American rhetoric continues to grow as a field of study and discourse. Gilyard and Banks offer six areas for future research. First, more scholarship is needed in out-of-school settings, such as analysis of the Black political speech writers, STEM workers, and digital-content creators. Additional scholarship is needed in the intersectionality of African-American rhetoric with various ethnic rhetorics and ethnic rhetorical traditions as a whole. The fourth call asks scholars to consider "questions of technology and rhetoric...to understand technology(ies) as a site of inquiry rather than as merely a site of production of discourse" (123). Fifth is the archival/curation of texts. And the sixth calls for additional study of visual rhetorics.

It is worth noting that in a contemporary era that spews post-racial rhetorics alongside Black Lives Matter, *On African-American Rhetoric* provides insight into the purposeful formation of Blackness in public discourse. Gilyard and Banks craft an artful and scientific analysis of Black cultural productions and its existing artifacts. In light of the text, those interested in alternative literacies and counter-languages must ask: How do Black speakers negate the tumultuous conversations surrounding Blackness in the hands of various power structures that continue to deny Black humanity? And what can we, as educators and scholars, do to support the legacy of Black rhetoricians in such a power struggle? Overall, *On African-American Rhetoric* proves an invaluable tool for educators, scholars, and students who wish to uncover the means through which meaning is made in African-American cultural productions.

Jacksonville, Florida

Works Cited

Banks, Adam, *Digital Griots: African American Rhetoric in a Multimedia Age*. Southern Illinois University Press, 2011.

Committee on CCCC Language Statement. Students' Right to their Own Language. *College English*, vol. 36, no. 6, 1975, pp. 708-726.

Unruly Rhetorics: Protest, Persuasion, and Publics, edited by Jonathan Alexander, Susan C. Jarratt, and Nancy Welch. U of Pittsburgh P, 2018. 336 pp.

Reviewed by Rebecca S. Haynes, University of Wyoming

Scholars of rhetoric and composition may be inclined to ask: what is the role of the unruly in public discourse? *Unruly Rhetorics: Protest, Persuasion, and Publics* answers this question in a series of essays that challenges the notion that the unruly has no place in civil discourse, and, indeed, that what is thought of as civil discourse is even particularly civil. Editors Jonathan Alexander, Susan C. Jarratt, and Nancy Welch apply the theories of Jacques Rancière and Judith Butler to build an unruly rhetoric, citing Rancière and Butler's claims that protest is not caused by temporary disenfranchisement and inequality, but persistent and fundamental inequality under which marginalized groups are expected to endure (29). Rhetoric concerning protest is, therefore, by its very nature unruly, because it disrupts a hegemonic status quo that consistently, not temporarily, fails to enfranchise citizens.

The essays within *Unruly Rhetorics* claim that the unruly not only has a place in discourse but that it is vital in a world of rampant inequality. *Unruly Rhetorics* examines the role of the physical body in discourse, not just as a tool of protest, but a reminder of what is at stake: the very lives and rights of those who are driven to protest. The body as a tool of protest also serves to illuminate the lived realities of those who are engaging in unruly rhetorics. In other words, how are they to avoid being unruly when their bodies are treated by the hegemony as being unruly by their very existence?

Contributors Jacqueline Rhodes, Dana L. Cloud, Diana George, Paula Mathieu, Joyce Rain Anderson, Londie T. Martin, and Adela C. Licona in particular reveal the ways in which the words of those in power villainize or pathologize the bodies of the disenfranchised. In chapter five of this volume, Jacqueline Rhodes examines the way Constable Michael Sanguinetti, while speaking at a safety forum at Osgoode Hall Law School in Toronto, indicated that women should avoid dressing "like sluts" in order to prevent violence against their bodies. Widely circulated reports of Sanguinetti's claim led to the birth of the SlutWalk protests (126). And though Sanguinetti cast himself as the voice of reason among unruly women who are complicit in the violence against them, readers will see the reclamation of a word used to degrade women through a protest that shines a light on the reality that women's bodies are frequently deemed unruly and problematic.

In chapter one, "Feminist Body Rhetoric in the #unrulymob, Texas, 2013," contributor Dana L. Cloud shines a light on women's responses to attempts to more stringently govern their bodies. In this case, a draconian Texas abortion bill was met by protesters who fashioned hats and accessories out of tampons. This was not just a symbolic and satirical protest, but a direct response to the ban on tampons in the state Capitol building (enacted, ostensibly, due to fear that protestors could use them as projectiles or lighters for Molotov cocktails).

These examples of bodies becoming action illustrates what contributor Kevin Mahoney argues is a vital component of rhetoric in action. Mahoney describes the practice of protesting as "the practice of occupying physical space, of throwing one's body on the gears" in order to effect social change (213). The metaphor of society as a system of gears illustrates that society functions regardless of whether the rights of all citizens are upheld, and that change occurs only if one puts his or her body on the line to disrupt the status quo functioning of the machine. Dissent and protest are then, by their very nature, unruly.

Diana George and Paula Mathieu's chapter, "Rewriting the life of James Eads How and *Hobo News*," underscores the inequities that exist even in a society with a free press. *Hobo News*, which circulated among the people James Eads How was attempting to organize, provided a dissenting voice that stood in stark contrast to the narratives of the mainstream press about "the fiction of poverty as personal choice" (175). These mainstream narratives, of course, were belied by the reality of economic inequality that perpetuates the precarity of life for many citizens (175). George and Mathieu analyze the ways in which the press pathologized poverty by framing How's choices as the actions of an eccentric rather than an activist. How threw his "body on the gears" by rejecting his inherited fortune and living among the homeless in order to organize for action. In this way, he put his body behind his words and his calls to action, a choice that illustrated his sincerity as much as it cast him as unruly in the eyes of the press.

Authors in *Unruly Rhetorics* consistently reveal hegemonic uses of language that cast marginalized peoples into "unruly" roles. In chapter two, Joyce Rain Anderson discusses how Indigenous Americans who protested the Dakota Access Pipeline were deemed "protesters" by the media and their hunger strikes were reconfigured as "liquid diets" (78). But Indigenous Americans identify as water protectors, and the unruliness of their rhetoric and action is a response to colonialism and an assertion of Indigenous Americans' rights to exist through a coalescing of bodies, speech, and action.

The coalescing of bodies, speech, and action is perhaps most salient in Londie T. Martin and Adela C. Licona's chapter, "Remix as Unruly Play and Participatory Method for Im/possible Queer World-making." In their examination of youth-produced digital videos coming out of the 2011 Nuestra Voz social justice summer camp, Martin and Licona reveal youth who are responding to the fundamental inequalities placed upon them, namely the marginalizing effects of abstinence-only sex education on queer youth and the school-to-prison pipeline (320). Of particular interest is how the youth use their already-unruly bodies to protest and reclaim speech that is used to define them: by writing troubling statistics about youth and sexuality in black marker directly on their skin (325). The ephemerality of the written numbers serves as a statement, a resistance of the reductive nature of treating groups of people as numbers.

Unruly Rhetorics doesn't sidestep the question of whether unruliness, particularly when considered uncivil, can reach the audience one is trying to persuade. Matthew Abraham, in examining Steven Salaita's controversial tweets criticizing Israel during the Gaza war, makes the claim that incivility can be utilized to highlight the manner in which the powerful have the privilege of defining incivility, and thus the ability to justify their own incivility. Specifically, Abraham makes the claim that Salaita's tweets were rhetorical choices that responded to military aggressivity and the discourse of historical anti-Semitism with linguistic aggressivity (113). These tweets enacted an unruly rhetoric that challenged the accepted hostility of military action by mirroring it. This example challenges the unruly/uncivil relationship and also returns to the recurring thesis that unruliness in rhetoric arises from consistent disenfranchisement.

Rhetoricians may take particular interest in chapter ten, where John Trimbur critiques James Berlin's criticism of the rhetoric/poetics binary and his own criticism of CCCC and NCTE's silence on the University of Illinois withdrawing an offer of employment to Steven Salaita based on the series of tweets discussed in the Abraham chapter. Trimbur asserts that relegating poetics in literary studies to a spiritual or ahistorical domain leaves no room for unruly poetics such as graffiti, hip hop, punk, reggae, Black Lives Matter, the Occupy movement, Dada, Brecht, and surrealism (256). These examples of poetics, given that they are not easily governable or definable, provide evidence that speech and action, performed by bodies that are deemed unruly (either by their existence or by stepping outside of the bounds of what is considered civil discourse), creates an unruly rhetoric.

Unruly Rhetorics was timely when it was published in 2018. At the time of this review writing in 2020, protesters continue to put their bodies on the line to decry the way the bodies of Black men and women are treated as unruly and expendable; others, also protesting, choose to put their own and others' bodies at risk to decry being required to wear protective masks. *Unruly Rhetorics* therefore remains highly relevant in light of this struggle for the power to put bodies on the line. It is a valuable resource for academics interested in the study of rhetoric and composition and an engaging book for instructors and students in these areas, particularly those who are interested in the area of social justice.

Laramie, Wyoming

Works Cited

Butler, Judith. *Notes Toward a Performative Theory of Assembly*. Harvard UP, 2015.
O'Reilly, Andrea. "Slut Pride: A Tribute to SlutWalk Toronto." *Feminist Studies*, vol. 38, no. 1, 2012, pp. 245-50.
Rancière, Jacques. *Disagreement: Politics and Philosophy*. Translated by Julie Rose, U of Minnesota P, 1999.
Rancière, Jacques. *The Politics of Aesthetics*. Bloomsbury Academic, 2013.
"Unruly." *Merriam-Webster Dictionary*. Accessed October 24, 2020.

Labor-Based Grading Contracts: Building Equity and Inclusion in the Compassionate Writing Classroom, by Asao B. Inoue. The WAC Clearinghouse, 2019. 334 pp.

Reviewed by Stephie Minjung Kang, Michigan State University

"If you use a single standard to grade your students' languaging, you engage in racism" ("How do" 359). Asao Inoue starts and ends his chair's address at the 2019 Conference on College Composition and Communication (CCCC) by problematizing White language preferences in writing classrooms. He calls on his colleagues to feel the discomfort—instead of think or study it as a subject—that raciolinguistically diverse students feel having to meet the standards set by White language habitus. He has argued that writing assessment is one of the most evident ways of promoting White language supremacy, and in his latest book, *Labor-Based Contracts: Building Equity and Inclusion in the Compassionate Writing Classroom,* Inoue continuously and compassionately urges readers to create labor-based grading contract ecologies as an anti-racist practice that not only moves teachers' focus on students' products to their labor in assessment but also has students engage with the politics of language. To exceptional effect, the book intertwines theories of labor and standard language ideologies with Inoue's reflection on his teacherly identity and experience.

Inoue begins the book by contextualizing White language supremacy as grounds for readers to problematize the current assessment ecology. Drawing on Bourdieu's notion of racial habitus, he argues that all performances, including judging writing, are reflections of our racial habitus—"structured dispositions associated with local racial formations" (26). The wicked, paradoxical nature of White racial habitus is that it is embedded as invisible, naturalized, neutral, objective, apolitical, and rational dispositions within larger structures that make up the society. Because these sets of White racial dispositions (i.e., Whiteness) are naturalized and neutralized, they have determined "standards" of various areas of the society, including literacy performances. What the framework of racial habitus allows us to see, then, is that "White language supremacy is a condition and outcome, not simply a trait, and is structured in assessment ecologies in such a way as to function simultaneously as an ideal and as the norm" (28).

Thus, White racial habitus is at the center of dominant academic discourses that dictate who gets the highest grades (53). Inoue turns to working-class, multilingual students of color who didn't have first-hand access to such discourses and often didn't receive an A-grade even though they tried hard. Seeking an answer to how teachers could create an assessment ecology that is fair and acknowledges student labor, chapter two offers the successes and misfires of variations of grading contracts over the years. One is Bill Condon's community-based assessment that uses peer evaluations as the only grading rubric. Although this model excludes teacher's judgement, peer evaluations were not free from racialized dynamics and hence the process itself created another structural way of policing non-standard languaging. Another is Jane Danielewicz and Peter Elbow's hybrid contract, which became the prototype of Inoue's grading contract. In Danielewicz and Elbow's contract, B-grades are given to all students who conscientiously participate and complete assignments, and A-grades are given under specific criteria of good literacy performance. Inoue finds problematic the idea of the teacher's judgment as the sole determinant in grading and reflects on the purpose of grades in the first place. Is this process a result of student learning outcomes or is it an institutional systematic marker? Inoue concludes the chapter by emphasizing that learning comes from the act of doing, not from grades. If grades are absent, students must ask: "What am I motivated by? What do I really care about in the learning?" (73). Grading without quality as the measurement, in other words, allows students to pay attention to what they do, not what teachers think about what they do.

Given these problems of writing assessment and a tendency to see work as a prerequisite of learning, Inoue further defends labor by drawing on Marxian theory in chapter three. Juxtaposing political economy with assessment ecology, Inoue finds that they share close similarity in the system of exchange—exchanging a commodity (habitus embodied in texts) with currency (grades, scholarships, degrees, jobs, etc.). One who doesn't have any commodity, then, has nothing to gain in exchange. However, if we look at labor as a commodity—here Inoue notes that Karl Marx considers labor power as a commodity because everyone, no matter the socio-economic status, "owns their own labor, the work that they can do" (82)—then everyone can exchange it for currency. As with labor power, labor-based assessment ecology allows *all* students to exchange their labor in a course—the "bodily work of reading writing and other activities associated with what it takes to engage in a writing course" (78)—with grades. In this exchange, Inoue reminds that "we can only labor at the paces we can," so measuring labor separate from its worth or rate must be followed (127).

All these discussions and theorizing of grading based on labor don't mean a thing if students don't believe in them. Therefore, in the last parts of the book, Inoue focuses on practicing labor-based grading contracts in classrooms. He includes his contract as an example assignment set-up that tracks labor, readings related to labor and White racial habitus, and mindful practices for both teachers and students. Among these resources, two things stand out as the core branches: (1) continuously introducing and discussing the philosophy behind grading on labor and (2) setting compassion as the core value of the class. In the first page of his sample contract, Inoue delineates the four key statements that open up conversations about the purpose of doing labor in learning, about agency in one's control over labor, about what absence of grading could mean, and about resisting White language supremacy. Throughout the semester, he brings in readings like Rosina Lippi-Green's *Linguistic Facts of Life* or Joseph Williams' "The Phenomenology of Error" to create a space for students to consider their "resistances, confusions, or concerns, respond[ing] to them, and find[ing] ways to have enough faith in the system" (146). Tasks are assigned with detailed step-by-step processes and then carefully documented to reflect time students have spent completing each step. As students understand the goal is labor, not product, they try new and unfamiliar things without fear of losing points. Most importantly, as Inoue emphasizes in chapter five, grounding the grading contract must be built upon students' understanding of practicing compassion in discussing politics of language. Through reading scientific research into the relation between compassion and collaborative learning, as well as peer-review practices that have compassion as a criterion, students are asked to think "how someone else's suffering in the world may be connected to their own" (182). This way of cultivating brave culture and an "uncomfortable yet safe space" prepares students for understanding racial, socio-economic power differential that comes with language ideologies (189).

In light of decades of calls for linguistic justice--from the 1974 CCCC "Students' Rights to Their Own Language" resolution to the 2020 "This Ain't Another Statement! This is a DEMAND for Black Linguistic Justice!"--*Labor-Based Grading Contracts* is a must-read for all writing teachers and scholars who seek to combat linguistic racism through real action. As a multilingual transnational teacher of color and writer, this book touches close to my heart by, one, providing consolation and acknowledging battles I went through in U.S. academia, and two, equipping me with literature against linguistic injustice. I also realize that I see students who are predominantly White and monolingual sitting across from me in the classroom, listening to my racial—and transnational—language habitus. Although the book does not address the role teacher identities play in practicing grading contracts in-depth, having to address the multiplicity of my positionality to navigate this power dynamic, creating the labor-based grading contract ecology opens up a space for not only students but for teachers by inviting students to actively interrogate White language supremacy and critically reimagine what "good" languaging is together.

East Lansing, Michigan

Works Cited

Bourdieu, Pierre. *The Logic of Practice.* Translated by Richard Nice. Stanford UP, 1990.

Committee on CCCC Language. "Students' Right to Their Own Language." *College Composition and Communication,* vol. 25, no. 3, Sept. 1974, pp. 1-18.

Committee on CCCC Statement on Anti-Black Racism and Black Linguistic Justice. "This Ain't Another Statement! This is a DEMAND for Black Linguistic Justice!" *National Council of Teachers of English,* July 2020, https://cccc.ncte.org/cccc/demand-for-black-linguistic-justice?fbclid=IwAR305_0URSbMIR5OVp0hLmm9osWbt20nGNf7H9IgqNkts8hNs_-tzpFmkDw

Danielewicz, Jane and Elbow, Peter. "A Unilateral Grading Contract to Improve Learning and Teaching." *College Composition and Communication*, vol. 61, no. 2, 2009, pp. 244-68.

Inoue, Asao B. "How do We Language So People Stop Killing Each Other, or What Do We Do about White Language Supremacy?" *College Composition and Communication,* vol. 71, no. 2, Dec. 2019, pp. 352-369.

Lippi-Green, Rosina. *English with an Accent: Language, Ideology, and Discrimination in the United States.* Routledge, 2012.

Williams, Joseph M. "The Phenomenology of Error." *College Composition and Communication*, vol. 32, no. 2, May 1981, pp. 152-68.

Counterstory: The Rhetoric and Writing of Critical Race Theory, by Aja Y. Martinez. National Council of Teachers of English, 2020. 201 pp.

Reviewed by Louis M. Maraj, University of Pittsburgh

As the inequitable racialized impacts of the global COVID-19 crisis raged on in the heat of midsummer 2020, I settled into Aja Y. Martinez's *Counterstory: The Rhetoric and Writing of Critical Race Theory*. I was worried about yet another presidential immigration ban, how these continuing mandates affect my status as a Black foreign worker in a temporality burgeoning with publicized xenophobia and anti-Blackness (that were always there, let's be all the way real, just way less lowkey these days). I could not watch the news; I refused to turn on the TV most days: images of Black death, protests, politicians' absurd denials, multinational corporations draping "Black Lives Matter" on repeat, political ads—a combo of "Defund the police? Who will protect you?" alongside "Black lives never mattered to Joe Biden." It remains, however, a privilege to quiet these representations for a minute, to read from a tablet screen with central air humming around me. Race, racialization, as always though, pulsates through this experience, as all else. And, yet, as Martinez rightly demonstrates, the permanence of race and racism—the first of eight, then nine, core tenets of critical race theory (CRT) highlighted in *Counterstory*'s introduction—still needs reiterating in the fields of rhetoric and writing studies. One might think that by 2021 these disciplines might have gotten it together well enough that our scholars, teachers, and students would not need a monograph like Martinez's. But here we are. And, yet again, a woman of color is doing the work.

Outlining key methods, principles, affects, and embodiments of CRT for use in rhetoric and writing studies, Martinez highlights the importance of groundbreaking scholarship by three "counterstory exemplars," Richard Delgado, Derrick A. Bell, and Patricia J. Williams, through a mobilization of counterstories via its various genres (2). "Counterstory," as Martinez explains, "is methodology that functions through methods that empower the minoritized through the formation of stories that disrupt the erasures embedded in standardized majoritarian methodologies" (3). Theorizing in practice, Martinez exercises CRT's foundational tenets through her experiences and those of her protagonist, Alejandra Prieto, showing us just how effectively these methods might enact possibilities for social justice work in rhetoric and writing studies—particularly for the racially marginalized. These precepts, culled from CRT and rhetoric and writing scholars, include: "Permanence of race and racism; challenge to dominant ideologies; interest convergence; race as social construct; intersectionality and antiessentialism; interdisciplinarity; centrality of experiential knowledge and/or unique voices of color; commitment to social justice" (9); to which Martinez adds "accessibility" (18).

Martinez immediately emphasizes *Counterstory*'s exigence. I clapped—I mean literally applauded—while reading the string of epigraphs to its introduction, "A Case for Counterstory." Excerpted from manuscript reader reviews from leading journals in rhetoric and writing studies, these epigraphs publicly attest to widespread ignorance of scholars in our field who ask for justification for CRT methods that have been around for decades. It's a shame for rhetoric and writing studies. As a Black migrant in a junior faculty job in these fields, I recall my own traumatic reception of similar reviews. Unfortunately, "this isn't research;" "maybe you should submit this to a creative nonfiction journal;" "here's a formula on how you write research essays;" and "do you have IRB approval for this?" all too often greet people of color's storying methods in these disciplines. While some experiences recounted in *Counterstory* at times mirror mine, sometimes they do not. But as endorsement of the strength and necessity of Martinez's work, I compose this review by consciously forwarding a combination of CRT strategies deployed by the monograph—the book review as space and autobiographic reflection as method for counterstory—though the author offers much more.

Martinez centers Delgado, Bell, and Williams in working through the construction of Prieto in proceeding chapters, while reminding readers of the specific CRT tenets from which each respective chapter draws. The second chapter, for instance, spotlights Delgado's use of counterstory as narrated dialogue by way of a discussion of perspective, racial history, and storytelling between Prieto and her daughter. Situating this kind of dialogue in a longstanding rhetorical tradition—stretching back as far as classical Greek thought—the chapter then deploys counterstory in relation to stock story as a form of critique for minoritized subjects to "offer alternate possibilities" for audiences (35). In conversation, the characters follow Delgado in a back-and-forth book review of Octavia Butler's *Kindred* and Margaret Mitchell's *Gone with the Wind*, demonstrating the distinct pedagogical capacities of narrated counterstory dialogue. Chapter three engages Bell's work on counterstory as allegory/fantasy. Again, drawing from a tradition dating back to Plato, but generated through CRT's principal concerns, Martinez here tackles "the politics of historiography" (64). By way of Prieto's teleportation as the character "Self" to a dramatized iteration of the 1988 Octalog at the Conference on College Composition and Communication, we witness imagined conversation between the Chicana scholar of racialized rhetorics and writing and canonized rhetoric and writing scholars James Berlin, Robert Connors, Sharon Crowley, Richard Enos, Susan Jarratt, Nan Johnson, C. Jan Swearingen, Victor Vitanza, and moderator James Murphy.

The subsequent chapter offers autobiographic reflection to make theory accessible in these fields via the foundational work of Black feminist, Williams. Martinez first sketches a genealogy of autobiographical reflection within rhetoric and writing studies, while narratively operationalizing that genealogy through another fantastical dialogue with members of it in an Octalog that this time practices "ancestorship" (87). This conversation features the fictionalized figures of Frankie Condon, Keith Gilyard, Carmen Kynard, Eric Pritchard, Elaine Richardson, Victor Villanueva, Vershawn Ashanti Young, and Martinez as her allegorized self, illustrating the varying potentials for the CRT method within our fields. Martinez then "crosses borders with counterstory" (99) through three vignettes narrating troubling experiences with different authority figures who question the narrator's presence as a Chicana woman in various U.S. spaces. The second, where a white male security guard effectively "checks the papers" of the protagonist and her father in Arizona, easily jars memories of my own many tense encounters with the U.S. Citizenship and Immigration Services (USCIS) officers. These kinds of confrontations all too often position marginalized subjects, whether in possession of official documents or not, to question our own sense of belonging and existence in the U.S.

Counterstory importantly offers insight into the pedagogical reverberations of CRT methods/methodologies in its fifth chapter, by considering CRT's quest toward social transformation in research and practice. Offering specific guidelines to educators who might pick up these methods/methodologies in crafting material (112-113), the chapter gives focused attention to what counterstory might do in educational spaces. By means of an email exchange between Prieto and her mentor V, we learn of several instances of racial violence that Prieto encounters in the classroom while teaching about decolonization, which gets us to crucial questions about the orientation of junior faculty to graduate teaching and how instructors of color continue to keep grinding in the face of continuing racial attacks from (often white male) students. Only a few months ago was I forced to begrudgingly and painstakingly explain to my own "Kyles and Connors" (128) that George Floyd did not—in no uncertain terms—ask for his own murder. The chapter's epistolary dialogue responds to these pressures by delving again into practical, pedagogical heuristics for engaging CRT work. *Counterstory*, as expected, walks the talk by providing material examples for doing so in its appendixes.

And although other paratextual matter like the beautifully written foreword by Carmen Kynard and afterword by Jaime Armin Mejía emphasize the importance of the book's contributions, Martinez's epilogue, "Birth Song," might have left the most lasting impression on me. Martinez's ode to her daughter Olivia—the latter's "baby story" of entering the world to an eighteen-year-old, first year college student mother facing the abuse of her father while navigating "blatant stares" in classrooms, plodding around campus with "feet painfully swollen" (140)—calls attention to the trials and survivals that people, and particularly women, of color aver through storytelling. *Counterstory* thus interrupts the status quo of rhetoric and writing studies theory to drive home the necessity for, and viability of, creative, narrative modes of analysis. It provides a practical trove of pedagogical material—for undergraduate, graduate, domestic, and public classrooms—for imagining more just futures. And yet again, a woman of color is doing the work. In solidarity with her, I call on these fields to incorporate *Counterstory*'s texts and paratexts not only on and into syllabi, practicums, and classrooms but also into frank everyday dialogue about who and what belongs in academic spaces.

Pittsburgh, Pennsylvania

Personal, Accessible, Responsive, Strategic: Resources and Strategies for Online Writing Instructors, by Jessie Borgman and Casey McArdle. The WAC Clearinghouse/UP of Colorado, 2020. 110 pp.

Reviewed by Kailyn Washakie, University of Wyoming

Online learning and instruction are far from new practices in the year 2021, but they have grown in significance and importance under the circumstances that the world has come to face. Many instructors and learners across the world have been forced to educate in the online realm due to the global COVID-19 pandemic, which continues to create uncertainties about the upcoming academic year. Jessie Borgman and Casey McArdle could not have published their book *Personal, Accessible, Responsive, Strategic: Resources and Strategies for Online Writing Instructors* at a more convenient time, as online instruction appears to remain a dominant mode of delivery for most educators. The book is written in a very personable style with references to golf, making it not only accessible but also feel as if the readers are having a conversation with their colleagues. The purpose of this book is to "provide a practical guidebook that includes a distinct approach to OWI [online writing instruction] for new and/or existing online writing instructors" (14). Borgman and McArdle also aim to provide resources and a space for an OWI community through the book, their website, and social media pages. The empirical PARS (personal, accessible, responsive, strategic) approach is intended to provide instructors with a distinct pedagogy based upon the user experience, that aims to make online writing instruction manageable for the instructor and student alike. Furthermore, when all four enactable elements are implemented simultaneously in the design, instruction, and administration of an online writing program, the process of online writing instruction and learning effectively becomes a cohesive experience for students, instructors, and writing department administrators.

As a secondary language arts educator, I found myself faced with the pitfalls of having to quickly move my congenial face-to-face instruction to the disconcerting online domain within a matter of days. Without any prior training or preparation, I, along with many other educators across the globe, had to learn how to implement online instruction while simultaneously delivering it. There have been approaches made available for implementing online instruction, including the CCCC's "A Position Statement of Principles and Example Effective Practices for Online Writing Instruction (OWI)," *Foundational Practices of Online Writing Instruction* by Beth L. Hewett and Kevin Eric DePew, and *Applied Pedagogies: Strategies for Online Writing Instruction* by Daniel Ruefman and Abigail G. Scheg. Borgman and McArdle draw inspiration from these sources, but none are as direct or easily enactable as the PARS approach. Borgman and McArdle's book holds an abundance of knowledge for this strategy to be implemented in the design, instruction, and administration of a writing program, but this review will focus solely on the ideas presented for the former two, due to the urgency that many inexperienced online instructors are currently faced with in learning and implementing this new style of teaching.

The first chapter focuses on the "Personal" element of the PARS approach, and how it is important for instructors to devote the same effort to making classes personal and inviting in the online setting as they would in face-to-face classes. When students experience this effort, it creates a safe space for them to reach out to the instructor and interact with classmates. For the design aspect of this element, Borgman and McArdle suggest that instructors use personal approaches and elements to set the inviting tone for the length of the course, and to display personality at every possible opportunity. Setting a personable tone for the course is important because "students are more engaged in courses that have a social sense of community, that include sensory details and engaging material and that pay attention to the entire experience, not just the content to be learned" (20). It is because of this notion that it is also important to deliver culturally sensitive and adaptive content so that all possible students from all possible backgrounds feel respected and included. The "Personal Instruction" facet underscores the importance of creating connections and relationships with students, but also confirms the challenges associated with this. In an online setting, it is important for instructors to step away from an authoritarian role and embody that of a coach or guide of the learning process instead. The ways in which Borgman and McArdle dissect the "Personal" element of the PARS approach at every level of implementation provides readers with a realistic and enactable ideology of how to create an inviting space for learners.

"Accessibility" is the elemental focus of chapter two, with Borgman and McArdle diving right into the fact that course management systems (CMS) and/or learning management systems (LMS) are built for the use of instructors rather than students. With this in mind, it is important for instructors to review all materials for the course and make alterations as needed, with the user experience in mind. When it comes to designing a course through the lens of accessibility, it is important for instructors to implement the American with Disabilities Act (ADA) guidelines and also be wary of the technical aspects. It is imperative for instructors to make assignments, lessons, instructions, and other important facets of the learning experience multimedia, in order to include multiple styles of learning that may not be of the "abled majority" (39). Accessible instruction means the instructor must plan and create points of contact for student-instructor interaction and student-student interaction. Students must be able to access the instructor, but they need clear and structured avenues for doing so. It is important for instructors to develop rapport with students and be intentional about sustaining it through consistent individual and whole-group communication (41). Borgman and McArdle offer their experienced advice on ways to make an online class accessible, but not how to clearly identify the extent to which to do so. The empirical research presented on the importance of doing so is compelling, but it would be helpful for inexperienced online educators to see this fleshed out with specific examples or methods.

Chapter three concentrates on the "Responsiveness" element of the approach, and how being responsive is much different than simply responding to students. It is vital for the instructor to create a structure and boundaries for when and how they'll respond to students and to make this clear to students from the very beginning. Feedback is the most important characteristic of responsiveness and should be done often throughout the writing process. It is important for the instructor to establish themselves as an audience and provide feedback from that lens rather than as the instructor, to help students successfully develop their skills and approach. Providing feedback can be done through text, audio, or video, but should always be done clearly and with encouragement. Designing this part of the strategy requires a lot of organization and time; one of the hardest things for new online instructors to adapt to is the workload. Borgman and McArdle suggest strategies to streamline this process; when students have questions, for example, it would be advantageous for the instructor to reply with an answer that is visible to all students and thereby avoid the possibility of repeating the response to multiple students with the same question. Creating a balance and schedule for how time will be spent in the course is also crucial for instruction and time management. Borgman and McArdle highlight that in an online setting it is easy for students and instructors to lose sight of a traditional class time structure for communication and may expect responses within minutes due to accessibility, but for the sake of sanity there must be a schedule and clear set of communication expectations set in place that are adhered to (59). The approach to responsiveness that Borgman and McArdle present is the strongest aspect of the PARS approach overall. Clear communication between instructors and students can make or break an online setting, and this strategy clarifies how to set boundaries and expectations that can be enacted as soon as possible.

The final element of the PARS approach is "Strategic." This element begins with planning and strategizing around the user experience by making a map of activities, assignments, timeframes, and learning objectives. Because "the instructor is responsible for architecting an experience for the student users in a very specific environment," it is important to solicit feedback on the design of the course and the course itself and to use that feedback to adapt to the learners (73). Creating a "strategic instruction" is one of the trickier parts of this element, due in part to the fact that instructor and student expectations are rarely the same. Learning who the students are and what motivates or distracts them is one of the best ways to design or adapt lessons for them. Not all students are going to be at the same starting line, so it is important to "strategize your content to meet them where they're at" (75). It is also imperative to understand where students will be learning from and whether or not any laws or access to specific platforms will impede their learning experience. Once again, Borgman and McArdle have offered a clear focus to an element of the PARS approach. Strategizing each facet of the learning experience from the perspective of the user may take more time but is undoubtedly one of the surest ways to create a successful course.

The PARS approach to online writing instruction proves to be a promising strategy for those who lack experience or direction in creating and navigating an online course. Although the PARS approach encompasses many facets of online learning, the book does little to address how to ensure that the cultural differences and needs of the students are met through an online pedagogy and learning platform. Culturally responsive teaching may not have been the focus of this book, but its addition would have strengthened the application of this approach to any online learning environment. However, Borgman and McArdle offer credible research to support each element of this approach along with their own empirical analysis, to show its reliability and that they do indeed practice what they preach. Their credibility within the specific field of online writing is furthered by their dedication in creating *The Online Writing Instruction Community* at www.owicommunity.org, which provides shareable resources for online writing instructors. The PARS approach offers suggestions and advice that can be used or adapted across all levels of online writing instruction, and it takes this form of education beyond theory by providing practical approaches and enactable ideas in the online setting. Although the near future of educational delivery remains uncertain, this practical approach to online teaching is invaluable for both novice online instructors and those looking to revamp their online pedagogy.

Fort Washakie, Wyoming

Works Cited

CCCC Committee for Effective Practices for Online Writing Instruction. "A Position Statement of Principles and Example Effective Practices for Online Writing Instruction (OWI)." *Conference on College Composition and Communication*, 14 Aug. 2018, cccc.ncte.org/cccc/resources/positions/owiprinciples.

Hewett, Beth L. and Kevin Eric DePew. *Foundational Practices of Online Writing Instruction*. The WAC Clearinghouse and Parlor Press, 2015

Ruefman, Daniel and Abigail G. Scheg, editors. *Applied Pedagogies: Strategies for Online Writing Instruction*. Utah State University Press, 2016.

Contributors

Sonja Andrus is Associate Professor of English and the Composition Coordinator at the University of Cincinnati Blue Ash College. She has been teaching a teaching-for-transfer curriculum for several years and has a deep interest in helping students learn how to learn and transfer their knowledge and skills to other contexts.

Zachary Beare is Assistant Professor of English at North Carolina State University. His research focuses on composition pedagogy, queer and feminist rhetorics, affect and emotion, and digital culture. His work has appeared in *College Composition and Communication*, *College English*, *Writing on the Edge*, *Reflections*, *Journal of Cultural Research*, and in various edited collections.

Mikayla Beaudrie is a writing instructor at the University of North Florida. She is also a poet and researcher. Her creative and scholarly work largely centers on the relationship between Blackness, nature, and the existence of a Black gothic rhetoric.

Diane Quaglia Beltran earned her PhD in Rhetorics, Communication, and Information Design at Clemson University. Her areas of research are at the intersections of rhetoric, memory in built environments, and composition.

Lauren Marshall Bowen is Assistant Professor of English and Director of the Composition Program at the University of Massachusetts Boston, where she teaches writing, literacy, composition theory, and composition pedagogy. Her work has appeared in *College Composition and Communication*, *College English*, *Community Literacy Journal*, *Literacy in Composition Studies*, and *Computers and Composition*.

John C. Brereton is Professor Emeritus from the University of Massachusetts Boston. He has published widely on many aspects of composition, including rhetoric, business writing, and critical reading. His books include *The Origins of Composition Studies*, *The Norton Reader*, and *Traditions of Eloquence*. He has taught at the City University of New York, Wayne State University, and Harvard University.

Wendy Chen is a PhD candidate in English at the University of Denver, where she works as a consultant in the University Writing Center. She is the author of *Unearthings* (Tavern Books), editor of *Figure 1*, and managing editor of *Tupelo Quarterly*.

Todd Craig is Associate Professor of English at Medgar Evers College (CUNY) and also teaches in the African-American Studies Department at New York City College of Technology (CUNY). He teaches courses in writing, rhetoric, and hip-hop studies. Not only did he raise the bar, the bar broke (Conway the Machine).

Eric Detweiler is Assistant Professor in Middle Tennessee State University's Department of English. His work has appeared in such journals as *Rhetoric Review*, *Pedagogy*, and *enculturation*. He runs the podcast *Rhetoricity*, and he is currently working on a book called *Responsible Teaching: A Case for the Rhetorical and Ethical Work of Higher Education*.

Claire Edwards is a PhD candidate in Public Rhetorics & Community Engagement at the University of Wisconsin-Milwaukee. She is originally from southern California and has several years of college teaching, tutoring, and administrative experience. She has also worked in editing and internal communications. Her scholarly interests include first year composition curriculum, linguistic diversity, and community colleges.

Gitte Frandsen is a PhD student in Public Rhetorics and Community Engagement at the University of Wisconsin-Milwaukee who came back to graduate school after years of teaching high school English and first year composition for native and non-native English speakers. Her research interests include translingual literacy studies, linguistic justice, cultural rhetorics, and writing program administration.

Cinthia Gannett is Professor Emerita at Fairfield University. She taught writing, linguistics, and the teaching of writing, and administered writing center, WAC, and writing programs for over forty years. Since retirement, she has continued her professional and scholarly work in historical and archival texts, Jesuit rhetoric, and international writing studies, all while supporting the next generation of teachers and scholars.

Rebecca Haynes is a classroom teacher in Rawlins, Wyoming and a graduate student of English at the University of Wyoming in Laramie. Her areas of research interest include representation of marginalized groups in young adult literature, social justice, feminist theory, and queer theory.

Stephie Kang is a PhD student in Michigan State's Writing, Rhetoric, and American Cultures program. Her research areas are standard language ideologies, multilingualism, and transnational non-native English-speaking teacher identities in writing classrooms. She also advocates for international students in the university as a graduate union representative.

Danielle Koepke is a PhD student in Public Rhetorics and Community Engagement at the University of Wisconsin-Milwaukee. She has an MA in Rhetoric and Composition, and her academic interests include multimodal composing practices, digital literacies, and feminist theories. Her current research applies these ideas to issues of reproductive justice.

Danielle Koupf is Assistant Teaching Professor in the Writing Program at Wake Forest University in Winston-Salem, North Carolina. Her research interests include composition pedagogy, invention, textual reuse, and rhetorics of making and crafting. Her previous scholarship has appeared in *Composition Forum*, *enculturation*, and multiple edited collections.

Louis M. Maraj is Assistant Professor of English at the University of Pittsburgh. He thinks/creates/converses cross-disciplinarily with theoretical Black studies, rhetoric, digital media, and critical pedagogies. He is the author of *Black or Right: Anti/Racist Campus Rhetorics* and essays in *Precarious Rhetorics*, *Prose Studies*, and *Women's Studies in Communication*.

Joni Hayward Marcum is a PhD candidate in Media, Cinema, and Digital Studies at the University of Wisconsin-Milwaukee. She is writing her dissertation about nonfiction films from the 1930s and what they can teach us about energy. She is also interested in the energy humanities and environmental communication.

Amanda M. May is Assistant Professor of English and director of the writing center at New Mexico Highlands University. She completed her PhD at Florida State University, where she taught first year and junior-level writing classes. She also served the institution's Reading-Writing Center and Digital Studio in numerous capacities.

Benjamin Miller is Assistant Professor of English/Composition at the University of Pittsburgh. He is a lead developer of the Writing Studies Tree (writingstudiestree.org), a crowdsourced, open-access academic genealogy for composition, rhetoric, and related fields, and one of the founding editors of the *Journal of Interactive Technology and Pedagogy*.

Sharon Mitchler is Professor of English and Humanities at Centralia College, a public community college located midway between Seattle, Washington and Portland, Oregon. She is a former chair of TYCA and teaches courses in composition, literature, introductory humanities, ethics, and film.

Beverly J. Moss is Associate Professor of English at The Ohio State University where she specializes in composition and literacy studies. Her scholarly and pedagogical interests include examining literacy in African American community spaces, composition theory and pedagogy, and writing center theory and practice.

Maria Novotny is Assistant Professor of English at the University of Wisconsin-Milwaukee. Trained in cultural rhetorics, she approaches community-engaged scholarship through the practices of relationality, care, and accountability. Her research has been published in *Computers and Composition, Communication Design Quarterly, Peitho, Reflections, Rhetoric Review,* and *Technical Communication Quarterly.*

Juli Parrish is Writing Center Director and Teaching Professor of Writing at the University of Denver. She has been published in *Transformative Works and Cultures, Across the Disciplines,* and *South Atlantic Review.* She is a co-editor of *Literacy in Composition Studies* and of the collection *Pedagogy and Literacy in an Age of Misinformation and Disinformation* (Parlor).

Laurie A. Pinkert is Assistant Professor of Writing and Rhetoric at the University of Central Florida. Her research has been funded by the National Science Foundation and has been published in journals such as *College Composition and Communication, College English, Reflections: A Journal of Community-Engaged Writing and Rhetoric,* and *WPA: Writing Program Administration.*

Chloe Robertson is an English native and has lived in America for three years. She is currently completing her coursework at Virginia Tech in pursuit of a PhD in Rhetoric. Focusing on interlocking systems of oppression, her work interrogates societal normativities couched in oppressive practices and beliefs.

Catalina Sepulveda is a first year undergraduate student at the University of Denver. She is an International Business and Management major, dreaming of starting her own high-fashion brand. She is from Santiago, Chile but has lived in the United States since 2015. Catalina is creative, funny, persistent, and empathetic. She hopes to bring more color into this world.

Jennifer Sheppard is Assistant Professor in the Rhetoric and Writing Studies Department at San Diego State University. Her research focuses on digital writing, visual and multimodal rhetoric, and professional communication. She has published in a variety of peer-reviewed journals and edited collections and is co-author of *Writer/Designer: A Guide to Making Multimodal Projects.*

Chloe Smith is a PhD student in Public Rhetorics and Community Engagement at University of Wisconsin-Milwaukee. Her research interests include linguistic justice, teacher training, and cultural rhetorics.

Angelyn Sommers is an MA student in the English department at University of Wisconsin-Milwaukee. She is pursuing a degree in Professional and Technical Writing. Her current research involves the rhetorical practices of online health communities and the user-generated technical communication that takes place in these virtual spaces.

Howard Tinberg is Professor of English at Bristol Community College in Massachusetts and former editor of the journal *Teaching English in the Two-Year College*. He is the author of *Border Talk: Writing and Knowing in the Two-Year College* and *Writing with Consequence: What Writing Does in the Disciplines*. He is co-author of *The Community College Writer: Exceeding Expectations*, and *Teaching and Learning and the Holocaust: An Integrative Approach*. He is co-editor of *Deep Reading: Teaching Reading in the Writing Classroom* and *What is "College-Level" Writing?*. He is a former Chair of the Conference on College Composition and Communication.

Turnip Van Dyke is a PhD student in the Rhetoric and Writing Studies program at the University of Texas at El Paso.

Victor Villanueva is a retired Regents Professor and Edward R. Meyer Distinguished Professor of Liberal Arts at Washington State University. He is a former writing program administrator, editor of the *Studies in Writing and Rhetoric* series, chair of CCCC, Rhetorician of the Year, Exemplar, and more. Scores of articles, books, and talks later, he remains concerned with rhetoric and racism.

Zhaozhe Wang has recently earned his PhD from the Department of English at Purdue University, where he teaches writing and communication. His work, broadly exploring multilingual literacy and non-Western/digital/public rhetorics, has appeared in *College Composition and Communication*, *Composition Forum*, *Rhetoric Society Quarterly*, and *WPA: Writing Program Administration*. He is also co-editor of *Reconciling Translingualism and Second Language Writing*.

Kailyn Z. Washakie is a middle school language arts teacher on the Wind River Reservation. She completed a BA in English/Secondary Education with a minor in Professional Writing at the University of Wyoming, where she is currently pursuing an MA in English with a minor in Native American & Indigenous Studies.

Madison Rose Williams is a graduate instructor and first year PhD student in Public Rhetorics and Community Engagement at the University of Wisconsin-Milwaukee. She earned her MA in Rhetoric and Professional Writing from UW-Milwaukee in 2020. Her research interests revolve around social justice, technical communication and rhetoric, and cultural rhetorics.

Kathleen Blake Yancey is Kellogg Hunt Professor and Distinguished Research Professor Emerita at Florida State University. She has served as the elected leader of several organizations, including CCCC and NCTE. A past editor of *College Composition and Communication*, she has published numerous articles and book chapters and has authored, edited, and co-edited sixteen books. She has won several awards, among them the CCCC Exemplar Award.

TCU PH.D. IN RHETORIC AND COMPOSITION

PROGRAM. One of the founding programs in rhetoric and composition. Scholarly innovation, professional development, excellent job placement, well-endowed library, state-of-the-art Center for Digital Expression, and graduate certificates in New Media; Women and Gender Studies; and Comparative Race and Ethnic Studies.

FACULTY. Nationally recognized teacher-scholars in literacy studies, composition, modern rhetoric, women's rhetoric, digital rhetoric, and writing program administration.

TEACHING. 1-1 teaching loads, small classes, extensive pedagogy and technology training, and administrative fellowships in writing program administration and new media.

FUNDING. Generous five-year graduate instructorships, competitive stipends, travel support, and prestigious fellowship opportunities.

EXPERIENCE. Mid-sized liberal arts university setting nestled in the vibrant, culturally rich Dallas-Fort Worth metroplex.

eng.tcu.edu

PARLOR PRESS
EQUIPMENT FOR LIVING

New Releases

Collaborative Writing Playbook: An Instructor's Guide to Designing Writing Projects for Student Teams by Joe Moses and Jason Tham

The Best of the Journals in Rhetoric and Composition 2020

The Art of Public Writing by Zachary Michael Jack

The Naylor Report on Undergraduate Research in Writing Studies edited by Dominic DelliCarpini, Jenn Fishman, and Jane Greer

Internationalizing the Writing Center: A Guide for Developing a Multilingual Writing Center by Noreen Lape

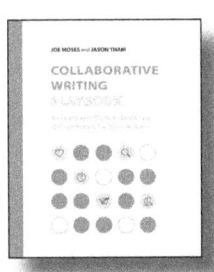

MLA Mina Shaughnessy Prize and CCCC Best Book Award 2021!

Creole Composition: Academic Writing and Rhetoric in the Anglophone Caribbean, edited by Vivette Milson-Whyte, Raymond Oenbring, and Brianne Jaquette

Check Out Our New Website!

Discounts, blog, open access titles, instant downloads, and more.

And new series:

Comics and Graphic Narratives
Series Editors: Sergio Figueiredo, Jason Helms, and Anastasia Salter

Inkshed: Writing Studies in Canada
Series Editors: Heather Graves and Roger Graves

www.parlorpress.com

Composition Stuides **Discount**: Use COMPSTUDIES20 at checkout to receive a 20% discount on all titles not on sale through June 15, 2021.

www.ingramcontent.com/pod-product-compliance
Lightning Source LLC
Chambersburg PA
CBHW031319160426
43196CB00007B/580